Making Peace

MAKING PEACE
Personal Essays

Eugene England

Signature Books   Salt Lake City   1995

Several of the essays in Making Peace, *sometimes in a different version or with a different title, first appeared in the following publications: "Healing and Making Peace, in the World and the Church," in* Sunstone, *Apr. 1992; "On Spectral Evidence, Scapegoating, and False Accusation" as "On Spectral Evidence" in* Dialogue: A Journal of Mormon Thought, *Spring 1993; "Perfection and Progression: Two Ways to Talk about God," as "Perfection and Progression: Two Complementary Ways to Talk about God," in* Brigham Young University Studies, *Summer 1989; "Making Peace at BYU, with the Help of Brigham Young," as "Becoming Brigham Young's University," in* On the Lord's Errand: The Purposes and Possibilities of Brigham Young University *(Provo, UT: Brigham Young University, 1985); "Why Utah Mormons Should Become Democrats: Reflections on Partisan Politics" as "On Saving the Constitution, Or Why Some Utah Mormons Should Become Democrats," in* Sunstone, *May 1988; "Why Nephi Killed Laban: Reflections on the Truth of the Book of Mormon" as "A Second Witness for the* Logos: The Book of Mormon and Contemporary Literary Criticism," in *By Study and Also by Faith: Essays in Honor of Hugh Nibley* (Salt Lake City: F.A.R.M.S. and Deseret Book Co., 1990); "'No Respecter of Persons': An Ethics of Diversity," in *Dialogue: A Journal of Mormon Thought, *Winter 1994; and "Monte Cristo" in* Wasatch Review International, *June 1993. "The Prince of Peace" was given as an Easter sermon in 1993 and remains in that form.*

COVER DESIGN: SCOTT KNUDSEN
COVER ILLUSTRATION: APRIL PERRY,
Tree of Life/Tree of Death, oil with mixed media on board.

Making Peace: Personal Essays was printed on acid-free paper and was composed, printed, and bound in the United States.

2000   99   98   97   06   95   7   6   5   4   3   2   1

Library of Congress Cataloging in Publication Information
England, Eugene.
        Making peace : personal essays / Eugene England.
              p.   cm.
        ISBN 1-56085-069-9
        1. Christian life--Mormon authors.   I. Title.
    BV4501.2.E575   1995
    248.4'893--dc20   94-40566
                                                             CIP

In Memory of
Howard W. Hunter,
Peacemaker

CONTENTS

PREFACE

And blessed are they who shall work to bring forth my Zion at that day, . . . if they endure unto the end they shall be lifted up at the last day, and shall be saved in the everlasting kingdom of the Lamb; and whoso shall publish peace, yea, tidings of great joy, how beautiful upon the mountains shall they be.

The passage above, from 1 Nephi 13:37, was quoted by Elder Boyd K. Packer in his March 8, 1995, sermon at the funeral of Latter-day Saint president Howard W. Hunter. Elder Packer commented on the vicissitudes, pain, and dangers that President Hunter had endured without complaint and with gentle grace and gratitude to all around him, to the very last seconds of his life.

Many have noted President Hunter's endurance and gentleness, his graciousness and integrity, and many of us have seen how beautiful upon our mountains he was because he published peace. We have felt perhaps an unusual grief at the passing of this prophet because his ministry was so brief and the qualities he possessed seem so important right now. I grieve especially because he was a peacemaker, focussed in his often-expressed devotion to his Savior as the Prince of Peace, and I yearn for peace with special longing right now—peace both in the world and the church.

President Hunter began his ministry as a peacemaker. His first public comments after being ordained president of the church focussed on what became his central theme, peace through Christ-like living:

I would invite all members of the Church to live with ever-more attention to the life and example of the Lord Jesus Christ, especially the love and hope and compassion he displayed.

I pray that we might treat each other with more kindness,

ix

more courtesy, more humility and patience and forgiveness. . . .
Our world cries out for more disciplined living of the commandments of God. But the way we are to encourage that, as the Lord
told the prophet Joseph in the wintry depths of Liberty Jail, is "by
persuasion, by long-suffering, by gentleness and meekness, and by
love unfeigned."

To those who have transgressed or been offended, we say
come back. To those who are hurt and struggling and afraid, we
say let us stand with you and dry your tears. . . . Feast at the table
laid before you in The Church of Jesus Christ of Latter-day Saints
and strive to follow the Good Shepherd who has provided it. Have
hope, exert faith, receive—and give—charity, the pure love of
Christ.

A few weeks later he made the remarkable promise that his other
great theme, the temple, was also linked to peace:

> May you let the meaning and beauty and peace of the tem-
> ple come into your everyday life more directly in order that the
> millennial day may come, that promised time when "they shall
> beat their swords into plowshares, and their spears into pruning-
> hooks: nation shall not lift up sword against nation, neither shall
> they learn war any more . . . [but shall] walk in the light of the
> Lord" (Isa. 2:4-5).

I pray fervently that the prediction and promise of our new
prophet, President Gordon B. Hinckley, that the influence of President Hunter will continue strongly and will be fulfilled as we try to follow his teachings and example in making peace through the pure love
of Christ.

My own faith in and understanding of peace have been energized
by the discovery that what, in my youth, troubled me about my inher-
ited religious thought and my own spiritual experience—the occasional paradoxes and contradictions—could also be exciting and
satisfying. As I have struggled with the contrary principles of justice
and mercy, I have found that the central element of my faith and experience, the atonement of Jesus Christ, did not make enduring sense
nor produce continuing power for change in my life if I neglected

either of those contraries. I found that my church service was sometimes exasperating, even bitter, because it brought into sharp conflict my idealism and my need to learn to love imperfect humans, including myself—and yet such service, like marriage, though it failed if I either withdrew from facing the daily struggles or sentimentalized them, could also produce profound joy as I learned how to love.

During a time of growing wonder at a universe of opposing forces and concepts that seemed to give existence its very tang and solidity, as well as its energy, I learned of Joseph Smith's remarkable statement, "By proving contraries, truth is made manifest." My heart and mind gave full assent. I remembered William Blake's claim that "Without contraries is no progression" and thought again of the teaching in the Book of Mormon about opposition "in all things." Lehi's unique effort to describe the foundations of being took on new power for me. I began to see all about me, in particle physics and organic evolution, in the history of literary movements and political struggles, in theological debate and the battle of the sexes, evidence that without the enlivening power of contraries "all things must be a compound in one . . . having no life" (2 Ne. 2:13). And I realized the added paradox that often our failure to accept this contrary, oppositional structure of all reality, physical and moral and spiritual, tended to produce much violence, to be a chief impediment to peace.

This book, then, is about ideas and ways of thinking that can help make peace. It is itself an effort to make peace. It brings together my most direct efforts, as a Christian, a literary critic, and a husband and father living in a violent yet marvelous century, to test and explore central contraries of my life. I begin with two essays about some of the most recent conflicts in both the world and the Latter-day Saint church. I have faith such conflicts can be resolved. Perhaps by resisting the temptation to judge others as evil based on "spectral evidence" and by applying the merciful, atoning love of Christ, we can experience the healing necessary to bring about peace.

The next three essays take up specific issues that we Mormons struggle with, ones that sometimes bring contention but actually, seen in new ways, could help produce peace: How can God be both perfect and progressing? How can church education both build and confirm orthodox faith and morals and also liberate from ignorance and prejudice? And how can Mormons, increasingly inclined to be Republicans, effectively improve the politics of a pluralistic democracy and avoid the sloth and poverty of new ideas in one-party rule and especially the peace-destroying (and recently increasing) fallacy that political opponents and their ideas are not only wrong but evil?

After a kind of breather—a very personal narrative about my daughter (and jacaranda trees) that records an effort to make peace through understanding others—there are three essays about some ethical and theological questions related to peace-making: How are we to respond when God asks us to violate the same moral principles that he himself has taught us? What could God mean when he asks Abraham to sacrifice his only child, or when he asks Nephi to kill Laban? How can we resolve the conflict between valuing moral agency and protecting life that the issue of legalized abortion raises? How are we to keep fully the commandment not to kill, if we still, as a nation, condone war and capital punishment? How are we to understand distinctions we still make between races, sexes, religions, and ideologies in light of God's love of diversity and constant reminder that *he* is "no respecter of persons"?

I end with a personal meditation about finding peace in the wilderness, in friendship, and in myself, and finally take a direct look at how Jesus, the Prince of Peace, provides, through his mercy, the ultimate strength and means to find and to make peace.

Provo, Utah
October 1995

HEALING AND MAKING PEACE,
IN THE CHURCH AND
THE WORLD

Just before Christmas, in 1955, Charlotte and I were living in Mapusaga, a small village in American Samoa. We had been married two years and had been missionaries to the Polynesians for a year and a half. Charlotte was six months pregnant. We were teaching a woman named Taligu E'e, who had Mormon relatives and had agreed to meet us each Wednesday afternoon. We would walk to her *fale*, her circular, open, thatch-roofed home, and teach her in far from fluent Samoan one of the lessons from the systematic missionary teaching guide. She would listen politely and impassively, her eyes looking down at the mats we sat on, and after we finished would serve us the meal she had prepared.

One Wednesday we discussed the plan of salvation. We told her how we had chosen to come to earth, with Jesus, who had offered himself as our Savior, and how important it was to follow him. Then we told her how, through temple ordinances, we could help those who had died without knowing Christ but would be taught about him in the spirit world. Her head came up as I told this story. Timidly she asked about her own ancestors who lived before Christian missionaries came to Samoa, who she had believed must be damned because they did not know Christ and were not baptized.

I repeated what I just then realized fully for the first time was indeed the *gospel*, the Good News. I assured her that God loves everyone equally who comes to earth and has provided a way for all, including her ancestors, to know about him and obey him and be saved. She kept her

1

eyes on my face, and they filled with tears. I sensed that a deep sorrow, a long-standing wound, was being healed, and I kept repeating, *"O le Atua, alofa tele 'ia i latou 'uma,"* which I hoped conveyed, "God really loves them all." Taligu was baptized the day after we left Samoa. Our mission president, we believe by inspiration, had transferred us to Hawaii for our baby to be born, and it turned out that the medical facilities there were necessary to save Charlotte's life during a very difficult delivery. We have heard that Taligu became the matriarch of a great church family in Samoa. We trust that she did the saving ordinances for her ancestors in the New Zealand temple built just a few years after her baptism.

What I *know* is that the gospel of Jesus Christ healed her and brought her peace. Truth is an essential part of healing and of peacemaking—though not just any truth administered in just any fashion. Paul talked about "speaking the truth in love" (Eph. 4:15). Mere "truth" can build weapons of mass destruction and motivate endless quarrels, even violence, over rights and wrongs. Truth can be a weapon to wound and increase animosity, to foster continuing adversarial escalation. Redemptive truth, the gospel, spoken in genuine love, can heal.

When I was bishop of a congregation of married students at Brigham Young University, one of them asked me to talk with a friend who had attempted suicide. When I met her, I found that, like many young Latter-day Saints I had counseled, this woman had a strong sense of justice and of self-condemnation, but a weak sense of Christ's mercy and love. She spoke quickly and harshly about her failings and her despair. I simply read to her from the Book of Mormon those passages that teach Christ's mercy in the Atonement and the spirit of reconciliation. After a while I could see peace visibly come over her, and she began to weep. When she left, she had perhaps been healed a little.

When John Taylor was president of the Quorum of Twelve Apostles, two men came to him for resolution of a bitter quarrel. President Taylor was an exceptionally good singer. He told the two, "Brethren, before I hear your case, I would like very much to sing one of the songs of Zion for you." When he had finished, he commented that he had never heard one of the church's hymns without wanting to hear another and so sang one more—and then another and another. Finally the two men were moved to tears and left, fully reconciled, without any discussion of their problem.[1]

Healing does happen; peace can come. These stories give me hope and direction: The redemptive truths of the gospel of the Prince of Peace can heal—*if* they are conveyed in a way consistent with their own nature and thus able to move others with their potential power. The central truth seems to be God's unconditional love, the unique power of mercy to heal our souls and bring peace to our lives—but it must touch our hearts and wills as well as our minds and understandings.

I remember one of the first sermons I heard Elder Marion D. Hanks give, shortly after he was called as a general authority over forty years ago. He told of two Mormon families who had been alienated from each other for years by an offense and then revenge. They would not speak to each other. They nursed their wounds and inflicted new ones. Finally the father who had been first and most sinned against went to the other father and asked forgiveness—and the two families were reconciled. I remember clearly how stunning it was for me to understand and feel for the first time, from that simple anecdote, the claim of Shakespeare's Portia, in *The Merchant of Venice*, that mercy blesses the giver as well as the receiver. Mercy is, in a phrase Elder Hanks may have learned, as I did, from Lowell Bennion, "the homeopathic medicine of the soul."

Such medicine does not work automatically or easily, though I believe it works directly and consistently when we really *work* at it. Again, understanding is not enough. Portia is a case in point. Disguised as a legal consultant in the court where Shylock has gone to claim his pound of flesh from Antonio for a defaulted loan, she admits that Shylock's claim is legal and in the name of justice must be honored, but she pleads nevertheless for mercy:

> The quality of mercy is not strain'd,
> It droppeth as the gentle rain from heaven
> Upon the place beneath. It is twice blest:
> It blesseth him that gives and him that takes.
> It is an attribute to God himself;

3

And earthly power doth then show likest God's
When mercy seasons justice. . . .
    . . . consider this
That in the course of justice, none of us
Should see salvation.
(*The Merchant of Venice*, 4.1.184-200).[2]

Shakespeare has Portia convey here the basic point of the atonement of Jesus Christ: We *all* sin beyond any ability to make amends, to
make anything like full restitution, if we are left only to the demands
of justice. These demands, which our consciences make on us and on
each other, as well as the unanswered demands of a just God, leave us
forever divided, unhealed, unatoned. The Atonement, which originally
meant and was pronounced At-one-ment, delivers the power from
Christ, through his self-sacrificing mercy, to reunite us to ourselves, to
overcome sin, which is the division within us between our knowledge
and our action. And in the same way we can only be reunited with each
other through similar acts of forgiveness for each other.

However, though Portia *speaks* of mercy brilliantly when she wants
it for her friend Antonio, she is not capable of *showing* it in a less self-
serving situation—when an enemy, Shylock, clearly deserves severe
punishment. By applying the letter of the law, she saves Antonio from
Shylock's revenge, but then she and Antonio use the law for revenge
against Shylock, not only threatening his life and fortune but, most
horrible crime of all, forcing him to renounce his Jewish faith and become a Christian. I believe that Shakespeare wanted us to see that
they thus miss their chance to be genuine peacemakers and are ultimately most un-Christian.

There are great wounds in the world that need healing. There is
continuing violence that needs genuine peacemakers. The hopeful de-
velopments in Eastern Europe of the past seven years were brought
about, I believe, not as much by military build-ups and threats as by
non-violent efforts of many people. Despite those develop-
ments—which ended the Cold War and suggested a great and marvelous possibility of a quick and relatively peaceful movement toward in-

ternational cooperation—great wounds remain. War continues in the Middle East, Africa, Northern Ireland, and the former Yugoslavia. The peace talks between Arabs and Israelis, Catholics and Protestants, Hutus and Tutsis, Bosnians and Serbs too often break down as both sides engage in violence and counter-violence even as talks begin; both sides stake out non-negotiable demands, couched in the language of justice, seeking a small advantage here or there. No one seems able to extend even the smallest act of trust, of giving up territory, or even old slogans and ancient grievances, as a way of changing the patterns of violence to something new. No one seems to be able to remember that tactics based on seeking advantage, on demands for justice, have *never* worked, certainly not permanently. No one seems to remember that the two occasions when nations tried something like mercy—the Marshall Plan, which rebuilt the economies of our former World War II enemies, and Anwar Sadat's sacrifices, which included eventually the giving of his own life—are the only two acts that have brought lasting peace between enemies in modern times.

There are also great wounds in the LDS church. The Mormon intellectual community seems riven in two, reduced to mutual alienation and public name-calling. Most of those in the Seminary and Institute system, along with many BYU religion faculty, are separated from those in the unsponsored or independent sector, including much of the BYU faculty outside of Religious Education. There is a scandalous lack of respect, isolation in effectively exclusive symposia and publications, with almost no learning from each other through dialogue or even sympathetic reading of each other's writings. The press has emphasized and perhaps created animosity by exaggerating or even misrepresenting controversial articles in the independent Mormon press and thoughtless or provocative expressions by independent symposia participants. In response, public statements by BYU professors and even church and university leaders seem to have hardened divisions and escalated antagonisms. In addition, there are deepening divisions over gender issues and the wounds that many Mormon women feel.

In the late 1960s, when there was turmoil in the church and anger and even action against the church over our discrimination against blacks, there was already evidence of potentially greater turmoil over women's issues. And that is what is happening. As Susan Faludi demonstrates in *Backlash: The Undeclared War against American Women*, the gains women made in the 1970s have been more than reversed in the 1980s. Abetted by government indifference and male anxiety, prejudice and discrimination have tended to *increase*, as was made dramatically visible in 1992 when it seemed to many people that fourteen male senators struggled and failed to deal either justly or mercifully with Anita Hill and her allegations. Now many women respond in despair and anger, and backlash escalates against backlash. We have great need for healing.

During this national period of gains for women and subsequent backlash, Mormon women seem also to have experienced gains and losses—certainly gains in general freedom and opportunity and in attention from church leaders but also what appears by some measures a reduction not only of their independence in their own organization and publications but even in their overt and formal healing role. In Samoa, when we were isolated as a missionary couple, Charlotte assisted me in administering to the sick. The official church handbook, Elder John A. Widtsoe's *Priesthood and Church Government*, quoted Joseph Smith as an authority that such a procedure was proper.[3] And of course many frontier women, like Eliza R. Snow and Patty Sessions, had healed by laying on hands. They spoke and sang in tongues and, up to the 1940s, administered a special ritual blessing to pregnant women.[4]

Charlotte no longer gives blessings with me. We are obedient to what seems to be an official withdrawal of the gift that LDS women once enjoyed to be formal healers. LDS women of course continue to bless each other in the temple ordinances and otherwise act as informal healers and peacemakers. In fact they bear for us all the central ideals and qualities of the healing arts, both symbolically and literally, and that function *must* not be lost in any backlash against women, in or out of the church.

Let me explain what I mean by that apparently sexist claim that women have a special healing role. French anthropologist René Girard has provided the most convincing theory about how violence and hatred begin in all cultures and relationships, how it perpetuates itself and spreads like a plague, and how cultures survive by ritualizing violence in duels and executions and football games and by focusing their violence on individuals or groups or even animals as scapegoats. He explains how cultures continue to harbor the plague of violence because they don't face the violence in themselves or go about healing it.[5]

Girard provides convincing analysis of a mechanism familiar to us all: Any two beings with desires inevitably focus on the same things—a toy, a piece of land, the highest office, global prestige, or academic honor. The intensity of each rival's desires increases out of envy—simply because the other desires the same thing. In the process, the two rivals become more and more like each other in their actions and emotions, literal doubles, imitative of each other in what they want and the violence they are willing to use—until there is all-out war or a scapegoat is found on which to discharge the violence, a process which only hides the violence for awhile until it breaks out again. Every childhood quarrel, if you'll think back to your siblings or cousins or playground friends, goes through this process—and so does every war in history. Imitative desire or jealousy leads to an offense which must be answered in the name of justice, often with additional blows or degrees of force for good measure to make certain justice is done, then reciprocation, revenge, again with added force in the name of justice. Meanwhile, the antagonists all adopt the same evil means, no matter who was most "right" at first or most self-righteously accuses the other of being evil.

For instance, by the end of World War II first the British and then the United States adopted high-level saturation bombing of civilian populations, though we had condemned this practice as evil and barbaric when the Germans used it earlier. Such imitative escalation culminated in the killing of hundreds of thousands at Hamburg and Dresden, and then at Hiroshima and Nagasaki in wholesale destruction that LDS apostle J. Reuben Clark called the "crowning savagery of the war."[6]

This mechanism of imitative rivalry and escalating violence seems inevitable. Yet Girard's study led him to a remarkable conclusion: There is one and only one successful way to stop it, and that is through the example and teachings of Jesus Christ. Girard, who was agnostic, came to believe the Bible is the truest book in the world, in fact divine. It alone reveals, rather than suppressing in rituals or scapegoats, the violence inherent in all humans—and it gives a solution: It shows God struggling against the universal violence mechanism through his chosen people and his divine son. God fails to make much headway throughout the Old Testament, much of which therefore is a record of human violence, even by the chosen people, and of human attempts to blame their violence on God. However, in the story of Joseph extending mercy and forgiveness to his brothers who sold him into Egypt, in the suffering servant passages (such as Isa. 53), and in other breakthroughs of the voice of God to prophets, and culminating in the life, teachings, and death of Christ, we have gradually been given the answer, which is simple to say but not at all simple to really believe and apply.[7]

The answer is contained in the Sermon on the Mount, which teaches the ethical solution; in Christ's maledictions against the Pharisees (Matt. 23:13-29), which required the Jews to recognize the violence in themselves—that they have always killed the prophets who bring the message of peace and will kill him also; and supremely and finally in Christ's death. Christ does *not* die as a traditional, guilty scapegoat, who *hides* the sins and violence of the community. Rather, Christ insists on being recognized as an innocent victim, a sacrifice whose perfect forgiving love clearly *reveals* the cost of our violence and the only way to stop it. He lived out his teachings and sealed his testimony with the divine authority of his perfectly innocent blood.

The teachings are crystal clear: "Love your enemies, bless them that curse you, do good to them that hate you, and pray for them which despitefully use you and persecute you; That ye may be the children of your Father which is in heaven" (Matt. 5:44-45); "Do good, and lend, hoping for nothing again; and your reward shall be great, and ye shall be the children of the Highest: for he is kind unto the unthankful and to the evil. Be ye therefore merciful, as your Father also is merciful" (Luke 6:35-36); "Resist not evil" (Matthew 5:39); "Be not overcome of evil, but overcome evil with good" (Rom. 12:21).

The Book of Mormon reinforces, as Hugh Nibley has pointed out, the crucial understanding that conflict, including war, occurs only when both sides have sinned.[8] When either side is willing to obey

Christ's commands, to lay down their weapons or angry words and stop fighting or competing, even if they thus sacrifice their lives, as Christ did, they stop the violence. And they sometimes even convert their enemies, as the great pacifist martyrs, the People of Ammon did (Alma 24:17-26).

Modern prophets have reinforced this answer. LDS president Spencer W. Kimball chose June 1976, during the height of the United States's self-congratulatory celebration of its bicentennial, to remind all Americans, including Mormons, of the violence in ourselves:

> We are a warlike people, easily distracted from our assign-ment of preparing for the coming of the Lord. When enemies rise up, we commit vast resources to the fabrication of gods of stone and steel—ships, planes, missiles, fortifications—and depend on them for protection and deliverance. When threatened we become anti-enemy instead of pro-kingdom of God.[9]

He then called on all of us to do the only thing that has ever brought peace: "to carry the Gospel to our enemies, that they will no longer be our enemies." President Kimball, of course, did not mean simply to send missionaries to countries like Russia or China, but to proclaim in all we say and do the gospel, the Good News that healed the Samoan convert Charlotte and I taught—that God loves us all un-conditionally and expects us to do the same. We are to take the gospel to our enemies by *acting* like Christians, by working for and showing consistent mercy.

Christ taught, "Blessed are the merciful: for they shall *obtain* mercy" (Matt. 5:7; my emphasis). I understand that to mean not only that our giving mercy will make it possible for God to give us mercy, but that extending mercy is the *only* hope we have for moving our enemies to give *us* mercy rather than responding to our violence with retribution until we have continuing and escalating war.

Modern prophets have reminded us not only of the *answer* to vio-lence but also of that mechanism Girard analyzes, by which escalating violence is unleashed. Hear the First Presidency of the LDS church in 1942, at the beginning of World War II: "There is an eternal law that rules war and those who engage in it. . . . The Savior laid down a universal principle [all they that take the sword shall perish with the sword] upon which He placed no limitations as to time, place, cause, or people involved [whether righteous or wicked]. . . . This is a universal law, for force always begets force."[10] Remember when the United States bombed Libyan leader Muammar Gadhafi's capital city in 1986, killing perhaps forty people, many civilians. That action, we claimed, was justified based on evidence that Libyans had killed five Americans in terrorist bombings in Europe—which was probably a response to our siding with Israel in its occupation of Arab lands. Though our government bragged that our raid on Libya had stopped Libyan violence, in 1992 evidence came to light that the airliner downed over Lockerbie, Scotland, in 1988, killing more than 250 people, was destroyed by a Libyan bomb. Our leaders then began talking about how we might achieve a "just" revenge. We had already gone from five Americans killed to forty Libyans killed to 250 people randomly killed. Force had not settled anything but had begotten even greater force.

Why is it so hard for us to learn what Tom Sutherland, one of the American hostages finally freed in Beirut, understood? In an interview in December 1991 on National Public Radio, he was asked how he felt about the call by some other former hostages for revenge and about government efforts to glean from the hostages information about their captors that would help achieve that. He responded, "I disagree totally with those who want to punish hostage-takers. Revenge or retribution of any kind is wrong." His wife, Jane, added, "We have prayed and worked for years for this resolution, an unconditional release. When people in the Middle East have been saying, 'You've done this to me and I've done this to you,' and this has been going on for thousands of years, it's time to just break it and stop!" Amen.

Girard claims that, next to the Bible, the clearest revelations of the violence mechanism are in the writings of William Shakespeare and Fyodor Dostoevsky. Think of how often Shakespeare shows rivals becoming antagonists and then becoming more and more alike and more violent, from the twins in the *Comedy of Errors* to Iago and Othello to Hamlet and his uncle to the Trojans and Greeks in *Troilus and Cressida*. My own careful study of Shakespeare convinces me Girard is right.

Most of Shakespeare's plays are concerned to show that revenge, in the name of justice, is always tempting, seems morally justified to the avenger and the audience, and always escalates in self-righteous violence. The revengers become more like their targets, though each first saw that target as a thoroughly evil perpetrator of crime. In the end, in the name of righteous justice, the revenger inevitably loads the stage with corpses. And the violence does not stop at that point but merely continues into the next generation in cycles of reciprocal revenge.

Shakespeare also knew how hard it is even for rational and religious people to stop this cycle. He developed a dramatic device of shaming his audiences into a change of heart—what might be called the "bandwagon effect." He portrays a wrong being done by some despicable character whom we in the audience love to hate and enjoy seeing get his comeuppance. As the victims and their friends begin to take revenge, say on the self-righteous prig Malvolio in *Twelfth Night* or the blood-thirsty Shylock in *The Merchant of Venice*, we cheer them on. We get on the bandwagon of "justified" revenge. However, a point comes when a sensitive, moral member of the audience feels that things have gone too far, that the revenge spirit has exceeded all possible justice, has perhaps inevitably done much more harm than good. We want to get off the bandwagon and wish we never had gotten on. Shakespeare's drama moves us to *feel*, not just understand, what it is like to approve violence—and to be ashamed that we have approved it. That point comes in *Twelfth Night* when Malvolio is put in a dungeon by the jovial mob of tricksters and begins to go mad. It comes in *The Merchant of Venice* at least by the time Shylock is forced to become a Christian. It should come in *Hamlet* by the time Hamlet refuses to kill the king at his prayers—because he realizes that if he does Claudius's soul will go to heaven! Hamlet delays not out of mercy or indecision but in what Elizabethan audiences would recognize as a blasphemous desire to destroy Claudius's soul as well as his life, by waiting to kill him when he is sinning. That was what the ghost of Hamlet's father had said was the most horrible thing Claudius had done to *him*, killed him in his sins before he could repent. So Hamlet becomes like his uncle, just as evil, just as poisonous and dangerous and soul-destroying.

But Hamlet also has a greater and more complex soul than

Claudius, and he has a moment of turning back that is crucial to our understanding of the role of women in healing I mentioned earlier. Near the end of the play, Hamlet confronts Laertes, whose father he has killed and whose sister Ophelia, whom he supposedly loved, he has destroyed in his obsession with revenge. For the first time Hamlet sees, as he struggles with Laertes at Ophelias's burial, exactly what he has himself become—a rash, bloody revenger in the name of justice, ranting and wrestling in an open grave and trailing death and hell in his wake. As a result of this insight I believe, in the next scene Hamlet says to Horatio, "I have a [mis]giving, as would perhaps trouble a woman. . . . —the readiness is all. . . . let be" (*Hamlet*, 5.2.215-24). "Be" is exactly the right word. Hamlet here experiences what men have, to their injury, relegated to the feminine and accordingly devalued in Western culture—that is, mercy, compassion, patience, a willingness to *be*. As he earlier states clearly in his famous soliloquy, "To be, or not to be" (3.1.57), he has struggled to determine whether it is nobler to "suffer / The slings and arrows of outrageous fortune," that is, to patiently accept God's world, to live in mercy (which is what, by direct grammatical parallel, Shakespeare is saying it means "to be") or on the other hand "to take arms against a sea of troubles, and by opposing, end them," that is, to take revenge in the spirit of justice and likely be justly killed—and thus *not* to be. The question whether to be or not to be is exactly the fundamental religious and moral question whether to live by "womanly" mercy or to die by "manly" revenge. Often, in *Hamlet*, men disclaim their tears as "women's weapons" and take heart that after weeping "the woman will be out," so then they can proceed with male honor to revenge.

In his speech about a "misgiving," Hamlet, for a moment, lets the woman in him turn him back, but it is too late: The mechanism of violence he has unleashed by killing Polonius and threatening Claudius soon catches him up again into the revenge spirit in the bloody ending of the play.

Shakespeare knew that the only solution to the revenge mechanism did in fact lie with "the woman" in us—or literally with women in Western culture, who have been left relatively free from the male cycles of violence and continuing war. For this reason Shakespeare's great healers are almost all women, true to our Western cultural symbolization of healing qualities as feminine. In *King Lear* Cordelia heals her sinful, proud, rash father, Lear, though he cruelly casts her off, by persisting in unconditional love for him. And Shakespeare makes the only ultimate source of healing perfectly clear. At one point Cordelia says, "O dear father,/ It is thy business that I go about" (*King Lear*, 4.3.22-3), invoking clearly in the audience's mind the young Christ in the temple. Later a gentleman says to Lear, as he runs away, "Thou hast one daughter/ Who redeems all nature from the general curse/ Which twain have brought her to" (4.4.53-55), which not only suggests the two evil sisters and Cordelia but also Adam and Eve and Christ and therefore unmistakably shows Cordelia's parallel to Christ as a healer. And Paulina, in *The Winter's Tale*, is given a unique Christian name in a Greek setting, one that invokes directly the *Pauline* Christian way of salvation. Paulina heals a sinful, violent man until he can participate in a stunning "resurrection" onstage of his supposedly dead wife.

Shakespeare's healers have much to teach us. Like Christ, they not only love but speak *the truth* in love. Cordelia refuses to play her father's public game of getting his daughters to flatter him for their inheritances; she is thus able to reveal to him his fundamental sin of equating love with quantity and *quid pro quo*—that is, with *justice* in some form. Her sharp refusal unleashes storms of guilt and madness in Lear that are finally healed only by her persistent mercy. Likewise, Paulina's tough accusations force the king in *The Winter's Tale*, Leontes, to face the harm his violent jealousy has done and to engage in a sixteen-year penance—until he is ready, and willing, to accept mercy. Shakespeare knew the final barrier to healing and peace: the shame that sinners feel because of the barbs of truth and justice. Lear, for instance, physically runs away from Cordelia's efforts to save him from her sisters' cruelty and his own madness because "a sovereign shame so elbows him: his own unkindness . . . these things sting his mind so venomously" (*King Lear*, 4.3.42-6). Only absolute mercy, eventually only the infinite mercy of Christ, has the power to break through the bands, the shame, of that sense of justice so we can be healed.

Clearly the art of healing involves helping someone through a painful process of both facing the truth and taking on new constructs, new ways of thinking and being. The 1991 winner of the Nobel Peace Prize was Aung San Suu Kyi, the non-violent leader of Burma's democratic opposition movement. Until recently under permanent house arrest, she once led a protest past kneeling soldiers aiming directly at her and was saved by a last-minute cease-fire. The military junta offered to let her leave the country if she would stay out of politics, but she refused. Remaining totally isolated, she apparently sells her belongings to pay bills. She has likened her dream, her vision of being a peacemaker, to a traditional Burmese poem: "Emerald cool we may be/ As water in cupped hands/ But oh that we might be/ As splinters of glass/ In cupped hands."[11]

"Splinters of glass" sounds like an image of violence, but I believe it captures one crucial element of the non-violent healing process that leads to genuine peace. Martin Luther King was often accused of inciting violence, but his disciplined non-violent direct action cast a spotlight on racial violence and provoked our consciences toward healing racism enough to prevent a terrible civil war that could easily have exploded.

Similarly the Mormon independent sector and non-Mormon press have been accused of opening wounds and inciting harsh and even violent antagonism through publishing information and opinions about people and issues we would rather not face. Indeed, when the September 1991 *Sunstone* appeared, detailing Elder Paul H. Dunn's embellishments of his famous war and baseball stories, I was offended. I have known Elder Dunn for many years and respect and love him as a kind and generous man and a moderate and sane theologian, and I wondered if he couldn't be spared all this. But as I read the extremely thorough and balanced package that the editors had put together, including Elder Dunn's own interview with the press and essays by William A. Wilson and Richard Poll which placed the matter of "improving on stories" in a traditional effective storytelling context, I changed my mind. Thinking this through could be—and was for me—a painful yet healing process. It has helped me be both more careful and more forgiving. On October 26, 1991, shortly after the *Sunstone* issue, Elder Dunn published a letter of apology in the *LDS Church News*, and I realized again how healing a simple admission and apology can be. I have seen evidence that the healing has multiplied throughout the church as many who before were angry have responded to Elder Dunn with mercy and increased love.

Besides requiring sharp truth, healing requires change. Shakespeare knew well a Renaissance tradition of healing the *soul* as well as the body, based on helping people imagine new possibilities for themselves. Therapists urged patients to try on new constructs, inventing dramas for them to literally or imaginatively participate in. For instance, Andre Du Laurens, in 1599, published a book on "Melancholike Diseases" that tells of various ruses therapists used to cure patients' delusions. One case tells of a man who was dying because he would not urinate for fear "all his towne would be drowned."[12] Rational arguments failed, but finally the physicians set a neighboring house on fire and had the town officials come in and plead with the man to urinate upon the fire, which he did—and thus was healed of his delusion. Other medical books of the time, which Shakespeare obviously knew, indicate this kind of therapeutic device was not only a common and accepted part of the healing tradition but that there was a theory to explain it. William Vaughan, in *Approved Directions for Health, both Naturall and Artificiall* (first published in 1604), clarifies the theory:

> Wherein consists the cure of the spiritual maladies? . . . The Physitian . . . must invent and devise some spiritual pageant to fortify and help the imaginative facultie, which is corrupted and depraved; yea, he must endeavor to deceive and imprint another conceit, whether it be wise or foolish, in the Patients braine, thereby to put out all former phantasies.[13]

Shakespeare's plays are full of such "spiritual pageants," plays within plays that various healers design to help cure their patients' souls. I think that Shakespeare saw his own plays themselves as spiritual pageants, designed to imprint new conceits upon the imaginations of audiences and thus cure their spiritual maladies. He was especially concerned about how to heal the spirit of revenge, the willingness to do harm in the name of justice, which I believe he saw as our chief human evil, the one that led to all the others, including sexism. I think he not only wanted us to see how Cordelia and Paulina heal sinful and vio-

lent men through telling them the truth and loving them unconditionally, even sacrificially; I think he wanted us, in Gloucester's words, to
"*see it feelingly*" (*King Lear*, 4.6.149), so that *we* would be healed as well.

How then can we be healers? One way is to create and repeat stories, dramas of the imagination, that enable us to imagine new possibilities for ourselves. Levi Peterson, one of our finest Mormon story-
tellers, does this. Rather than preaching, he tells us stories that drama-
tize the consequences of believing in a harsh God as opposed to a God
of tender mercy.

From such stories we can learn about *imaginative* mercy. Some
years ago I saw the results of a *failure* to be imaginative. A bright, young
state department official, on a visit back to BYU, was telling me, with
some pride, how he had been selected to be part of a two-hour session
held before the Reagan-Gorbachev Summit in Iceland to plan strate-
gies for Reagan. My friend related how the group discussed various bar-
gaining gambits for Reagan to use to get some small advantage or even
trick Gorbachev into a disadvantage. I finally asked my friend if anyone, during those two hours, had suggested a way our two nations
might *cooperate*. Had anyone suggested a unilateral offer that might reduce tensions, some act of pure mercy in hopes of a similar response?
With surprise and then remorse, he said no to both questions.

Girard has given us a theory for what the scriptures and modern
prophets say plainly: force, even "righteous," justified force, almost always begets force; mercy at least sometimes begets mercy. Shakespeare has dramatized the consequences of revenge, of any kind of adversarial undertaking, even in the name of "justice," and shows us how
to heal by telling the truth in love and by being inventive, creating new
imaginative constructs, rather than being confrontive and adversarial.
For instance, I thought, even before President Gordon B. Hinckley's
advice against them in the fall of 1991, that public prayers to Mother in
Heaven tended to be taken—and perhaps offered—as political statements rather than as a means of uniting believers in worship. But what
a wonderful alternative, an imaginative new construct, that Carol Lynn
Pearson reports a Relief Society president in California practices. She
prays, sometimes even publicly, to Heavenly Father *about* Heavenly

Mother, expressing love to her through him and asking for more knowledge about her. Certainly no one could be offended, and I believe her prayers will be answered. Such imaginative devices, developed through inspiration and the merciful spirit of peace, can help heal us and bring peace in this difficult time.

There are other practical means. We can *all* try to practice, even when others do not, the fundamental counsel of the scriptures for handling differences or perceived offenses: Go to thy brother or sister alone and talk it through, in prayer, in love, with a song, with apologies, with whatever it takes. This means we do not write to higher authority or go to the press with adversarial, escalating responses. We work it out, between each other and in a spirit of mercy. In church circles of all places we should be able to confront each other truthfully and kindly.

But we must be *willing*. Kenneth Godfrey, a fine Mormon historian and Seminaries and Institutes area supervisor in northern Utah, relates that when he was about five he would walk out each night to meet his father, who drove a school bus and had to park it a mile from their home, which was on a small farm. One night, just as Ken ran the last few yards to his father's arms, a large high school senior came up out of hiding in the weeds near the road and started calling Ken's father names. He had kicked the young man off the bus that evening for causing trouble, and now he was intent on revenge. He threatened Ken's father, who first held him down and tried to talk quietly and quell his anger, but then let him up. Suddenly the boy hit him in the face. Ken remembers how terrified he was and then how amazed when his father simply stood and let himself be hit in the face again before the boy turned and ran away. He remembers his dad, with the blood drying on his face, taking him by the hand and walking home. He remembers hearing for a long time the gossip that spread through town about his father's cowardice, and he remembers feeling ashamed for him. For years, as he passed the house where the boy lived after he married, he felt helpless rage, hoping that some day he could grow large and strong enough to avenge his father, but he never did.

When Ken was a high school senior himself, eating in a cafe with his date after a dance, the man who had hit his father long before came into the cafe drunk. He went to Ken's booth and sat by him and began to cry. "Your father gave me the worst beating of my life twelve years ago," he said, "and some day, when I am sober, I am going to be man enough to tell him how sorry I am for what I did and ask him to forgive me." However, it was Ken's father, ten years after that, when he was called as a patriarch and felt he could not function in his office until he had completely forgiven and been forgiven, who went to the man who had hit him, asked to be forgiven, and was reconciled.

Another fine Mormon historian told me about a similar healing person. A few years ago their stake presidents were instructed to call in the editors and some writers for *Sunstone* and *Dialogue* and talk with them about their activities. Stake presidents responded in a variety of ways, some with threats and sanctions. The historian's stake president called him on a Sunday afternoon and asked if he could visit. My friend, who himself had recently finished a term in the stake presidency, wondered if he was to receive a new call. The new stake president arrived, with his counselors—and asked him if they could give him a blessing. The stake president blessed my friend that he could continue to do his important work as a historian with integrity and skill and continue to be an asset to the church. And he has.

In the fall of 1990, shortly after attending our stake conference, I received a letter from a BYU faculty member who lives in my stake. He reminded me of the powerful spiritual presence that was in our Saturday evening session and then told of a particular impression that had come to him when he saw me there. He had felt simultaneously scolded and blessed: scolded because he had let his differences from me in doctrinal perception keep him from feeling and expressing the kind of gospel love we ought to have for each other; blessed to feel that love for me right then, along with a desire to express it and put other things in perspective. He reported to me that he first thought, "But Gene believes and teaches doctrines which I think have serious, even dangerous implications for those with tender or unsettled spiritual roots," and then felt a quick response to that thought: "That is not the issue here. The issue is love. All people have doctrinal misperceptions that will some day need correcting." He told of pondering that experience again and again and finally deciding to share it with me—"acknowledging my own inadequacies, and seeking to do what is right." I say, God give us all the courage to be as honest and pure as this dear colleague and thus to make the church a place of healing and peacemaking, not by ignoring differences or errors, but by loving and talking despite them.

Emma Lou Thayne, Mormon poet and essayist, is a constant laborer for peace who has written a book about healing and being healed.[14] Ten years ago, in *Exponent II*, she shared an example of peacemaking despite religious differences that was experienced by her friend Jan Cook:

> She and her husband were for three years in Africa, in "deepest Africa, where *The Gods Must Be Crazy* was filmed." His work had taken them and their three small children there, and any meetings attended were in their own living room with only themselves as participants. By their third Christmas, Jan was very homesick. She confessed this to a good friend, a Mennonite; Jan told her how she missed her own people, their traditions, even snow. Her friend sympathized and invited her to go with her in a month to the Christmas services being held in the only Protestant church in the area, saying that there would be a reunion there of all the Mennonite missionaries on the continent.
>
> It took some talking for Jan to persuade her husband, but there they were being swept genially to the front of the small chapel. It felt good, being in on Christmas in a church again. The minister gave a valuable sermon on Christ; the congregation sang familiar carols with great vitality. Then, at the very end of the meeting, a choir of Mennonite missionaries from all over Africa rose from their benches and made their way to stand just in front of Jan and her family. Without a word, they began singing. Without a leader, without music, without text, they sang, "Come, Come Ye Saints." Every verse.
>
> Disbelieving, totally taken by surprise, Jan and her husband drenched the fronts of their Sunday best with being carried home on Christmas. . . . When they finished, Jan's friend said simply, "For you. Our gift."
>
> Jan's Mennonite friend had sent to Salt Lake City for the music to the hymn that she knew Jan loved, had had it duplicated and distributed to every Mennonite missionary in Africa; they in

turn had learned it very carefully to bring the spirit of Christ to their own reunion where foreigners to their faith would be waiting to hear.[15]

I believe that apostles are indeed special witnesses for Christ and for his healing, peace-making mercy. One of the men who served as an apostle during my boyhood, Elder George F. Richards, bore witness about mercy in a general conference right after World War II. Many who heard him had lost sons or husbands in the war, and all had suffered in various ways and still had reason to be bitter. I remember vividly the feelings of fear and hatred that the words "Jap" and "Nazi" evoked in me as a young teenager, conditioned by the propaganda movies and newsreels during and even after the war. Elder Richards chose this time to put aside his prepared manuscript and talk instead about "Love for Mankind." He reviewed the teachings and example of Jesus Christ, "in life and in death, a voluntary gift for us, a manifestation of love that has no comparison." He professed love for all who could hear him, "in the Church or out of the Church, . . . good or bad, whatever their condition of life," and reminded his hearers that in the pre-existence we lived in love together and "ought to love one another just the same here."[16] Then he said, "The Lord has revealed to me, by dreams, something more than I ever understood or felt before." He first told of a dream from forty years earlier, in which he stood in the presence of the Savior and felt such "love for him that I have not words to explain." Then he told of a dream from just a few years previous, toward the end of the war, in which he and some of his associates were in a courtyard where German soldiers led by Adolf Hitler were preparing weapons to slaughter them. Then a circle was formed, with Hitler and his men on the inside facing inward. Elder Richards dreamed he stepped inside the circle, faced Hitler, and spoke to him "something like this":

> "I am your brother. You are my brother. In our heavenly home we lived together in love and peace. Why can we not so live here on the earth?"
> And it seemed to me that I felt in myself, welling up in my soul, a love for that man, and I could feel that he was having the same experience, and presently he arose, and we embraced each

other and kissed each other, a kiss of affection.

Then the scene changed so that our group was within the circle, and he and his group were on the outside, and when he came around to where I was standing, he stepped inside the circle and embraced me again, with a kiss of affection.

I think the Lord gave me that dream. Why should I dream of this man, one of the greatest enemies of mankind, and one of the wickedest, but that the Lord should teach me that I must love my enemies, and I must love the wicked as well as the good?

Now, who is there in this wide world that I could not love under those conditions, if I could only continue to feel as I felt then?[17]

I must confess that that is a difficult lesson for me. I feel like the older brother in Jesus' parable, who resented the returning prodigal. Hitler unleashed on our world the most extensive and penetrating horror we know about in human history, including a war that killed tens of millions and extermination camps of unimaginable degradation and suffering. I have read the diaries of those who suffered and have tried to write about them, to preserve the memory of their anguish. To think of a "kiss of affection" for Adolf Hitler brings me close to nausea.

Yet I want to believe Elder Richards, a humble apostle of the Lord Jesus Christ. I want to believe that even Hitler is my brother, that we once lived in love and peace and that through the power of mercy we can do so again. I want to believe that the very worst is redeemable, that anyone can be healed through mercy—because then I can be too.

NOTES

1. See *Improvement Era* 43 (Nov. 1942): 522.

2. All Shakespeare references are from *The Riverside Shakespeare*, ed. G. Blakemore Evans et al. (Boston: Houghton Mifflin, 1974).

3. John A. Widtsoe, *Priesthood and Church Government*, rev. ed. (Salt Lake City: Deseret Book Co., 1954), 357.

4. Linda King Newell, "Gifts of the Spirit: Women's Share," *Sisters in Spirit: Mormon Women in Historical and Cultural Perspective*, ed. Maureen Ursenbach Beecher and Lavina Fielding Anderson (Urbana: University of Illinois

Press, 1987), 111-50.

5. René Girard's main ideas can be reviewed at length in *Violence and the Sacred* (Baltimore: Johns Hopkins University Press, 1977) and *Deceit, Desire, and the Novel* (Baltimore: Johns Hopkins University Press, 1965).

6. J. Reuben Clark, "Demand for Proper Respect of Human Life," *Improvement Era*, Nov. 1946, 689.

7. For a short and accessible summary of this conviction, see Girard's "The Bible Is Not a Myth," *Literature and Belief* 4 (1984): 3-12; this was a forum address given at BYU in the fall of 1983. For a thorough analysis of the Bible as a testament against violence, see Girard's *Things Hidden since the Foundation of the World* (Stanford, CA: Stanford University Press, 1987).

8. Nibley develops this insight most thoroughly in chapter 12 ("Good People and Bad People") of *Since Cumorah* (Salt Lake City: Deseret Book Co. and FARMS, 1988), esp. 342-46. See also his "If There Must Needs Be Offense," *Ensign* 1 (July 1971): 54, and "Scriptural Perspectives on How to Survive the Calamities of the Last Days," *Brigham Young University Studies* 25 (Winter 1985): 7-27.

9. Spencer W. Kimball, "The False Gods We Worship," *Ensign* 6 (June 1976): 4.

10. The First Presidency, *One Hundred and Twelfth Annual Conference of the Church of Jesus Christ* (Salt Lake City: Deseret Book Co., 1942), 95.

11. Quoted in *Newsweek*, 28 Oct. 1991, 80.

12. Andre Du Laurens, *A Discourse of the Preservation of Sight; of Melancholike Diseases; of Rheume; and of Old Age* (London: Felix Kingston, 1599), 103.

13. William Vaughan, *Approved Directions for Health, both Naturall and Spirituall*, 4th ed. (London: T. S. for Roger Jackson, 1612), 89.

14. Emma Lou Thayne, *Things Happen: Poems of Survival* (Salt Lake City: Signature Books, 1991).

15. Emma Lou Thayne, "The Gift," *Exponent II*, Fall 1982, 6.

16. George F. Richards, *Improvement Era*, Nov. 1946, 694.

17. Ibid., 758.

two

ON SPECTRAL EVIDENCE, SCAPEGOATING, AND FALSE ACCUSATION

And then shall many be offended, and shall betray one another, and shall hate one another. . . . And because iniquity shall abound, the love of many shall wax cold.
—Matthew 24:10-12

Though I admitted in my feelings and knew all the time that Joseph [Smith] was a human being and subject to err, still it was none of my business to look after his faults. . . . It was not my prerogative to call him in question with regard to any act of his life. He was God's servant, and not mine.
—Brigham Young

October 3, 1992, the first day of the 162nd semi-annual LDS general conference, also marked the 300th anniversary of the action that finally stopped the Salem witch trials. Those trials, perhaps the greatest blot on American religious devotion, resulted in the deaths of twenty people, all of whom vigorously proclaimed their innocence to the end.

On October 3, 1692, Increase Mather ended the legalized murders of "witches" by circulating an essay, *Cases of Conscience*, in which, drawing on his authority as perhaps the most prestigious minister in New England, he unequivocally condemned the use in the trials of what was called "spectral evidence." The governor of Massachusetts, Sir William Phips, at last accepted his duty, excused the court, and annulled the warrant that had been signed for eight more deaths.

On October 3, 1992, in remembrance of what can happen when suspicion and criticism based on spectral evidence run wild—and in contrition for my own sins in that regard, I fasted and, between sessions of conference, reread Perry Miller's account of the trials and their causes.[1] I also read again Nathaniel Hawthorne's story "Young Goodman Brown," his own act of remembrance and contrition (his ancestor, John Hathorne, had been one of the Salem judges).[2] That story tells of a young Puritan in Salem who enters the devil's territory by accepting spectral evidence. It powerfully shows the loss of faith, of joy, even of life, that can follow.

"Spectral" was the term for evidence based on the commonly held Puritan doctrine that once witches covenanted with Satan they were rewarded with a servant devil, a specter, who took on their likeness and did their bidding, especially in hurting their enemies. If someone testified they had observed such a specter trying to harm someone, that constituted a fair presumption of the witch's guilt. Some seventeenth-century New England thinkers and leaders recognized the danger that a specter might well be imagined, especially by an enemy, or that Satan might himself create a counterfeit specter of an innocent person to bring damnation to their credulous accusers, or even that unusual or misunderstood actions or words could be assumed to be from a specter. But the Salem Village court, despite objections by some ministers, took the position that God's providence would not allow innocent people to be so represented and accepted testimony by their enemies that their specters had afflicted them.

Increase Mather's son Cotton, another of the colony's prestigious thinkers, had warned against spectral evidence early in the trials which began in March. On May 31 he had begged the court in a letter not to depend too much on such testimony: "It is very certain that the divells have sometimes represented the shapes of persons not only innocent, but also very virtuous." Cotton prophesied that if credit was given to such representations by the devil, "The Door is opened!" Miller comments, "Had the court heeded his recommendation, there would have been no executions; if, having made it, he had thereafter kept his mouth shut, he would be a hero today."[3]

Miller traces the tragic record of a man of insight and good heart whose fear and ambition—and especially his excessive loyalty to civil authority—led him to equivocate his earlier good counsel. Mather thus contributed to the scapegoating—for which he in turn became a major scapegoat in popular world memory. He did not, as many continue to assume, condemn or burn witches. But when Governor Phips, in the face of growing doubts, on June 15 asked the association of ministers for advice, Mather authored for them *The Return of Several Ministers*. Despite restating his rejection of spectral evidence as adequate to condemn, he ended that document by reinforcing the position that civil authority should vigorously punish those the devil has led astray. The court took that latter advice, ignoring the warning about spectral evidence, and the killings continued until Cotton's father read his emphatic essay to the ministers on October 3.

Clearer vision and greater courage by the ministers might have stopped the trials in June, before any deaths. Without their intervention, in Miller's words, "a reckless use of spectral evidence gave rein to the seething passions and festering animosities of New England. Prisons became crowded, every man's life lay at the mercy of any accuser, brother looked sidewise at brother, and the friend of many years' standing became a bad security risk."[4]

No wonder Arthur Miller was able to set in the midst of that madness his powerful drama of frenzied suspicion and imitative violence, *The Crucible*. The play was written as a parable, an indictment of the McCarthyism of the 1950s but universal in its haunting relevance to every period and place when multiplying fears during a time of great change or external threat suddenly focus irrational fears on one person or group—a scapegoat—and, on the basis of spectral evidence, people condemn, exclude, and even kill each other. It happened in Missouri when the old settlers turned on Mormons; it happened when Mormons turned on Missourians at Mountain Meadows; it happened after the Civil War when Southern whites turned on blacks; it happened to Jews in Germany and Kulaks in the Soviet Union; and such demonization continues to happen today around the world and seems to be increasing in our nation and even in the church.

As I listened to general conference and that night watched the priesthood session on satellite television at a stake center, I thought of the increasing passions and anxieties, jealousies and name-calling, low morale and scapegoating, the tide of judgments and even punishments based on spectral evidence I had seen in the church lately—mainly at Brigham Young University and along the Wasatch Front but beginning to extend elsewhere. I mean by "spectral evidence" something somewhat different than the Puritans but similar enough that the parallel is instructive: We too make judgments of other human beings based on static, partial, even merely reported images of them that we take to represent their whole beings and therefore to constitute the basis for a fair presumption of their evilness or guilt which we and others must act on. When we do so we use evidence that is as spectral and devilishly dangerous as that which condemned the Puritan "witches."

When church members write to the First Presidency complaining about an action of their bishop or a speech by a high councilor, they are, I believe, using something like spectral evidence—and the letter is rightly sent back to them. When BYU students or their parents complain to church or university leaders because they are offended by a teacher or administrator, rather than discussing the offense directly with them (or their immediate supervisor), that is also spectral evidence—and should be simply dismissed. When persons are rejected from a teaching position, or denied publication, simply because of an unusual belief or controversial reputation, they are victims of spectral evidence. When anyone is denied due process, the right to face their accusers directly—or treated in any way that disregards their rights and feelings as long-standing, proven, virtuous members of the church, they are victims of the kind of irrational fears that gripped Salem and killed some of its best people through spectral evidence. And when any of us stereotype religion teachers as being reactionary or narrow-minded or criticize, in public or in private conversations, our church or university leaders, we are guilty of using spectral evidence.

Of course, criticism and judgment are proper—even required—to carry out certain responsibilities and in the right circumstances, but they are deeply flawed and dangerous, I believe, when they do not include direct response to whole persons but are an indirect and punitive response to specters of them.

The great evil of spectral evidence, of course, even when it stops short of punishment, is that it reduces the most precious eternal beings in the universe, children of God with infinite capacity who are constantly changing, to static, partial beings. A specter can never properly represent the whole person—which is one reason we are warned not to judge and that we will be judged (that is, will judge ourselves) the same way we judge: partially. Human beings cannot be reduced to an action, a political or intellectual position, a quotation in a newspaper, an essay or story they have written. Each of those, even if clearly and fully seen (which is impossible, since we always see only partially, from a particular point of view), is still only part, a static part, of what is a constantly dynamic, complex, failing, and repenting potential god. We are never less—and actually much more because of our infinite potential—than the complete sum of our history, our stories, a sum which is constantly increasing, changing, through time.

The weekend of October 3 and 4 was a perfect Utah Indian summer. Though it cooled off to freezing at night, it was quite warm in the day, emphasizing the colors that filled the canyons and contrasted with the cool, dense blue of the sky. We have a cabin a few miles up the South Fork of Provo River, in an area of narrow canyon that angles generally southeast, leaving no large northern slopes for pines. The steep mountain walls on both sides are covered with deciduous shrubs and trees which because of the dry summer in 1992 had already dropped most of their leaves—mainly the soft reds of mountain maple and soft yellows of box elder mixed with bronze scrub oak. The masses of leaves had completely covered the hillsides and had blown down across the lawns and fields to the river: "worlds of wanwood leafmeal lie."[5] Like Hopkins, it was not for them I mourned.

Our cabin is surrounded by aspen and cottonwoods whose leaves were just turning bright gold and lime yellow. As I looked up from reading or listening to the conference radio broadcast or walked out for a few minutes, I was surrounded, from ground to sky, with golden-yellow light, heavy and falling even as it lifted me.

On Saturday, October 3, at about 5:30 p.m., when I traveled down Provo Canyon to watch the broadcast of priesthood meeting, I drove through air thick with falling motes of gold. Across from Upper Falls, where the traffic was shifted sharply from the two left lanes to the right lanes of the new freeway being built (the place where a BYU professor, Marek Kaliszewski, would be killed driving up the canyon just two weeks later), one last beam from the setting sun made the reflector strips on the center dividing lines disappear long enough that I drifted straight into the oncoming lane. I wrenched the wheel just in time to miss a car, then drove slowly, my heart pounding, to the stake center in north Provo.

As I watched what might be called the "specter" of Elder Dallin H. Oaks during the session—the electronic image of him sent out from the tabernacle through the air and projected before me, larger-than-life, on a screen—I thought of the other specters of him that I had heard at times from both liberals and conservatives, reducing him to a partial, static version of himself.

The terms "liberal" and "conservative" are themselves examples of the mischief that reliance on spectral evidence can do to a community. These terms once identified two equally ethical and valued political perspectives; they stood for the two main different, but honorable, positions from which people could seek to improve society—arguing, developing programs, compromising, voting, and then respecting each other as that process worked to provide better ideas than either position by itself could have produced. But in the last dozen years, especially the right wing of what has been my own party, the Republicans, has tried to make these labels, these specters which before were simple and rough guides to political tendencies, stand for the whole identity of people as good (conservatives) or evil (liberals). It is a great tragedy that this poisoning of the traditional political process at the national level has succeeded in my own state and religious community—and also provoked in some liberals an equal and opposite reaction, so that "conservative" becomes a term of dismissal of others as ignorant or heartless.

In current philosophical and literary jargon, to use spectral evidence is to "totalize," to accept and promote, or even to act punitively on the basis of, a specter—a real or imagined part that is made to stand for the whole—of someone who seems to be dangerous or unorthodox. It is *not* to open oneself up to the "other" as a whole person directly and continuously, critically but also receptively, in the personal give-and-take, mutual calling-to-account and forgiving, that may be the heart of eternal life. Totalizing on the basis of spectral evidence is to deny the perspective insisted on by Joseph Smith in the King Follett Discourse: "All the minds and spirits that God ever sent into the world are susceptible of enlargement and improvement."[6] It is to refuse Christ's clear instruction, "If thy brother shall trespass against thee, go and tell him his fault between thee and him alone" (Matt. 18:15), which he reemphasized in modern revelation: "If thy brother or sister offend thee, thou shalt take him or her between him or her and thee alone" (D&C 42:88).

I know this is difficult. Often when we make the supreme effort and, rather than responding in kind, go in humility to a person who has offended us and seek understanding we are still rejected. I know that many feel they have acted in good faith, opened themselves up to others—and been totalized, even betrayed. I have heard some say, "I just don't trust so-and-so any more," or, "I'm certain feminists [or conservatives or whoever], no matter what I do, will not respond to me kindly, as a whole person, so I protect myself."

I reject such counsel—even if the perception of unkindness by others that produces it is accurate. Just as it is wrong to let good ends justify evil means, so it is wrong to let failure to succeed justify bitterness. As Lowell Bennion reminds us, quoting the words of a Hindu proverb: "To action alone thou hast a right, not to its fruits"[6]—that is, we must do good whatever the response. To put it bluntly, none of us has any right to use spectral evidence, even if it seems clear that others are determined to. Especially in a religious community, trust, like Christ-like love, is to be extended not because others *deserve* it but because they *need* it, because they can *become* trustworthy (or loving) by being nurtured in a community of trust and love. We need to extend trust, even if doing so makes us vulnerable to pain and great cost, in order to save our own souls.

As I watched the image of Elder Oaks on television, I became aware of a way to get beyond the dangerous temptation to use spectral evidence—a danger I knew I had succumbed to recently in a very damaging way. I went to priesthood meeting that night, after a day of fasting, with a prayer that I might feel the confirmation of the Spirit as I listened to the Brethren. I prayed again during the songs and prayer and the opening speeches and felt some comfort and reassurance, but I felt most directly what I was seeking when Elder Oaks, departing from his usual clear, carefully reasoned, sometimes rather stern doctrinal messages, began to talk about the heroic Bible stories that had inspired him in his youth with a sense of God's care. I remembered those stories and my own youthful yearnings to be on God's side and to enjoy his acceptance and blessings.

Then Elder Oaks told of an occasion, while he lived in Chicago in the 1960s, when he was confronted by an armed young man who demanded his money and car and endangered Sister Oaks, who was locked inside the car with the keys. During a momentary diversion when a bus stopped nearby, Elder Oaks, who had his hands raised, was tempted to strike down the smaller man's arm and overpower him, but he had a clear impression from the Spirit that he should not—in fact, he was given a vision of what would happen in the struggle: he would accidentally kill the man. He obeyed the Spirit, put his hand on the young man's shoulder and talked to him, so that he was dissuaded and turned and ran away.[7]

Hearing this full story, opening myself to the whole person, and being unusually open to the wholesome and completing power of the Spirit, I could not see Elder Oaks as any of his specters. I saw him as a human being, one I could privately and humbly disagree with at times but openly love and respect and submit myself to. I saw him as an apostle, called by God as a special witness of Jesus Christ and an authority over God's church, to which I belong by covenant, a person I should obey and not criticize.

Hugh Nibley, in a discourse called "Criticizing the Brethren," talked about the shift in perspective that would allow one to say what I have just said. He told about being assigned as a young faculty member in the 1950s to accompany Elder Spencer W. Kimball to a stake conference to recruit students for BYU. As their train made a stop in Los Angeles, Nibley, who knew the bookstores near the old Los Angeles station, hopped off, bought a rare ten-volume set of books, and barely made it back to the train by running across a vacant lot:

> As we sat talking about the books, Brother Kimball casually took an immaculate linen handkerchief from the breast pocket of his jacket, and, stooping over, vigorously dusted off my shoes and trousers. It was the most natural thing in the world, and we both took it completely for granted. . . . but ever since, that has conditioned my attitude toward the Brethren. I truly believe that they are chosen servants of God.[8]

My own experience that produced a similar life-long conviction was in some ways more dramatic, but it has been reconfirmed a number of times by simple human experiences like Brother Nibley's. When I was twelve, our family moved from Downey, in southeast Idaho, where we continued to raise dryland wheat, to live the winter months in Salt Lake City. My father was called during that first year to serve on the high council of the new Hillside Stake, formed from the Sugarhouse Stake. During the Sunday session of the first conference of the new stake, on March 24, 1946, when my father was being sustained, I sat on the front row of the chapel in the old Wasatch Ward on Emerson Avenue, with my younger sister and mother right behind me.

The visiting authority was Elder Harold B. Lee, a young apostle called five years before. During his address, when I was leaning back over the pew to tease my sister, I felt something throughout my body that was forceful enough to turn me around to look up at Elder Lee, perhaps ten feet away. After the meeting I learned from my parents that he had suddenly interrupted his speech and had begun to give the congregation an apostolic blessing. I don't remember what he said but the feeling was like a burning deep inside me but also sweet like honey—and an idea was connected with that feeling: that he was a person called of God as an apostle of the Lord Jesus Christ, one of a body of such persons appointed to direct Christ's church. That feeling and idea have sometimes waned and waxed a bit over the years since, but they remain grounded in the deepest part of me, the part that I recognize as my eternal intelligence and the awareness of which is more real to me than anything else.

In late September 1992 our family celebrated the sixtieth wedding anniversary of my parents, who were living with my sister in Smithfield, Utah. We children, grandchildren, and assorted spouses met for dinner at the marvelously preserved old Bluebird Restaurant in Logan. We had a short program honoring my parents, and then my mother stood and, with remarkable energy, given her declining health and 83 years, bore her testimony to her family. She told of feeling directly guided by the Spirit as she led the women's auxiliaries when my father was president of the North Central States Mission, of being healed from illness by the power of the priesthood, so immediately that she could feel the illness move out of her body through her arms and legs. And she told, the first time I could remember her mentioning it since it happened, about the feeling she had had in that meeting with Elder Lee, how everyone she talked to had felt it with us, that it had been like a day of Pentecost to the people of the stake.

What did that day mean to me? A fundamental shift in the way I saw my relationship to the church. Since then I have no anxiety that the leaders would lead the church astray, have felt no need to set them straight. I have had no reason to think them infallible and plenty of reason, including the frank admissions of some, to know they make mistakes. But I have not felt it my business to correct or to criticize them. I have felt about them as Brigham Young felt about Joseph Smith:

> Though I admitted in my feelings and knew all the time that Joseph was a human being and subject to err, still it was none of my business to look after his faults. . . . It was not for me to question whether Joseph was dictated by the Lord at all times and under all circumstances. . . . It was not my prerogative to call him in question with regard to any act of his life. He was God's servant, and not mine.[9]

I believe that the apostles are called by God to be special witnesses of Christ and to bear testimony that is potentially saving to all the world—including me—and, as prophets, seers, and revelators, to proclaim the official doctrines and policies of the church. This means that as long as I claim to be part of the church I obey them—and that I am anxiously engaged in the work of the church they direct and in bearing my own testimony of Christ and his restored gospel wherever and however I can.

My calling is to be a teacher and writer, to use my gifts to seek and promote truth and virtue, and to build up the Kingdom of God (including the one that Jesus said was within each of us) with all my means. What happens, then, if I am asked by the Brethren to believe something or do something I think is wrong, even after careful thought and prayer? If the matter in question is a policy about church procedure and I am not obliged to do or say anything that in itself violates my integrity, I can quietly obey and wait for further understanding.

Certainly it is possible for an individual among the Brethren to ask me to do or believe something I simply could not, at least in good conscience. As Elder Boyd K. Packer explained in a devotional address at BYU in 1991, safety lies in the motto, "'Follow the *Brethren*,' not 'Follow the *Brother*.'"[10] He told how the presiding councils go to great effort to make certain they function that way, how he as a BYU trustee had been careful to observe that principle, and testified, "If ever another course has been followed, trouble has followed as surely as night follows day."[11]

It is not always easy for us who are not in the presiding councils to distinguish between the Brother and the Brethren, so I have come, through careful study and prayer and trial, to the following approach: I am bound by my beliefs to be attentive and receptive to everything any of the Brothers says—to listen charitably and invite the Spirit to confirm, to be fundamentally believing and submissive. I am bound by covenant to obey the official directions of the president, the First Presidency, and the Quorum of the Twelve—and to obey according to the best understanding that plain sense and the confirmation of the Spirit can give me *and not according to the interpretation or claimed understanding of any other person than those who give the direction.*

This is not simple or easy. It requires constant attention and response. It exacts the costs of discipleship—sacrifice, discipline, sometimes humiliation—and it means that I must daily risk my salvation as I choose to follow the Brethren's ethical and spiritual leadership. To do this authentically, in good faith, I must constantly renew that faith at its source: my deepest feelings and sense of knowing that come from my full life experience and thought and spiritual confirmations. I must constantly try to be true to *both* kinds of integrity: (1) my convictions based on careful thought and carefully considered experience—both worldly and spiritual—and (2) my convictions about the principles, covenants, and authority in Christ's church that I have accepted on the basis of such thought, experience and witness. I cannot shift that responsibility to any person or authority or dogma—nor can I avoid the consequences for my integrity of not being true to covenants I have made and authority I have accepted in good faith. Finally, I must constantly test and renew these covenants and convictions as Paul directed and Joseph Smith exemplified: "Prove all things; hold fast that which is good" (1 Thess. 5:21).

One of the most troubled times of my life came about when I failed to make the distinction between Brother and Brethren. In 1979, as associate director of the Honors Program at BYU, I gave a talk to honors students on the LDS ideal of continuing, life-long education in which I used, among other examples, the doctrine of eternal progression in knowledge. I mentioned that one of the reasons our ideal of becoming like God is so attractive is that if we do we will be able to experience the joy of learning forever—as he does. I had been taught that doctrine all my life and believed it to be perfectly orthodox—in fact, in my research for my talk I had located many references by Brigham Young and other church leaders that also exulted in the doctrine.

In the summer of 1980 Elder Bruce R. McConkie gave an address at BYU entitled "The Seven Deadly Heresies" in which he ranked the belief that God is progressing in knowledge as heresy number one.[12] I was surprised and confused, as were a number of students who came to me pointing out the discrepancy between his view and those of various prophets. I studied the matter carefully and found that there were other leaders besides Elder McConkie, including Hyrum Smith and Joseph Fielding Smith, who had expressed the belief that God is absolute, perfect, and not progressing.

I also found that Brigham Young and B. H. Roberts had developed a concept that could explain such an apparent contradiction: God is perfect in relation to our mortal sphere, has all knowledge regarding it, but is learning and progressing in spheres beyond ours that have nothing to do with ours—thus not endangering in any way his perfect redemptive plan and power in *our* sphere. It thus was possible to talk of God as perfect and unchanging when praising him in regard to us and our sphere—or to speak of him as developing and enjoying new ideas and experiences in spheres beyond ours—and to be right and orthodox in both cases.

I wrote Elder McConkie explaining all this and how it had helped me resolve students' anxieties about seemingly contradictory teachings by the prophets. In the meantime I left for London on a term abroad program for BYU. I heard nothing for six months, when I received a phone call from a friend from Provo asking if a letter being circulated, purportedly from Elder McConkie to me, was authentic. I was shocked as my friend read the letter to me and could not confirm it as genuine until weeks later when the original arrived in England by surface mail. The letter rejected my position and the sources I had cited and instructed me not to speak or write about the subject again. I wrote back saying I would comply.

Unfortunately, a copy of Elder McConkie's letter had somehow been taken from his office or circulated by someone he may have sent a copy to, and it was reproduced by anti-Mormons and became widely read. I was deeply embarrassed and concerned about the damage it might do, but I did not criticize Elder McConkie and I objected when others did so in my presence. I listened carefully to his speeches and opened my heart to believe all I could that he taught, and I was careful to be obedient to my promise not to teach a progressing God. I was especially moved, along with many others, by his very personal and humble testimony of Jesus Christ in his last address, in April 1985 general conference.

But I hurt inside, a hurt which increased after Elder McConkie's death until I spent some time considering that nagging pain and concluded that I had violated my integrity in agreeing so readily to obey, against my convictions, a single Brother rather than the Brethren in so important a matter. I knew the First Presidency and Quorum of the Twelve, in one of their very first joint statements, August 23, 1865, had denounced the idea that God is *not* progressing in knowledge as heresy,[13] and no subsequent official statement had reversed that position.

It was not my prerogative to publicly challenge or oppose Elder McConkie's ideas, especially while he was serving as an apostle. But neither did it any longer seem right for me to remain silent about what I understood to be an important and official teaching of the Restoration affecting the education of my students. So in 1989, four years after Elder McConkie's death, I published an essay in *Brigham Young University Studies*, exploring as objectively as possible two complementary ways of talking about God—as perfect and as progressing. (See the following essay in this book.)

An even more painful experience occurred in the summer of 1992. This time I felt the pain both of being a victim of spectral evidence and of using it myself—and found myself, though unaware of it at the time, actually criticizing the Brethren. If I had thought a little more calmly at that time, I would have recognized the universal and almost irresistible tendency, when a variety of tensions and mutual offenses are growing like a plague, for all the fear and anxiety suddenly to focus on a scapegoat.

During my anger in August I should have remembered what I reread on October 3—Perry Miller's description of what led up to the witch trials: the growing anxieties of Puritans about their children, who had not had the original conversion experience of the founders; increasing concerns about changing political conditions as their original charter was revoked after the return of Catholic Royalists to power in England; and the increasing worry of the ministers that the community had "abysmally degenerated." Miller describes Cotton Mather's attempt to explain what had happened:

> There is something both appealing and repulsive in Cotton's frantic clutching at the old array of sins in order to explain this affliction, at those village vices so long since arraigned: back-biting, scandal-mongering, talebearing, suits-at-law—precisely that cave of winds into which anthropologists of today would search for "causes" of the saturnalia that overwhelmed Salem Village.[14]

This seems to me to describe my own community in the past few years, at least along the Wasatch Front: people accusing others of being

Korihors or traitors or Nazis, rumors of persecution flying throughout the Mormon intellectual community, people denied positions or opportunities on spectral evidence, and back-biting concerning the Brethren. I am ashamed that into this cave of winds I boldly and angrily stepped and committed a gross error based purely on spectral evidence.

It happened this way: Lavina Fielding Anderson gave a presentation at the August 1992 Sunstone Symposium on how we might go about healing the breach that seemed to be growing between church authorities and Mormon intellectuals and feminists. My anxiety and pain increased during her catalogue of events I knew about and in which I knew people had been badly hurt, hurt at the heart of their faith, and I suddenly became convinced that the Strengthening Church Members Committee (which I had recently heard about from a BYU administrator) was behind most of those events. My general hurt and fear focused in anger, and during the question-and-answer period I accused the committee of undermining the church and invited the audience to use their influence to stop it.

I had in mind that people would write to church leaders they knew and that thus the committee, which I assumed was ad hoc and mid-management, would be quietly discontinued. But in my heart was also a desire to punish, and the powers of darkness were glad to oblige—that is, the natural laws of reciprocal violence that are always unleashed by growing, unresolved animosities based on spectral evidence and by the scapegoating that suddenly focuses that growing plague. Television cameras captured and replayed the scene on the news; an Associated Press reporter went right out, called the church spokesman, and got a confirmation of the existence of the committee and some of its activities in question, which was reported nationwide.

Meanwhile I went home to Provo in a welter of emotions (still angry, sometimes glad, even a bit self-righteous about speaking out, but then doubtful, increasingly aware that I had violated the principle that offenses should be dealt with personally and privately). As the publicity continued, much of it negative, I felt much anguish; I remembered a comment to me the night after the *Sunstone* session from one in the audience who may have been alluding to my recent book, *The Quality of*

Mercy: "Well that was brave, but it wasn't very merciful." Indeed, I felt like a hypocrite, and when I learned from the First Presidency statement the next week that the committee consisted of two apostles, James E. Faust and Russell M. Nelson, I felt despair that I had, however unwittingly, criticized them and possibly invited others to do so. I immediately wrote an apology to them, at the same time doing what I should have done before if I had been patient enough to find out how: I told them directly and personally what concerned me about the committee's actions as I now understood them, of the hurt I felt those actions had caused me and others I knew.

On October 3 I read again not only Perry Miller's account of the witch trials but also Hawthorne's "Young Goodman Brown," the best piece of American literature I know for conveying what it feels like to be, not a victim, but a *victimizer* through spectral evidence. I identified closely with that brash young Salem Village Puritan, newly married and thus required by law to be a newly covenanted member of his religious community, who adventures forth into the forest to test his faith against the devil. The devil turns out to look much like his father—and thus like himself! He accepts the devil's spectral evidence that all others in the community, including his wife, are given over to evil, are even participants with him in a witches' Sabbath, and returns to a life of gloom—having lost faith, hope, and charity. Goodman Brown makes the same mistake that the Salem court made; he judges people and defines his own life on the basis of what are merely specters, probably illusions from the devil.

Hawthorne creates a clear sense that the devil can be a projection of ourselves, our deepest fears and animosities, and that as we move into his territory and accept his evidence, he is able to tell truths in order to convey lies that besmirch the character of whomever we wish to scapegoat—ultimately even everyone. The devil, for instance, reminds Goodman Brown that individual Puritans whipped Quakers and burned Indian villages—but in order to condemn Puritans universally and to promote a false belief in universal evil. As David Levin writes in his excellent essay on this matter, "At the witch meeting, the 'shape of evil' invites Goodman Brown to 'the communion' of the human 'race,' the communion of evil, but we have no more right than Brown himself to believe the Father of Lies."[15]

When Young Goodman Brown becomes convinced that his wife, Faith, whom he foolishly left behind that night, is present at the devilish Sabbath, he suddenly finds himself alone, the evil vision gone, and Hawthorne asks the reader to consider whether he had "fallen asleep in the forest and only dreamed a wild dream of a witch meeting." Whatever the case, the gloom that darkens his life from then on is his inverted "faith" in spectral evidence. Hawthorne turns the issue to the reader, to me and you: "Be it so if you will." *We* must choose whether to believe in the divine wholeness and potential of people or in the reductive partiality of spectral evidence about them. Levin reminds us of the personal and social implications of this psychological allegory: "Hawthorne condemns that graceless perversion of true Calvinism which, in universal suspicion, actually led a community to the unjust destruction of twenty men and women."[16]

It is just such a "graceless perversion" of honorable motives and of true Mormonism and true Americanism that I fear is increasing now in our church and nation—and may yet lead to much destruction of faith and love, in addition to the pain many already feel. I feel the fear so deeply in part because I have felt in my bones what it is like to be part of the perversion. Between my "outburst" (as the AP reporter rightly called it) on August 6 and my day of humiliation and repentance on October 3, I went through another shift in perspective.

On the one hand I became conscious that people in the church, even in an organized way, were willing, in the name of honorable ends, to use hearsay evidence to judge, hurt, intimidate, and even punish people. Perhaps most troubling of all, I learned that others, even though disagreeing with such means, were willing to stand by and let those things happen, even participate to some extent.

On the other hand I became more fully aware that *I* could participate in the same kind of activity—with gusto. In my own hurt and desire for revenge I could use spectral evidence to judge and try to punish people, even risking harm to the church I believe is as true as the gospel and risking violation of my sacred covenants and deepest commitments.

It is time to stop. The risk is enormous. We may be at the period prophesied by Christ: "Then shall many be offended, and shall betray one another, and shall hate one another" (Matt. 24:10). We must stop listening to, accepting, or passing on to others spectral evidence. We must, I believe, specifically stop dealing indirectly, spectrally, with offenses. We must stop writing to people in authority with our complaints; stop using church authority to intimidate or punish rather than dealing face-to-face with those who offend us in speech or writing; and stop criticizing the Brethren.

I believe there are some positive things to do, as well. We can speak out against spectral evidence and extend trust even when we feel it is not deserved or has been betrayed—which seems to me exactly the ultimate vulnerability that Christ exhibited and asks of us. I believe that, just as there is naturally the kind of escalation of imitative hurt and revenge which I have seen recently in the communities I know best, so there can be an escalation of love and trust. The recent statements on academic freedom at BYU, whatever their faults, convey a remarkable degree of trust from the Board of Trustees to the faculty and administration. The board, which holds absolute power to fire and hire at will, has consciously given up some of that power: First, it has agreed in principle to a statement on academic freedom that recognizes the unique nature of a university, its need for unfettered inquiry and for the atmosphere of love and trust that *should* govern our behavior. Second, it has accepted a procedure of judgment in cases of termination for cause which is essentially lodged in faculty committees. I wish to respond to that trust with reciprocal expressions of trust and of my desire to be a responsible holder of the unique freedoms I have at BYU, especially the freedom to relate the gospel and my testimony to my study of literature, as both a teacher and writer.

President Gordon B. Hinckley in his devotional address at BYU on October 13, 1992, expressed his confidence that "never in the history of [BYU] has there been a faculty better qualified professionally nor one more loyal and dedicated to the standards of [the church]."[17] I feel certain from my own observation that he is right. I invite my colleagues to feel that way about themselves and each other—and invite the church membership at large to accept that vote of confidence from one who is now our president and prophet.

President Hinckley quoted the first section of the Doctrine and Covenants, "But that every man might speak in the name of God the Lord, even the Savior of the world," and continued: "We trust you to do so. We love you. We respect you."[18] As one faculty member said in a meeting two days later in which gathering tensions about academic freedom were discussed, "That address was like having a stone lifted from my heart."

As for me, my job is to teach students in ways that can improve the moral quality of their lives, including using what I learn from the Brethren and from literature and experience and the Spirit—and to try meticulously never to resort to spectral evidence myself. My role is certainly not to use the imagined weaknesses of others or problems in the church as an excuse for my own failings or to lash out in kind.

I can also, as Nibley suggests, talk my griefs over with the Lord, so that things bottled up do not lead to the kind of explosion I have learned that *I* am as capable of as others are:

> Be the importunate widow and complain. Itemize your griefs, your doctrinal objections, your personal tastes. Lay them out in full detail and get it out of your system. . . . With this understanding—you will do all this before the only Person qualified to judge either you or your tormentors. As you bring your complaints, be fully aware that he knows everything already—including everything there is to know about you.[19]

Good advice for all, "from the highest to the least and last ordained" (as my grandfather used to pray). In Christ's prophecy concerning our day, he held out some hope even for us: "Because iniquity shall abound, the love of many shall wax cold. But he that shall endure unto the end, the same shall be saved" (Matt. 24:12-13).

NOTES

1. Perry Miller, *The New England Mind: From Colony to Province* (Boston: Beacon Press, 1961).

2. Nathaniel Hawthorne, "Young Goodman Brown," in *Great Short Works of Hawthorne* (New York: Harper and Row, 1967).

3. Miller, 194.

4. Ibid., 195.

5. Gerard Manley Hopkins, "Spring and Fall" ("Margaret, are you grieving/ Over Goldengrove unleaving?"), in *The Poems of Gerard Manley Hopkins*, ed. W. H. Gardner and N. H. Mackenzie (New York: Oxford University Press, 1967), 89.

6. Lowell L. Bennion, *Selected Writings of Lowell L. Bennion: 1928-1988*, ed. Eugene England (Salt Lake City: Deseret Book Co., 1988), xxii.

7. Dallin H. Oaks, "Bible Stories and Personal Protection," *Ensign* 22 (Nov. 1992): 39.

8. Hugh Nibley, *Criticizing the Brethren* (Provo, UT: FARMS, 1989), 24.

9. *Manuscript History of Brigham Young, 1801-1844*, comp. Elden J. Watson (Salt Lake City: the Compiler, 1967), 96-97.

10. Boyd K. Packer, "'I Say unto You, Be One'," in *Brigham Young University 1990-91 Devotional and Fireside Speeches* (Provo, UT: Brigham Young University Press, 1991), 84.

11. Ibid.

12. Bruce R. McConkie, "The Seven Deadly Heresies," in *Brigham Young University Speeches of the Year* (Provo, UT: Brigham Young University Press, 1980), 74-80.

13. *Deseret News*, 23 Aug. 1865, 372-73.

14. Miller, 202.

15. David Levin, "Shadows of Doubt: Specter Evidence in Hawthorne's 'Young Goodman Brown'," in *American Literature* 34 (Fall 1963): 351.

16. Ibid., 352.

17. Gordon B. Hinckley, "Trust and Accountability," BYU Devotional Address, 13 Oct. 1992, 2, available through BYU Alumni Association.

18. Ibid.

19. Nibley, 24.

three

PERFECTION
AND PROGRESSION: TWO
WAYS TO TALK ABOUT GOD

On April 6, 1844, Hyrum Smith, older brother and counselor to the prophet Joseph Smith, speaking at the general conference of the Latter-day Saint church, claimed, "I would not serve a God that had not all wisdom and power."[1] Yet on January 13, 1867, speaking as president of the church in the tabernacle, Brigham Young stated, "According to [some men's] theory, God can progress no further in knowledge and power, but the God that I serve is progressing eternally, and so are his children."[2]

It is difficult to imagine a more stark contradiction in authoritative statements about the Mormon concept of God. Hyrum Smith says that God has all wisdom and power; Brigham Young says that he does not. How could there be such a dramatic reversal in doctrine? Isn't it certain that either God is perfect, with all knowledge and power, or he is not?

My thesis is that, in fact, the statements by Hyrum Smith and Brigham Young are *not* necessarily contradictory.[3] These leaders emphasized two different aspects of the Mormon understanding of God, both of which, I believe, are essential to our theology and must be maintained. With the help of a basic concept—that of different, progressive *spheres* of development and of possible perfection within each sphere—one can believe in God's perfection of knowledge and power in relation to our sphere and in his progression in these attributes in his own and higher spheres. This concept was first articulated by Brigham Young, but it was suggested earlier in some of Joseph Smith's discourses and in the Doctrine and Covenants. It has been employed by many church leaders from the beginning to the present.

The Book of Mormon and Doctrine and Covenants, consistent with the traditional Christian scriptures, refer to God as having all knowledge and all power (2 Ne. 9:20; Alma 26:35; D&C 38:1-2, 88:7-13; 93:21, 26). The earliest Mormon doctrinal exposition, the Lectures on Faith, uses the traditional Christian categories of omnipresence, omniscience, and omnipotence in describing God. It makes the explicit claim that "without the knowledge of all things God would not be able to save any portion of his creatures . . . and if it were not for the idea existing in the minds of men that God had all knowledge it would be impossible for them to exercise faith in him."[4]

Joseph Smith's part in composing the lectures is still uncertain. They seem mainly the work of Sidney Rigdon, and some readers suspect they reflect a very early stage of doctrinal expression about God that was still heavily influenced by traditional creeds.[5] For instance, God is described as a personage of spirit, Christ as a personage of tabernacle, and the Holy Ghost as a kind of unifying mind. Those who quote the Lectures on Faith have had to editorialize to make it conform to later orthodox Mormon thought, as, for instance, Joseph Fielding Smith does at the beginning of *Doctrines of Salvation*. Church authorities added a qualifying footnote to the lectures in the early 1900s and then excluded them entirely from the Doctrine and Covenants in 1921.[6] Joseph Smith never repudiated them, but it is likely that if they had been written later, he would not have used some of the terms and concepts used there. Still I think he saw no inherent contradiction between them and his later understanding.

That understanding was received and amplified over a number of years before it was most clearly, comprehensively, and publicly declared in the famous King Follett Discourse given at the same April 1844 general conference at which Hyrum Smith emphasized God's perfection. Although the discourse was recorded in rather sketchy longhand, the notes of the four scribes were later amalgamated. Nowhere in those notes does Smith state definitely that God progresses in knowledge and power, but both there and in the Doctrine and Covenants he makes it clear that God is not everywhere supreme and does not have all power. He states, for instance, that there are gods above God and that even God himself cannot do all things: he cannot create elements out of nothing, he cannot create eternal intelligences, and he cannot force salvation or damnation upon his children. Joseph clearly describes an eternal process of learning and growth by which godhood is attained, and he implies that that process continues for God himself:

> First God Himself who sits enthroned in yonder heavens is a Man like unto one of yourselves—that is the great secret! . . . The first principle of truth and of the Gospel is to know of a certainty the character of God, and that we may converse with Him . . . that He once was a man like one of us. . . . You have got to learn how to make yourselves God . . . and be kings and priests to God, the same as all Gods have done by going from a small capacity to a great capacity, from a small degree to another, from grace to grace . . . from exaltation to exaltation. [Jesus said], "I saw the Father work out His kingdom with fear and trembling and I am doing the same, too. When I get my kingdom. I will give it to the Father and it will add to and exalt His glory. He will take a higher exaltation and I will take His place and also be exalted, so that He obtains kingdom rolling upon Kingdom.". . .
>
> All the minds and spirits that God ever sent into the world are susceptible of enlargement and improvement. The relationship we have with God places us in a situation to advance in knowledge. God Himself found Himself in the midst of spirits and glory. Because He was greater He saw proper to institute laws whereby the rest, who were less in intelligence, could have a privilege to advance like Himself and be exalted with Him, that they might have one glory upon another in all that knowledge, power, and glory.[7]

Notice the lack of traditional Christian absolutism here. The emphasis seems rather to be on God's similarity to humans, on making available to us a process of growth God has been engaged in, "whereby the less intelligent . . . could have a privilege to advance like Himself." The verb structure implies that God is still advancing. God is "greater" but not absolute; he is moving to "higher" and "higher" exaltations; one glory is added to another "in all that knowledge, power, and glory."[8]

In the winter 1978 issue of *Brigham Young University Studies*, which contains a newly amalgamated text of the King Follett Discourse, Van Hale demonstrates that Smith had taught the concept of a plurality of gods from 1835 on. Hyrum Smith is quoted in George Laub's journal as having taught, on April 27, 1843, that there is "a whole train and lineage of gods."[9] In fact, in that very sermon Hyrum provided the basic shift in perspective I mentioned, which makes it possible to talk about many gods, of ascending spheres of power and intelligence, and then to turn around and talk of one God, our God, perfect in intelligence and power and thus able to save his children. He began his discussion with a quotation from 1 Corinthians 8:5-6: "There be gods many and lords many. But to us there is but one God the Father." Despite the context of this scripture—a discussion of idolatry—Brigham Young, B. H. Roberts, Joseph Fielding Smith, and others used it to explain how it is possible to be both a Christian polytheist (technically a henotheist) and a monotheist. And Roberts specifically used it to justify how we can talk sometimes in an adventuresome mode about multiple orders of progressive godhood and yet at the same time, without contradiction, talk in worshipful language about our one God and his perfect knowledge and redemptive power.

With this perspective we can understand Hyrum Smith's later concern that the Saints have faith in Christ's sufficient power to save, which had perhaps been undermined by too exclusive a focus on polytheism: "I want to put down all false influence. If I thought I should be saved and any in the congregation be lost, I should not be happy. . . . Our Savior is competent to save all from death and hell. I can prove it out of the revelations. I would not serve a God that had not all wisdom and power."

Brigham Young, like Hyrum Smith, used both ways of talking about God. At times, when he felt his audience most needed the emphasis, he spoke in classical Christian terms of God's sovereignty in our world. He often emphasized God's perfections, his knowledge and power absolutely sufficient to save us. But at other times, especially in his ongoing debates with Orson Pratt, he spoke forthrightly about multiple gods, rejoicing in the expansive vision received from Joseph Smith of "eternal progression," which he claims is at the heart of all existence because it motivates all action:

> The first great principle that ought to occupy the attention
> of all mankind, that should be understood by the child and the
> adult, and which is the main spring of all action (whether people
> understand it or not), is the principle of improvement. The prin-
> ciple of increase, of exaltation, of adding to that we already possess,
> is the grand moving principle and cause of the actions of the chil-
> dren of men . . . the main spring of the actions of [all] people, . . .
> Those who profess to be Latter-day Saints, who have the privilege
> of receiving and understanding the principles of the holy Gospel,
> are in duty bound to study and find out, and put in practice in their
> lives, those principles that are calculated to endure, and that tend
> to a continual increase in this, and in the world to come.
> All their earthly avocations should be framed upon this principle.
> This alone can insure to them an exaltation; this is the starting
> point, in this existence, to an endless progression.[10]

It is clear from other sermons that Brigham Young does not mean
by "progression" mere *quantitative* increase in spirit children or kingdoms, as we sometimes now hear the term "eternal increase" used. He
said, "We shall never cease to learn, unless we apostatize. . . . Can you
understand that?"[11] And this was not a unique or peripheral notion for
him. It was central to his theology:

> Let us not narrow ourselves up; for the world, with all its variety
> of useful information and its rich hoard of hidden treasure, is before
> us; and eternity, with all its sparkling intelligence, lofty aspirations,
> and unspeakable glories, is before us.[12]

> . . . when we have passed into the sphere where Joseph is, there is
> still another department, and then another, and another, and so on
> to an eternal progression in exaltation and eternal lives. That is the
> exaltation I am looking for.[13]

> . . . when we have lived millions of years in the presence of God
> and angels . . . shall we then cease learning? No, or eternity ceases.[14]

Brigham Young delighted in his expansive vision of continued, unlimited learning and experience. It was, for him, both the reason for and the means of continued existence, of eternal life. It led him to exult in the inclusiveness of the gospel:

> Every accomplishment, every grace, every useful attainment in mathematics, . . . in all science and art belongs to the Saints, and they should avail themselves as expeditiously as possible of the wealth of knowledge the sciences offer to the diligent and persevering scholar.[15]

> As Saints in the last days we have much to learn; there is an eternity of knowledge before us; at most we receive but very little in this stage of our progression.[16]

Such enthusiasm led President Young completely to reverse the medieval Dr. Faust legend, which implies that too much learning leads a Christian to blasphemy. Brother Brigham, on the other hand, claimed that only when we blaspheme, when we sin against the Holy Ghost, do we *stop* learning:

> If we continue to learn all that we can, pertaining to the salvation which is purchased and presented to us through the Son of God, is there a time when a person will cease to learn? Yes, when he has sinned against God the Father, Jesus Christ, the Son, and the Holy Ghost—God's minister: when he has denied the Lord, defied Him and committed the sin against the Holy Ghost. That is the time when a person will cease to learn, and from that time forth, will descend in ignorance, forgetting that which they formerly knew....
> They will cease to increase, but must decrease. . . . These are the only characters who will ever cease to learn, both in time and eternity.[17]

Belief in endless progression in knowledge was not a speculative matter with Young, as some other matters were. About some things, such as the exact status of Adam in relation to God, he frankly said, "I guess," or this subject "does not immediately concern your or my welfare." He clearly felt that Joseph's doctrine of eternal progression was so important that it needed to be kept alive in Mormon theology. He reprinted the King Follett discourse a number of times and referred often to teaching only what he had learned from Joseph. Only a few months before his death he testified,

> From the first time I saw the Prophet Joseph I never lost a word that came from him concerning the kingdom. And this is the key of knowledge that I have today, that I did hearken to the words of Joseph and treasured them up in my heart, laid them away, asking my Father in the name of his Son Jesus to bring them to mind when needed.[18]

The testimony of those who knew both men—and who like Brigham were taught and trained by Joseph in a concentrated way in the last two years of his life—was that he indeed remembered and taught what Joseph taught.

A major motivation for Brigham Young's public doctrinal disagreements with Orson Pratt was his concern not only that Elder Pratt was wrong in insisting without qualification on God's absolute perfection and the impossibility of his further progression, but that such an influential speaker and writer would convince many to follow after him and leave to posterity the impression that only his view and emphasis was part of Mormon thought. President Young felt it so crucial to keep before the Saints his own and Joseph's emphasis that he pushed Pratt to a public recantation in 1865.[19] Then he published Pratt's recantation in the *Deseret News* and later in the *Latter-day Saints' Millennial Star*, along with a denunciation of specific doctrines of Elder Pratt, signed by the First Presidency. When these documents were reprinted, signed also by the other Apostles, Brigham Young specifically condemned a number of assertions Elder Pratt had taught in his book *The Seer*. The following beliefs of Elder Pratt were identified as *not* true:

> [1] There will be no being or beings in existence that will know one particle more than we know, then our knowledge, and wisdom, and power will be infinite; and cannot from thenceforth be increased or expanded in the least degree.
> [2] There will be nothing more to be learned.

[3] The Father and the Son do not progress in knowledge and wisdom because they already know all things past, present and to come.

[4] None of the Gods know more than another and none are progressing in knowledge; neither in the acquirement of any truth.[20]

Part of Brigham Young's concern was with the presumption of actually *limiting* God while seeming to describe him as having limitless power and knowledge. In October 1856 he commanded the Saints, "Now do not lariat [rope off] the God that I serve and say that he cannot learn anymore; I do not believe in such a character."[21] President Young's counselor, Jedediah M. Grant, developed the same image later that month: "[If God] is lariated out, as Orson Pratt lariated out the Gods in his theory, his circle is [only] as far as the string extends. My God is not lariated out."[22] It was this concern which motivated the statement of Brigham Young I began with, the one that seems to contradict Hyrum Smith:

> Some men seem as if they could learn so much and no more. They
> appear to be bounded in their capacity for acquiring knowledge, as
> Brother Orson has, in theory, bounded the capacity of God. Accord-
> ing to his theory, God can progress no further in knowledge and
> power, but the God that I serve is progressing eternally, and so are
> his children; they will increase to all eternity, if they are faithful.[23]

Brigham Young's concern was also with spiritual psychology, the importance, in motivating humankind toward salvation, of their retaining a certain vision: that what was most rewarding in earthly progression—increasing in knowledge and gaining power over new experience in order to serve others better—would continue forever and would make celestial life, or Godhood, attractive. Godhood is not a mysterious stasis or endless repetition of creating spirits and saving them. Apostle Wilford Woodruff, in 1857, gave pointed expression to this concern: "If there was a point where man in his progression could not proceed any further, the very idea would throw a gloom over every intelligent and reflecting mind. God himself is still increasing and progressing in knowledge, power and dominion, and will do so world without end. It is just so with us."[24] In his journal for 11 March 1860 Woodruff wrote in rebuttal to what he had heard about Pratt's teachings, "The moment that we say that God knows all things, comprehends all things, and has a fulness of all that He ever will obtain, that moment Eternity ceases. You put bounds to Eternity and space and matter and you make an end and stopping place to it."[25]

Elder Lorenzo Snow, who like Brigham Young and Wilford Woodruff knew Joseph Smith's teachings firsthand, provided the famous Mormon couplet which summarizes memorably the concept of eternal progression for both God and humans: "As Man now is, God once was; as God now is, Man may be."[26] While president of the church in 1901, he also spoke clearly about eternal progression *after* Godhood is reached:

> We are immortal beings. . . . Our individuality will always exist . . . our identity is insured. We will be ourselves and nobody else. Whatever changes may arise, whatever worlds may be made or pass away, our identity will always remain the same; and we will continue on improving, advancing and increasing in wisdom, intelligence, power and dominion, worlds without end.[27]

In the twentieth century some church leaders began to emphasize the mortal sphere in talking about God. President Joseph F. Smith, like his father Hyrum, was concerned that some were inclined to demean God, to reduce too much the distance between God and humankind, and thus to undermine confidence in God's saving power. (I remember some Mormons in my own youth who were so caught up with the vision of eternal progression that it seemed to me they could hardly wait to die to be like God!) Speaking in 1914 about those who would limit God's power and majesty, President Smith said:

> Beware of men who come to you with heresies of this kind, who would make you to think or feel that the Lord Almighty, who made heaven and earth and created all things, is limited in his dominion of earthly things to the capacities of men. . . . They would, if they could, make you believe that the Son of God, who possessed all

power . . . power to raise the dead, power to unstop the ears of the dead . . . did not do such things. . . . There are just a few ignoramuses, "learned fools," if you please, who would make you believe, if they could, that the Almighty God is limited in His power to the capacity of man. . . . Don't you believe it, not for one moment.[28]

Joseph F. Smith's son, Joseph Fielding Smith, took a similar position. In his extremely influential book, *Doctrines of Salvation*, he quotes the passage from his grandfather Hyrum about God being absolute and also passages from the Lectures on Faith about God's perfections. It is clear that his concern, like that of his father and grandfather, was with God's power in relation to humans. He asks, after the quotation from Hyrum, "Do we believe that God has all wisdom? . . . Does he have all power? If so then there is nothing in which he lacks. If he is lacking in 'wisdom' and in 'power' then he is not supreme and there must be something greater than he is, and this is absurd."[29]

Clearly, Elder Smith is here speaking in the single, mortal sphere mode, the one bounded by the idea that *to us* there is only one God the Father. We know he is doing so because, of course, he knew that both his grandfather and Joseph Smith clearly taught that there *is* "something greater" than God—that God is (if we speak in terms of the multiple, eternal spheres) *not* supreme, that there are Gods above God, a Father of God who gave him salvation and a Father of that god and so on, apparently to infinity.

One reason we know that Joseph Fielding Smith, despite the statement above, believed there is "something greater" than God is that in response to a question about "plural gods" in the second volume of his *Answers to Gospel Questions*, he quoted a long passage from Joseph Smith's discourse of June 16, 1844, the one most explicit about the doctrine. In this sermon we can see Joseph Smith at ease with two modes of thinking, multiple and single spheres, because he uses in support and explanation that same passage from Corinthians that his brother Hyrum had used the year before. In the passage quoted by Joseph Fielding Smith, Joseph Smith states, "Paul says there are Gods many and Lords many. I want to set it forth in a plain and simple manner; but to us there is but one God—that is *pertaining to us*; and he is in all and through all. But if Joseph Smith says there are Gods many and

Lords many, they cry, 'Away with him! Crucify him!'"[30] After some analysis of the Hebrew original of Genesis 1:1, Joseph Smith continues,

> In the very beginning the Bible shows there is a plurality of Gods beyond the power of refutation. It is a great subject I am dwelling on. The word *Eloheim* ought to be in the plural all the way through—Gods. The head of the Gods appointed one God for us; and when you take that view of that subject, it sets one free to see all the beauty, holiness and perfection of the Gods.[31]

After this long quotation from the prophet, Joseph Fielding Smith shows his own understanding of the two perspectives:

> It is perfectly true, as recorded in the Pearl of Great Price and in the Bible that to us there is but one God. ... This Godhead presides over us, and to us, the inhabitants of this world, they constitute the only God or Godhead. There is none other besides them. To them we are amenable, and subject to their authority, and there is no other Godhead unto whom we are subject. However, as the Prophet has shown, there can be, and are, other Gods.[32]

Joseph Fielding Smith clearly recognized both the multiple sphere and single sphere modes of expression and the basis of both in Joseph Smith's teachings, but he also shared, it seems to me, his father's concern about belittling God and his grandfather's concern about Mormons losing faith in God's absolute power to save. He seems to have chosen to focus his own writing and sermons about God in the single sphere mode, which influenced Bruce R. McConkie to do the same. Elder McConkie, in his influential *Mormon Doctrine* (1958, p. 221), stated unequivocally that God does not progress in knowledge or power and cited as authority the passage from President Smith's *Doctrines of Salvation* that I have discussed above.

During the same period as Joseph Fielding Smith's early writings, others chose to emphasize the larger view of God as dwelling in multiple spheres of progressive existence, particularly elders B. H. Roberts and John A. Widtsoe. This is not surprising, since these were the two twentieth-century general authorities most influenced by Brigham Young and most influential in preserving and developing the basic philosophical ideas, what Elder Roberts called the "eternalism," of Joseph Smith.

In his most lengthy discourse on the nature of God, Elder Roberts, after quoting extensively from Joseph Smith, states:

> Of course, such views as those expressed above involve us in the reality of a pluralistic universe, and a plurality of Gods; . . . there have been appointed certain exalted, glorified and perfected intelligences, who have attained unto a participation in, and become partakers of, "the Divine Nature" (II Peter 1:4), who have been appointed as Presidencies over worlds and world systems, who function in the dignity of Divine intelligences, or Deities, even as to our world and its heavens there has been appointed a Godhead, as taught by St. Paul.[33]

He then goes on to quote that same passage from Corinthians used by Joseph and Hyrum Smith to demonstrate the two perspectives, the two modes of discourse: ". . . as there be Gods many and Lords many—but to us (i.e., pertaining to us), there is but one God."

In Elder Roberts's mind, the passage from Corinthians is strong support for his belief in a realm where there are many gods, all progressing eternally, as a complement rather than contradiction to his belief in a realm where, to us mortals, there is but one God, perfect in every way. Earlier, Elder Roberts, in an essay in the church's *Improvement Era*, had taught,

> Even with the possession of [the Holy Spirit] to guide us into all truth, I pray you, nevertheless, not to look for finality in things, for you will look in vain. Intelligence, purity, truth, will always remain with us relative terms and also relative qualities. Ascend to what heights you may, ever beyond you will see other heights in respect of these things and ever as you ascend, more heights will appear, and it is doubtful if we shall ever attain the absolute in respect of these qualities. Our joy will be the joy of approximating them, of attaining unto ever-increasing excellence without attaining the absolute. It will be the joy of eternal progression.[34]

In Roberts's famous and influential *Seventies Course in Theology*, used as an official priesthood manual and published by the church, he argued, harking back to Brigham Young's concern about limiting God:

> God's immutability should not be understood as to exclude the idea of advancement or progress of God . . . an absolute immutability would require eternal immobility—which would reduce God to a condition eternally static . . . which from the nature of things, would bar him from participation in that enlargement of kingdom and increasing glory that comes from the redemption and progress of men. And is it too bold of a thought, that with this progress, even for the Mightiest, new thoughts and new vistas may appear, inviting to new adventures and enterprises that will yield new experiences, advancement and enlargement even for the Most High?[35]

Elder Widtsoe, the brilliant immigrant convert who wrote the important 1903 work *Joseph Smith as Scientist*, emphasized the prophet's naturalism and teachings on God as organizer according to natural law, not as an absolute creator out of nothing and thus not truly omnipotent in the traditional absolutistic sense. In his book *A Rational Theology*, Widtsoe was even more explicit about the similar capability of both humans and God for eternal progression:

> The essential thing is that man has to undergo experience upon experience, to attain the desired mastery of the external universe; and that we, of this earth, are passing through an estate designed wholly for our further education. Throughout eternal life, increasing knowledge is attained, and with increasing knowledge comes the greater adaptation to law, and in the end an increasingly greater joy. Therefore, it is, that eternal life, is the greatest gift of God.
>
> . . . if the great law of progression is accepted, *God must have been engaged from the beginning, and must now be engaged, in progressive development.* As knowledge grew into greater knowledge, by the persistent efforts of will, his recognition of universal laws became greater until he attained at last a conquest over the universe which to our

finite understanding seems absolutely complete.[36]

That last sentence shows that Elder Widtsoe was also concerned to give the single sphere mode of thought, which fits the natural human inclination to awe and worship, its proper due. He goes on with that single sphere emphasis even while talking of multiple spheres:

> As more knowledge and power are attained, growth becomes increasingly more rapid. God, exalted by his glorious intelligence, is moving on into new fields of power with a rapidity of which we can have no conception, whereas man, in a lower stage of development, moves relatively at a snail-like though increasing, pace. Man is, nevertheless, moving on, in eternal progression. In short, man is a god in embryo. He comes of a race of gods, and as this eternal growth is continued, we will approach more nearly the point which to us is Godhood, and which is everlasting in its power over the elements of the universe.[37]

An emphasis on the multiple spheres mode, focussing directly on our adventure in forever progressing to higher realms, continued in the writings of President David O. McKay: "A man's idea of the significance of the words 'eternal progression' will largely determine his philosophy of life. . . . The great secret of human happiness lies in progression. Stagnation means death. . . . The doctrine of eternal progression is fundamental in the Church of Christ."[38] President McKay quoted the passage from Brigham Young I gave earlier on the principle of improvement as the main spring of all action and continued:

> Somebody has said, "Show me a perfectly contented man and I will show you a useless one." So there must be some other element with contentment, some other virtue. What is it? Progress. Contentment and progress contribute to peace. If we are no better tomorrow than we are today, we are not very useful . . . so we want to experience two things: contentment and progress—progress intellectually, progress physically, but above all, progress spiritually; and the cognizance that we grow contributes to peace. You cannot remain stationary.[39]

Hugh B. Brown, President McKay's counselor in the First Presidency (1962-69), also emphasized this multiple spheres mode:

> The time will come when all men will know something of the glory of God. But the time will not come when I or any other man will arrive at a point in knowledge, experience or understanding beyond which we cannot go. In other words, we believe in eternal progression.[40]

> When we speak of eternal increase, we speak not only of increase of posterity, we speak of increase of knowledge and the power that comes with knowledge, the increase of wisdom to use knowledge and power wisely; increase of awareness and the joy that comes through understanding; increase of intelligence, which is the glory of God; increase of all that goes to make up Godhood.[41]

President Brown carried on the multiple spheres, adventuresome mode of talking about God prominently in modern Mormon thought until his death in 1975. Younger Mormon thinkers have continued to explore the implications of the unusual Mormon belief in a finite, learning God for our concepts of evil, time, prophecy, etc.[42] At the same time other voices emphasize the single sphere, worshipful mode, especially Elder McConkie[43] and his son, Joseph McConkie,[44] a professor of religious education at Brigham Young University. These two, and others, have thought of the two modes as opposed, as mutually exclusive; but it seems more useful to recognize the authoritative base for both modes in Mormon thought and the evidence that advocacy of both modes by the prophets provides that God is not to be limited to mutually exclusive human categories.

The Doctrine and Covenants contains the key idea (including the very word "sphere") that was used by Brigham Young to describe the harmony between these seemingly competing views. Section 93, a revelation to the prophet Joseph Smith in 1833, tells us that "all truth is independent in that sphere in which God has placed it, to act for itself, as all intelligence also; otherwise there is no existence" (v. 30). This seems to be not only a statement of the free agency of intelligences but to evoke a universe of co-existent (perhaps concentric, or more likely hyperspatial, multidimensional) spheres of truth and intelligent activity. In such a universe, a statement such as that God has all knowledge and power can be taken to be true when applied to our sphere alone, in which God is *not* progressing, but it is not completely true when applied to larger or more advanced spheres, where God *is* progressing.

Brigham Young had this precise understanding. This is from a sermon on June 13, 1852, in the old tabernacle:

> We can still improve, we are made for that purpose, our capacities are organized to expand until we can receive into our comprehension celestial knowledge and wisdom, and to continue worlds without end. . . . if men can understand and receive it, mankind are organized to receive intelligence until they become perfect in the sphere they are appointed to fill, which is far ahead of us at present. *When we use the term perfection, it applies to man in his present condition, as well as the heavenly beings.* We are now, or may be, as perfect in our sphere as God and angels are in theirs, but the greatest intelligence in existence can continually ascend to greater heights of perfection.
>
> We are created for the express purpose of increase. There are none, correctly organized, but can increase from birth to old age. What is there that is not ordained after [such] an eternal Law of existence? *It is the Deity within us that causes increase.*[45]

B. H. Roberts, fully aware of the emphasis throughout the scriptures on a worshipful mode of discourse, the almost exclusive focus on God's perfection, developed a careful explanation of why the other mode, the expansive vision beyond this sphere, is used so rarely, even in modern scriptures. He quotes the Doctrine and Covenants reference to many kingdoms, greater and lesser ones, filling all space (88:37), then points out that when God speaks to Moses—though he also mentions these other kingdoms, the many heavens that "cannot be numbered unto man"—he informs him that he will give him only an account "concerning *this* heaven and *this* earth" (Moses 1:37; 2:1; my emphasis). Elder Roberts concludes that virtually all the revelations relate to our earth and its heavens alone:

In other words, our revelations are local; they pertain to us and our limited order of worlds. It is only here and there that a glimpse of things outside of our earth and its heavens is given. . . . This limited knowledge, these glimpses of the universe, were doubtless displayed by the Lord to these prophets at the heads of dispensations of truth, because of the influencing power which this knowledge of the nature of the universe upon man's conception of God would have; for undoubtedly such knowledge clearly influences conceptions of God.[46]

Elder Roberts also cites the expanding modern scientific awareness of a limitless universe and concludes:

this universe must be more than a mere creation for definite relationships to our earth . . . and God must be conceived of as having larger interests and immensely greater objectives than the affairs of the race inhabiting our world. . . . the very limited revelations given concerning our earth and its heavens are not adequate as an explanation of the universe at large.[47]

Such an expansive vision of the cosmos, a vision also worshipful and deeply ennobling in its ultimate humility, seems to me vital to the Mormon spirit and to Mormon thought. It must not be lost in our very proper emphasis on the equally true and important vision of God's perfections and on human dependence. I appreciate the influence of Mormon theologians who, speaking in the single sphere mode, might help correct, as Joseph F. Smith and Joseph Fielding Smith did, any tendency to belittle God or reduce faith in his saving power. But it is also important not to polarize Mormon doctrine about God or to obscure the grand vision of eternal progression that has traditionally energized it.

I do not expect that to happen. Modern writers as diverse as Gerrit de Jong, Jr., in his 1956 Sunday school manual, *Living the Gospel*,[48] and Hyrum Andrus, in his *Doctrinal Commentary on the Pearl of Great Price*,[49] have managed to reconcile the two views. With a little discussion, perplexed students who encounter what seem to them contradictory statements by their church leaders and other authorities can be helped with analogies. For instance, a being who is learning and progressing in a four dimensional realm, or hyperspace, can at the same time have *all* knowledge and power that is available in only three dimensions—and thus all that is necessary for the salvation of us in mortality.[50]

There is genuine anxiety sometimes voiced against the idea that God is still learning: that God might therefore err or be unable to save us. This anxiety can be calmed with the analogy that a person can know algebra perfectly and make absolutely no mistakes but can still be learning new things in calculus without endangering the realm of algebra—and so God can have all knowledge and power in our realm or sphere and still be learning in higher spheres, without in any way endangering his absolute ability to save us in this sphere. To rephrase Paul's letter to the Corinthians: "In the cosmos there is a multitude of progressing Gods, but pertaining to us there is one God, with all knowledge and power."

Students can be taught to hear and appreciate the emphasis and the apostolic witness of both Hyrum Smith and Brigham Young, of both Hugh B. Brown and Joseph Fielding Smith. Mormon thinkers of various orientations can unite in this task, while continuing to use whichever way of talking about God is more appropriate to what they choose to emphasize in their ongoing struggle to know God—adventure or worship, potential or dependence, progress or perfection, the multiple spheres of our ultimate vision or the single sphere of our immediate concern.

NOTES

1. Quoted in Joseph Fielding Smith, *Doctrines of Salvation*, comp. Bruce R. McConkie (Salt Lake City: Bookcraft, 1954), 5; from Joseph Smith, *History of the Church* (Salt Lake City: Deseret News Press, 1912), 6:300 (hereafter *HC*).

2. *Journal of Discourses*, 26 vols. (London: Latter-day Saints' Booksellers' Depot, 1854-86), 11:286 (hereafter *JD*).

3. James R. Harris quotes conflicting statements in parallel columns and tries to explain how it can be that God is able "to 'know all things' and at the

same time to progress eternally in 'light and truth,'" but he does this with a move (see n9 below) that seems to me untrue to the clear meaning of various leaders' statements (see James R. Harris, "Eternal Progression and the Foreknowledge of God," *Brigham Young University Studies* 8 [Autumn 1967]: 37-46).

4. Lectures on Faith, 44, in all editions of the D&C before 1921.

5. On authorship and decanonization, see Leland H. Gentry, "What of the Lectures on Faith?" *Brigham Young University Studies* 19 (Fall 1978): 5-19, and Richard S. Van Wagoner, Steven C. Walker, and Allen D. Roberts, "The 'Lectures on Faith'; A Case Study in Decanonization," *Dialogue: A Journal of Mormon Thought* 20 (Fall 1987): 71-77. For a consideration of apparent changes in doctrine that may have led to the decanonization, see Thomas G. Alexander, "The Reconstruction of Mormon Doctrine," in *Line upon Line: Essays on Mormon Doctrine*, ed. Gary James Bergera (Salt Lake City: Signature Books, 1989), 53-66, and for a critique of Alexander, see Robert L. Millett, "Joseph Smith and Modern Mormonism: Orthodoxy, Neoorthodoxy, Tension, and Tradition," *Brigham Young University Studies* 29 (Summer 1989): 49-68.

6. In editing the *History of the Church*, B. H. Roberts noted that the Lectures on Faith were "not of equal authority in matters of doctrine" compared with the regular sections of the Doctrine and Covenants because when they were originally presented to the Church for acceptance, they had been separately designated as not inspired revelation, though "judicially written and profitable for doctrine" (*HC*, 2:176).

7. Joseph Smith, "The King Follett Discourse: A Newly Amalgamated Text," *Brigham Young University Studies* 18 (Winter 1978): 200, 203, 204.

8. Harris quotes one of these passages from the King Follett Discourse that implies progression but then goes on to define "eternal progression" as meaning *God's* progression, or God's perfect union with "the Patriarchal order of Exalted Fathers" and thus perfect access to their absolute power and knowledge. This removes the crucial element of change in any useful notion of "progression" (37, 43-4). For more on Brigham Young's belief, see Boyd Kirkland, "Eternal Progression and the Second Death in the Theology of Brigham Young," in Bergera, *Line upon Line*, 174-75.

9. "George Laub's Nauvoo Journal," ed. Eugene England, *Brigham Young University Studies* 18 (Winter 1978): 176.

10. *JD* 2:90, 6 Feb. 1853.

11. Ibid. 3:203.

12. Ibid. 8:9.

13. Ibid. 3:375.

14. Ibid. 6:344; these quotations were compiled by Hugh Nibley, "Edu-

cating the Saints," *Nibley on the Timely and the Timeless*, ed. Truman Madsen (Salt Lake City: Bookcraft, 1979), 235.

15. *JD* 10:224.

16. Ibid. 3:354.

17. Ibid., 302.

18. *Deseret News*, 6 June 1877.

19. This experience is thoroughly reviewed in Gary James Bergera, "The Orson Pratt-Brigham Young Controversies," *Dialogue: A Journal of Mormon Thought* 13 (Summer 1980): 7-49, and in Breck England, *The Life and Thought of Orson Pratt* (Salt Lake City: University of Utah Press, 1985), 209-17.

20. *Deseret News*, 25 July 1865, 162-63; this statement, together with additional comments and signed as well by the apostles, was reprinted in *Deseret News*, 23 Aug. 1865, 372-73.

21. *Deseret News Weekly* 22:309.

22. *JD* 4:126-27.

23. Ibid. 11:286, 13 Jan. 1867.

24. Ibid. 6:20, 6 Dec. 1857.

25. Wilford Woodruff Journal, 11 Mar. 1860, archives, Historical Department, Church of Jesus Christ of Latter-day Saints, Salt Lake City, Utah (hereafter LDS archives).

26. The origin of this couplet is explained in Eliza R. Snow Smith, *Biography and Family Record of Lorenzo Snow* (Salt Lake City: Deseret News Co., 1884), 46, 47.

27. *Conference Report, April 1901* (Salt Lake City: Church of Jesus Christ of Latter-day Saints, 1901), 2.

28. *Conference Report, April 1914* (Salt Lake City: Church of Jesus Christ of Latter-day Saints, 1914), 5.

29. Smith, *Doctrines of Salvation*, 1:5.

30. Joseph Fielding Smith, *Answers to Gospel Questions* (Salt Lake City: Bookcraft, 1958), 140.

31. Ibid.

32. Ibid., 142.

33. *Discourses of B. H. Roberts* (Salt Lake City: Deseret Press, 1948), 93-94.

34. B. H. Roberts, "Relation of Inspiration and Revelation to Church Government," *Improvement Era*, Mar. 1905, 369.

35. B. H. Roberts, *Seventies' Course in Theology* (Salt Lake City: Deseret News Press, 1911), 69-70.

36. *A Rational Theology* (Salt Lake City: General Priesthood Committee of the L.D.S. Church, 1915), 30-31, my emphasis.

37. Ibid., 23-25.

38. *Pathways to Happiness* (Salt Lake City: Bookcraft, 1957), 260.

39. Ibid., 292.

40. *The Abundant Life* (Salt Lake City: Bookcraft, 1965), 116.

41. *Continuing the Quest* (Salt Lake City: Deseret Press, 1961), 4.

42. See, for example, Gary James Bergera, "Does God Progress in Knowledge?" *Dialogue: A Journal of Mormon Thought* 15 (Spring 1982): 179-81; Blake Ostler, "The Concept of a Finite God as an Adequate Object of Worship," in Bergera, *Line upon Line*, 77-82; and Kent E. Robson, "Omnipotence, Omnipresence, and Omniscience in Mormon Theology," in Bergera, *Line upon Line*, 67-75.

43. See "The Lord God of Joseph Smith," *Brigham Young University Devotional Addresses* 55 (Provo, UT: Brigham Young University Press, 1972), Jan. 1972, in which Elder McConkie stated that God "has attained a state where he knows all things and nothing is withheld" (7); and "The Seven Deadly Heresies," in which he listed belief in God's progression as one of the heresies, *BYU Speeches of the Year* (1980): 74-80.

44. See Robert L. Millett and Joseph Fielding McConkie, *The Life Beyond* (Salt Lake City: Bookcraft, 1986), 148-49: "Our Father's development and progression over an infinitely long period of time has brought him to a point at which he now presides as God Almighty, He who is omnipotent, omniscient, and, by means of his Holy Spirit, omnipresent: he has all power, all knowledge, and is, through the light of Christ, in and through all things."

45. From a sermon by Brigham Young, 13 June 1852, quoted in Hugh B. Brown, *Continuing the Quest* (Salt Lake City: Deseret Press, 1961), 4.

46. *Discourses of B. H. Roberts*, 91.

47. Ibid., 93.

48. *Living the Gospel* (Salt Lake City: Deseret Press, 1956), 138.

49. *Doctrinal Commentary on the Pearl of Great Price* (Salt Lake City: Deseret Press, 1967), 507.

50. See Robert P. Burton and Bruce F. Webster, "Some Thoughts on Higher-dimensional Realms," *Brigham Young University Studies*, Spring 1980, 281-96.

f o u r

ON BRINGING PEACE TO BYU, WITH THE HELP OF BRIGHAM YOUNG

Suppose that someone acquired the old BYU Academy buildings in downtown Provo and announced that the campus was being restored and developed as a liberal arts college. Suppose again that this person, a graduate of the University of Utah and Stanford, offered the following prospectus:

> The central purpose of this college is to improve the minds of its students, to teach them to think clearly and make their own informed judgments rather than depending on tradition, authority, or popular opinion. To this end we intend to expose them to the thinking and research offered by all branches of human knowledge and the challenges posed by all the various scholarly, religious, and moral positions.
>
> We will place before them, so they can actually know by their experience and make their own decisions on a fully informed basis, the main principles concerning truth and error, virtue and vice, that have continually perplexed human beings. We will particularly emphasize the fundamentals of our own language and require facility in at least one additional language, including careful study of the customs, laws, politics, and literature of the people who use that other language, so they can escape the provincial blindness of being bound by one language and culture. We will focus on the great radical thinkers, like Galileo and the early geologists, who have reexamined the received ideas of their culture, even the great discoverers, in art, science, and practical life who have been called

"fanatic" and "crazy" by their contemporaries.

We will renounce biblical literalism in favor of rational efforts to understand how prophets received and understood the traditions of their fathers. We will renounce puritanic restrictions on students' dancing, music, and reading but instead encourage them to feel free and unfettered in body and mind.

This prospectus would be greeted with complacent approval by our imaginary founder's friends at Stanford, perhaps even, by some at the University of Utah, welcomed with a little unholy joy at the prospect of such a challenge to BYU under its very nose. I suspect there would indeed be some apprehension in certain Latter-day Saint circles over such a prospect. But suppose the prospectus continued in this way:

This college will be named Joseph Smith College, in honor of the person who the founders believe has done more for the salvation of humankind than anyone except Jesus Christ. We will strongly encourage all our students to study the life and thought of this prophet of God and also the book he translated by divine power, the Book of Mormon, providing our best teachers and resources to this end. Our purpose in this primary effort is to combat the increasing secular, even atheistic, influences in higher education and to further Joseph Smith's vision for building the Kingdom of God on earth by challenging students with the great ideas and patterns for enlightened living that Jesus Christ and his prophets have revealed to us but which are generally neglected elsewhere.

We believe that the study of religion is queen of all the liberal arts and sciences and will hire teachers on the basis of their ability to use the Bible, as well as modern revelation, as a source of critical perspectives on every subject matter; indeed we believe that the best education occurs when nothing, not even computer graphics or nuclear fusion, is taught without teachers and students having an eye single to eternal values and thus being open to the influence of the Holy Ghost.

Imagine the outcry now from this poor turncoat's friends and colleagues at Stanford and the U—and the rejoicing in BYU's administration building! But wait, the prospectus continues:

> We believe that next to development of the mind and eternal
> spirit, our basic purpose should be to develop practical skills both
> for self-sufficiency and for service to others. We also believe that
> the pride that comes from riches and from unequal standards of
> living, as well as from differences in educational opportunity and
> academic and social rank, is the main obstacle to learning. We will
> therefore strive, as a central goal, to build a true community based
> on the principles of consecration and humility taught by Jesus
> Christ and Joseph Smith.
>
> Students, faculty, and administration will work together to
> maintain the school and its properties, all sharing a variety of tasks
> assigned according to skills and the need for new kinds of experi-
> ence—sometimes simply jobs that need to be done, however me-
> nial. We will develop handicraft projects, farming, light industry,
> etc., to provide laboratories for practical application of all kinds of
> knowledge and to help support our community economically, and
> we will have, as a regular part of our curriculum, participation in
> service projects for the community of Provo and, where possible,
> beyond. We will do everything we can to remove the distinctions
> among most educational communities that are created by rank,
> titles, and differences in property; we will set salaries and tuition
> as much as possible by need and by ability to pay.

Now if you will listen in your imaginations, you can hear polite
screams of opposition from both the University of Utah and BYU. Here
is a vision of higher education that offends across the board. Yet all
three of these visions—the liberal, secular one that emphasizes freedom and comprehensiveness; the conservative, almost sectarian one
that emphasizes defined religious purpose and order; and the radical
one that no one has tried at least since the 1960s—all of these come
from the same person: Brigham Young.

The entire prospectus was composed from carefully compiled
and only slightly altered statements by Young, statements that are consistent within their contexts and with other statements by him over a
thirty-year period. But, you say, they contradict each other. The purpose of this essay is to argue that they do not, that they instead accu-

rately and consciously reflect a powerful, inherent paradox in the very idea of church-sponsored higher education—a paradox that has productively, if painfully, informed Mormon-sponsored higher education throughout its history.

Brigham Young's philosophy of education is more sophisticated and ultimately more visionary—and in my judgement more *true*—than his critics and praisers alike realize. And the most serious challenge BYU faces is not the criticism or pressures of those who can see and value only one part of that philosophy but our own failure to understand completely and then measure up to our founder's radical vision—in its entirety. He is still the victim, even inside the church, of a stereotype: the tough, practical administrator, energetic but rather simple-minded; an ill-educated, confused, and contradictory, even seriously misleading, thinker. Hugh Nibley has taken Brigham Young's mind seriously enough to read him completely and carefully, and here is his report:

> No man ever spoke his mind more frankly on all subjects; all his days he strove to communicate his inmost feelings, unburdening himself without the aid of notes or preparation in a vigorous and forthright prose that was the purest anti-rhetoric. It has been common practice to dismiss any saying of his of which one disapproves (and he makes no effort to please) by observing that he said so many things that he was bound to contradict himself, and therefore need not be taken too seriously all the time. No view could be more ill-advised, for there never was a man more undeviatingly consistent and rational in thought and utterance. . . . Granted that Brigham would admonish the Saints to wear overcoats one day, so to speak, and the next day turn around and advise shirtsleeves, the element of scandal and confusion vanishes if we only get the main idea, which is, that it is not the rulebook or the Administration but the weather that prescribes the proper dress for the day. All the other apparent contradictions in Brother Brigham's teachings likewise vanish when we grasp the main idea behind them.[1]

It seems to me that traditional histories have idealized the Mormon pioneers' enthusiasm for education and claimed that that enthusiasm was energized by clear prophetic support for whatever kind of education—from liberal to utilitarian to religious—that *the historian* favored. Historians have explained the twentieth century prominence of citizens of Mormon-dominated Utah in various educational categories as a simple result of that pioneer enthusiasm and have prophecied a glorious future for BYU on the same basis. On the other hand revisionist historians have detailed a troubled history of what seem anti-intellectual, even suppressive, incidents and policies at BYU; they have tended to see the conflicts operating in BYU's history—faith versus reason, freedom versus order—as merely a problem to be overcome when enlightened faculty and administrators rid themselves of a backward and limited philosophy of education, rather than as unavoidable and ultimately productive paradoxes. Though I perhaps have not studied the primary sources as thoroughly as Nibley, I have studied them enough to sense that he is right: most of the critics, and the apologists, have simply not grasped the prophet's main idea.

To provide a measure of objective support, let me quote from a non-Mormon scholar who has seen that main idea. Ernst Benz, then a distinguished professor of religion at the University of Marburg, Germany, in the mid-1970s studied this issue carefully. He demonstrated considerable insight by discussing Brigham Young's role in keeping Mormonism from the increasing "false secularization"[2] or worldliness that not only threatens Christianity, and all the world's religions, but diminishes the influence of religion in all areas of modern thinking and behavior.

Brigham Young, Benz asserts, led Mormons in developing, with unique effectiveness, the "positive secularization" of involving the divine in the world. Mormonism invests all of our honorable but mundane activities with sacred meaning by making them part of God's active penetration into the realities of the world in order to use it to develop humankind, for "building up His kingdom." But Benz also shows how Mormons have uniquely managed to avoid the dangers of such an approach. All other millenarian groups, as well as openly secular ones, have succumbed to the tendency, after successfully building a literal physical kingdom, to "proceed so far into worldliness, that it comes in the advanced state of it to be an interruption or a loss of contact with the original or heavenly source and with the heavenly aim."[3]

With rare insight into Mormon theology and experience, Benz points to three basic Mormon concepts which he believes will continue to prevent the ideal of the Mormon kingdom from declining into a "social gospel" effort merely to solve our material problems—concepts which he claims Brigham Young is mainly responsible for articulating and transmitting permanently into modern Mormonism. First, the concept of the "Everlasting Gospel," a body of truth that Joseph Smith called the "ancient order of things," which, unlike the usual forms of academic knowledge, does not evolve inevitably—or even through determined effort—but can be lost through neglect, and thus must be revealed again and again from God. This body of truth includes the permanent duty of mission—the divine call and power to spread that gospel throughout the whole earth, by every means, including the schools supported by the kingdom. Second, Benz cites "the permanent presence of the gifts of the Holy Spirit" as guiding and validating elements in all of the activities of the believers as they prepare for the coming kingdom of God. Third, and most important in Benz's opinion, for keeping Mormons from "false secularization" as they build a literal, worldly, as well as spiritual, kingdom, is their unique understanding of the origin and destiny of humanity—the "incarnation of pre-existing spirits in human bodies" as part of a God-given opportunity "to advance in the grand scale of being, in which he is to move in the eternal worlds":

> Denying his heavenly origin, man would deny himself, would deny the sense of his life, the meaning of the community of man in which he lives, the sense of the universe in which he dwells. . . . The will of developing this image of God, the will to perfection, the will to reach the end of the development of all his power given him from above, is deep-rooted in man's life; hope and aim of perfection is a basic element of life itself.[4]

Benz shows he thoroughly understands President Young's philosophy of education, which he credits for energizing BYU and motivating its construction under more trying circumstances and greater sacrifices compared to other religious schools, including Benz's own. He shows that this philosophy is consistent with Brigham Young's under-standing of the highest aims of humankind, first quoting his early statement, "Intelligent beings are organized to become Gods, even the Sons of God, to dwell in the presence of Gods, and become associated with the highest intelligences that dwell in eternity. We are now in the school, and must practice upon what we receive," and then comment-ing:

> So his concept of education, and with it his concept of the aim of a university, is included in his concept of perfection, which opens the human mind and fills it with a real love of knowledge and joy of wisdom. In our time, where all kinds of reform programs of education are elaborated all over the world, based on a more or less totally secularized understanding of human nature, I find it quite inspiring to discover in the discourses of the founder of [BYU] words which encourage students, teachers, and scholars to study and learning as an essential element of perfection of man and of human society with its outlook on the kingdom of God, the king-dom of heaven. Let me close with this really ecumenical statement of Brigham Young, underlining the right way of secularization and preserving from its going wrong.

Benz then ends with another quotation from Brigham Young, one that captures perfectly the paradox, the equal and sometimes conflict-ing values, that the founder of BYU supported:

> How gladly would we understand every principle pertaining to science and art, and become thoroughly acquainted with every intricate operation of nature, and with all the chemical changes that are constantly going on around us! How delightful this would be, and what a boundless field of truth and power is open for us to explore! We are only just approaching the shores of a vast ocean of information that pertains to this physical world, to say nothing of that which pertains to the heavens, to angels and celestial beings, to the place of their habitation, to the manner of their life, and their progress to still higher degrees of perfection.[5]

Benz concludes, "This concept of education is unique for this Brigham Young University and is worthy to be celebrated forever."[6]

If Benz is right, BYU was founded, very consciously, to further the most intellectually exciting goal a university could have—the full development of individuals in terms of all our possible capacities, now and forever. However difficult to translate into specific curricular arrangements and administrative structures and social rules—however painful to contemplate, and even more painful to experience, the real history of the actual human institution which struggles with those paradoxical possibilities—we would do well to try to catch the vision and engage wholeheartedly in the struggle.

Certainly we have no reason to be dissuaded by those who would polarize the paradox into either a seminary for religious indoctrination or a wholly secularized institution. Neither kind of institution has proven by actual success that it can surpass the invigorating complexity—the inclusion of practical, humane, aesthetic, moral, and spiritual all together—of Brigham's definition of education which he gave to the territorial legislature in 1850 as they contemplated founding a university only three years after colonizing a desert: "Education is the power to think clearly, to act well in the day's work, and to appreciate life."

The academic revolution of the late nineteenth century, which Brigham Young saw at its beginning, diverted the somewhat unified humane questioning of meaning and value on the part of whole faculties to the new and powerful mode of asking pragmatic and finely reduced questions manageable through empirical means. The power of the land-grant colleges and research-oriented universities, and of their faculties as individuals, dramatically increased with the market for their salable knowledge in an increasingly technological world. There have been periodic outcries against the resulting independence and detachment of faculty from their students and from traditional student yearnings for ultimate meaning and moral challenge in their education, and there have been periodic curricular reforms to try to recapture those values. However, all these efforts have essentially failed because of a lack of any truly unifying vision, which in my view must be in some sense religious.

The 1960s marked the most dramatic disillusionment with higher education's secularization, not only voiced by students but by distinguished faculty such as Princeton's history professor James Billington, who in a widely circulated article in 1968 declared that the "humanistic heartbeat has failed" and as a result "liberal education is largely dead."[7] He cited trivializing diversification of curriculum, specialization by faculty, and loss of passionate commitment to values in the teaching environment and quoted a student at Michigan: "There is a drift towards something worse than mediocrity—and this is absolute indifference. An indifference towards perhaps even life itself." Many men and women, religious or not, have noted this increasing emptiness in all the whirl of secular higher education. The idolizing of freedom and specialism and detachment has produced mere anomie or at worst a "pagan melancholy" that issues in suicide or barely suppressed violence. The power to reduce human questions to the more accessible limits of the experimental method alone has produced many who have given themselves to what Daniel Bell calls the "religion of science."[8] An increasing number of so-called humanists are seduced by the reductionist techniques of science—to merely providing better and better answers to smaller and smaller, more spiritually void, questions, while neglecting tentative but heartfelt answers to the large questions that impassion and give meaning to our lives.

To succumb at BYU to critics' insistence that we "grow up," come into the wonderful twentieth century, and become a "real university" can be one way to sell our birthright for national rankings. It would be to adopt a depreciated, one-sided view of the possibilities of education. One commentator has asserted, "BYU can claim to be a university only if it acts as one and follows a basic rule of inquiry: no truth claim is so absolutely final and certain that it cannot be exposed to the processes of rational inquiry."[9] Despite the trouble some might have with that assertion, I am convinced that Brigham Young would accept it with alacrity. But he would also insist on the other side of the paradox, something like this: "No process of rational inquiry is so certain it cannot be exposed to the challenge of absolute truth claims revealed by prophets of God." Despite the opposition of modern secularist educators in and out of the church, President Young would insist that a complete higher education, worthy of that name and of the tithing resources of the church must try, however difficult it will always be, to maintain *both* values.

Let me review in his own words some of Brigham Young's most clear and powerful statements that establish both poles of the paradox as a basis for evaluating where BYU is right now in reaching that complex and radical vision and how we might do better. Probably the first time the title "Brigham Young University" was used was in a letter to President Young from his devoted friend, Thomas Kane, who was not a Mormon but who wrote in terms he knew the prophet would appreciate of hearing that he planned to found an educational institution:

> It is impossible to deprecate too seriously the growing practice of sending your bright youth abroad to lay the basis . . . of their lives on the crumbling foundations of modern unfaith and specialization. . . . The young fledglings who would resort to our Eastern seminaries of learning—to learn what you will hardly be able to unteach them all their days—should even now be training in the Brigham Young University.[10]

"Modern unfaith and specialization" seem to me very accurate terms for what was wrong with higher education then and still is. Two years after receiving that letter, in the fall of 1875, Brigham Young deeded property to a board of trustees for the purpose, as he wrote his son Alfales at Michigan law school, "of endowing a college to be called 'Brigham Young's Academy of Provo' . . . at which the children of the Latter-day Saints can receive a good education unmixed with the pernicious atheistic influences that are found in so many of the higher schools of the country."[11] Recent critics have read this as an excuse for censorship of particular subjects, a clear decision to limit education to purely utilitarian matters and to a set of narrowly defined values. But I think the statement means just what it says, "pernicious atheistic *influences*," that is, perspectives limited by a *wholly* materialistic and utilitarian view of the world.

Brigham Young opposed supporting public schools with the Saints' taxes, since those schools left Mormons with an education based on a process of inquiry which ignored spiritual values. By the same token Brigham Young would today, I believe, oppose our spending tithing monies to subsidize schools merely to gain nothing better than the kind of education they could receive in secular institutions which the Saints also subsidize. He would, I think, be particularly scandalized at what seems to me an increasing tendency on the part of BYU students themselves, abetted by some faculty, to substitute for his vision of eternally responsible education the fostering of ambition, status, and wealth. He would, for instance, oppose elitist standards and curricula prescribed, especially in engineering and business, by external and wholly secular professional organizations that in turn influence decisions at BYU about our own academic standards and curricula.

President Young, I believe, would deplore the use of sacred tithing funds merely to make possible for faculty and students a higher standard of living than that available to those around the world who sacrifice to pay for those students' education and those faculty members' salaries. If you have any doubt of that, listen to his own voice:

> While the inhabitants of the earth are bestowing all their ability, both mental and physical, upon perishable objects, those who profess to be Latter-day Saints, who have the privilege of receiving and understanding the principles of the holy Gospel, are in duty bound to study and find out, and put in practice in their lives, those principles that are calculated to endure, and that tend to a continual increase in the world to come.[12]

In other words, our chief duty is to achieve what church president Spencer W. Kimball once called, in defining BYU's central goal, "education for eternity."[13] To fulfill Young's famous, brief founding instruction to Karl Maeser, "not to teach even the alphabet or the multiplication tables without the spirit of God,"[14] is not merely to begin class with prayer or teach religion at one end of the campus or to try to develop a Mormon physics or psychology or literature or a Mormon pedagogy. It simply means that everything should be done for eternal, not worldly, values, for the lasting development of mind and spirit, and for useful service to other people, especially *redemptive* service and service that is in turn educational, helpful in others' lasting development of mind and spirit. Brigham knew this would be difficult because, as he said, "There are hundreds in this community who are more eager to become rich in the perishable things of the world than to adorn their minds."[15] He was talking specifically about clothing fashions and costs, but he specifically broadened his point to include economic "cooperation" and improving oneself "by every good book and then by every principle that has been received from heaven." He went on to assert, "It is beneath the character of the Latter-day Saints that they should have no more independence of mind or feeling than to follow after the grovelling customs and fashions of the poor, miserable wicked world."[16] He saw the issue in educational terms: Those who are seduced by the world will therefore not *learn*; they will "remain fixed with a very limited amount of knowledge, and like a door upon its hinges, move to and fro from one year to another without any visible advancement or improvement. . . . Man is made in the image of God, but what do we know of him or of ourselves when we suffer ourselves to love and worship the god of this world—riches?"

In a letter to his son Willard, just a year before his death, Brigham deplored the growing tendency in Utah to "teach the false political economy which contends against cooperation and the United Order."[17] It may surprise modern Mormons that that "false political economy" was not socialism or communism but free enterprise capitalism, the lack of which in Utah was being used by gentiles as evidence that Mormons were un-American barbarians in need of the salvation of public schools controlled purely by secular standards.

Brigham Young was not interested in limiting the subject matter of our studies. "God has revealed all the truth that is now in the possession of the world," he said, "whether it be scientific or religious."[18] He advocated teaching every imaginable subject, from agronomy to military science and geology, from law to liberal arts and philosophy. However, he did not see all knowledge as equally or intrinsically valuable: "It matters not what the subject be, *if* it tends to improve the mind, exalt the feelings and enlarge the capacity."[19] Even the study of religion, by itself or narrowly conceived, could fail to fulfill those purposes: "Shall I sit down and read the [scriptures] all the time? says one. Yes if you please, and when you have done you may be nothing but a sectarian after all. It is your duty to study everything upon the face of the earth in addition to reading those books."[20]

How, then, could the Saints make certain their education was for eternity, whatever the subject? And what education should come first in a busy life? Brigham Young, believing that "there is an eternity of knowledge before us; at most we receive but very little in this stage of progression,"[21] knew that subjects were not the key but rather the development of the mind's intrinsic qualities and of a moral, eternal perspective on any subject or issue. He saw these basics as connected. Genuine intelligence, because it is a fundamental attribute of God, is intrinsically connected to the spiritual and moral: "If men would be great in goodness they must be intelligent."[22] Brigham clearly saw that one basic reason for this is that the essence of moral development, which is free exercise of agency, depends completely on knowledge: "Every mortal being must stand up as an intelligent, organized capacity, and choose or refuse the good, and thus act for himself . . . All must have the opportunity, no matter if all go into the depths of wickedness."[23]

That is strong doctrine, wholly unacceptable to some who are presently at BYU, but President Young did not flinch: "It would be useless for anybody to undertake to drive me to heaven or hell. My independence is sacred to me—it is a portion of that same Deity that rules in the heavens."[24] He recognized that such freedom would bring disagreements and diversity, but again he did not flinch: "Interchanging our ideas and exhibiting that which we believe and understand affords an opportunity for detecting and correcting errors."[25] And again, "I am not a stereo-typed Latter-day Saint, and do not believe in the doctrine. . . . Are we going to stand still? Away with stereo-typed Mormons!"[26]

But, you say, isn't stereotyping precisely what BYU does to students and faculty, abetted by Young's narrow vision of "useful" knowledge and of eternal (meaning Mormon-defined) purposes? When I first considered a teaching position at BYU, having taught at state universities and a secularized private university, I was often asked if I might not find BYU lacking in freedom and diversity. It is sponsored by a church with a strong central authority and definite, even dogmatic, beliefs, they would say, as if the consequences should be obvious. Already familiar with Brigham Young's vision of independent thought, I did not expect such an environment, and I have indeed found, as I had hoped, that Brigham Young's university allows me *greater* freedom in my teaching and challenges me with greater diversity of student and faculty thinking than any other place I have taught, including Stanford and the University of Utah. That is because I am free here (as are my students) to explore the rich, diverse, and positive issues of religious and moral faith as well as the questions and challenges and skepticism that predominate elsewhere.

Brigham Young had no illusions about the superior wisdom and morality of secular institutions. He was grateful that the Saints had not been "educated in the devilry and craft of the learned classes of mankind,"[27] to hold them back. They could, in the words of Apostle Parley P. Pratt that Brigham admired, "receive and extend that pure intelligence which is unmingled with the jargon of mystic Babylon." Brigham Young shared the understanding of his younger contemporary, Herman Melville, who, writing about the time of Brigham's death in 1877, praised Shakespeare for being "so advanced a modern" that he was "utterly without secular hypocrisy, superstition, or secular cant."[28]

However, we have enough problems trying to work through the paradox of Christian higher education that we need not point fingers at secular institutions. I am, indeed, grateful to our recent and future secular critics for pointing to our problems, but they need to be somewhat patient while we continue to work on those problems, which are not, given the conflicting but important values at stake, at all simple. In my view the critics actually need to be *more radical* in their criticism. Brigham Young's vision provides a much more demanding standard than that provided by secular universities. He would not worry as much (though I trust he would be disappointed) about occasions of spying and pressure on faculty at BYU as he would that we are not finding inventive ways, through cultural and institutional change, to help our younger faculty and administrators solve the increasingly terrible dilemma of contemporary couples: how to achieve genuine equality of opportunity for self-development and service, maintain a reasonable standard of living, and still be nurturing and responsible parents. I think he would be less worried about the occasional bouts with censorship as he would that we are not aggressively and creatively working to find ways to fulfill a central principle of his vision:

> There is not, has not been, and never can be any method, scheme, or plan devised by any being in this world for intelligence to eternally exist and obtain an exaltation, without knowing the good and the evil—without tasting the bitter and the sweet. Can people understand that it is actually necessary for opposite principles to be placed before them, or this state of being would be no probation . . . we cannot obtain eternal life unless we actually know and comprehend by our experience the principle of good and the principle of evil.[29]

If the complexities of that paradox are such—given the tenderness of young undergraduates and the concern of our largely conservative constituency for their protection—that Brigham Young's ideals cannot now be fulfilled through direct confrontation of ideas and actual experience, then we must find ways to use the power of art, literature, film, and drama, where experience is less direct because it is filtered through a moral imagination, to achieve those crucial purposes having to do with salvation. We could more thoroughly prepare students, with both aesthetic and ethical training from our best teachers, to deal with difficult and challenging movies and books and plays, in a closed environment where the non-university public, with its own unprepared perspective and often politicized agenda, would not be invited. This is already happening to some extent in the International Films program and the dramas presented only in the small, experimental theaters at BYU. But we need a more thorough preparation and discussion of works of the kind that would educate us morally and in terms of our salvation in the ways Brigham suggests.

I think President Young, given his broad, paradoxical vision, might be worried that we welcomed General Westmoreland and Howard Ruff on campus, without serious debate of their very controversial values, but were uneasy about having the head of the Soviet Supreme Court here, merely because he was a communist, or about allowing a visit from Christian pacifist Jean Hutchinson, merely because she has been arrested (like Joseph Smith) for peacefully advocating her beliefs, or about having Pulitzer-prize-winning historian Laurel Thatcher Ulrich speak to us, apparently because she is a feminist. I think President Young would be less worried about the comparatively more expensive education we give potential lawyers and entrepreneurs than whether, as he put it, law and business students are led "to study the decisions and counsels of the just and the wise, and not forever be studying how to get the advantage of their neighbor."[30] I think he would be less worried about whether we should sponsor a medical school than whether we should have the courage to discuss the profound moral issues that increasingly confront the medical profession.

Finally, Young would be less concerned about whether our critics, or we at BYU, agreed about these judgments I have just made than that we continue working with the paradoxes that stimulated them, and that we do so in a spirit of respect and cooperative adventure. I am afraid that at BYU, an institution of "higher learning," differences of opinion make people uncomfortable. Too many students and even faculty hunger for the devil's bread of easy and final answers without disagreement or struggle. Some, both conservatives and liberals, excommunicate one another in their hearts over differences of approach or perception. Too many of us fall far short of the spirit and vision of our founder, a man without formal education who knew the Greek myth of the Bed of Procrustes better than too many current Ph.D.s:

> The world is before us, eternity is before us, and an inexhaustible fountain of intelligence for us to obtain. Every man, and more particularly my immediate associates who are with me daily, know how I regret the ignorance of this people—how it floods my heart with sorrow to see so many Elders of Israel who wish everybody to come to their standard and be measured by their measure. Every man must be just so long, to fit their iron bedstead, or be cut off to the right length: if too short, he must be stretched, to fill the requirement.[31]

Brigham Young cared about BYU and, I believe, continues to watch over it. He is patient, perhaps amused by our struggles, hoping we can slowly come up to his vision. I have learned that despite his close supervision of the building of the St. George temple, he was not its designer and disliked the small original tower which offended his

carpenter's eye as badly out of proportion. He did not embarrass the local craftsmen by directly insisting on a change, but on August 16, 1878,
about one year after his death, his voice was heard. The tower was
struck by lightning and, though the temple was miraculously preserved
from burning, the tower was damaged. It was replaced by a much larger
one.

Also, in 1878, not long after his death, Brigham Young visited Karl
Maeser in a dream and took him on a tour of a large building with many
rooms and a spacious assembly hall. Maeser, on waking, drew the floor
plans for the building in some notes about the dream and put them
away until six years later when the old building on Center Street was
destroyed by fire. He remembered the notes and used them to design
the new Academy Building[32] that became the center of BYU for fifty
years. These are parables for those with ears to hear.

Let me close by turning again to Hugh Nibley:

Brigham Young's educational concepts stand out in brilliant con-
trast against the background of everything that is practiced and
preached in our higher schools today. But . . . as administrative
problems have accumulated in a growing Church, the authorities
have tended to delegate the business of learning to others, and
those others have been only too glad to settle for the outward show,
the easy and flattering forms, trappings and ceremonies of education. Worse still, they have chosen business-oriented, career-
minded, degree-seeking programs in preference to the strenuous,
critical, liberal, mindstretching exercises that Brigham Young recommended. We have chosen the services of the hired image-
maker in preference to unsparing self-criticism, and the first question the student is taught to ask today is John Dewey's golden
question: "What is there in it for me?". . . . Whether we like it or
not, we are going to have to return to Brigham Young's ideals of
education; we may fight it all the way, but in the end God will keep
us after school until we learn our lesson.[33]

NOTES

1. Hugh Nibley, "Educating the Saints—A Brigham Young Mosaic," *Brigham Young University Studies* 11 (Autumn 1970): 61-87; reprinted in Richard Cracroft and Neal A. Lambert, eds., *A Believing People: The Literature of the Latter-day Saints* (Salt Lake City: Bookcraft, 1979); the quotation is from p. 62.

2. See Ernst Benz, "Mormonism and the Secularization of Religions in the Modern World," *Brigham Young University Studies* 19 (Summer 1976): 627-40.

3. Ibid., 628.

4. Ibid., 636.

5. Benz is quoting from the *Journal of Discourses* (hereafter *JD*), 26 vols. (Liverpool: Latter-day Saints' Bookseller's Depot, 1854-86), 5:256, 20 Sept. 1857.

6. Benz, 638-39.

7. *Life*, 23 Feb. 1968, 11; I review and quote liberally from this fine essay in my "The Quest for Authentic Faculty Power," *Soundings: An Interdisciplinary Journal* 52 (1969): 196-217.

8. Ibid., 199.

9. Fred Buchanan, "Education among the Mormons: Brigham Young and the Schools of Utah," paper given at the Pacific Coast History of Education Society, May 1979, and the American Educational Studies Association, Nov. 1980; copy in my possession.

10. Cited in *Brigham Young University: The First One Hundred Years*, 4 vols., ed. Ernst L. Wilkinson (Provo, UT: Brigham Young University Press, 1976), 1:63.

11. Brigham Young to Alfales Young, Oct. 20, 1875, cited in *Brigham Young University*, 1:67.

12. *JD* 2:91.

13. See Spencer W. Kimball, "Second-Century Address," *Brigham Young University*, 4:555.

14. Reinhard Maeser, *Karl G. Maeser, A Biography by His Son* (Provo, UT: Brigham Young University, 1928), 79. This seems to be the main source for this often-quoted statement.

15. *JD* 8:9.

16. Ibid. 13:4

17. Cited in Dean C. Jessee, ed., *Letters of Brigham Young to His Sons* (Salt Lake City: Deseret Book Co., 1974), 199.

18. *JD* 8:162.

19. Ibid. 1:335.

20. Ibid. 2:93-94.

21. Ibid. 3:354.

22. Manuscript History of Brigham Young, 22 Sept. 1851, archives, Historical Department, Church of Jesus Christ of Latter-day Saints, Salt Lake City, Utah.

23. *JD* 8:352.

24. Ibid. 10:191.

25. Ibid. 6:95.

26. Ibid. 8:185.

27. Ibid. 6:60.

28. Manuscript, Melville Papers, Houghton Library, Harvard University, Cambridge, Massachusetts.

29. *JD* 7:237.

30. Ibid. 16:9.

31. Ibid. 8:8. I am grateful for this quotation and other insights to Bruce B. Clark, *Brigham Young on Education* (Provo, UT: Brigham Young University Press, 1970).

32. R. Maeser, 112.

33. Nibley, 65.

five

WHY UTAH MORMONS SHOULD BECOME DEMOCRATS: REFLECTIONS ON PARTISAN POLITICS

Over one hundred years ago, in September 1891, there occurred in Huntsville, Utah, a strange incident. In this American town on a bright late summer morning with young cottonwoods and Lombardy poplars turning bright yellow along the streets and pockets of gold aspen and deep-red maples visible on the surrounding hills, Mormon church leaders went from door to door, assigning one family to be Democrats, the next to be Republicans. Thus were Mormons attempting to accommodate gentile political ways as a prerequisite for Utah statehood. David O. McKay, one of the most openly Republican of church presidents, confirmed this story of how his hometown of Huntsville had once been divided by alternate houses, while Joseph Nelson, head of the Saltair Corporation, reported that in his Salt Lake City ward his bishop stood and declared all the Saints on one side of the aisle Democrats and all those on the other Republicans.[1] In Rockville, in southern Utah, leaders divided the community down Main Street.[2] Whatever the mechanism, in the early 1890s Mormon leaders, from the First Presidency through stake presidents down to bishops and other local leaders, were energetically engaged in a remarkably paradoxical enterprise. They went about proving that the rank-and-file was independent of political influence from the church hierarchy by directing many Mormons, against their inclinations, to join the Republican party.

As everyone in Utah knew, a wholesale onslaught on Mormon beliefs had been led by the national Republican Party. Its initial platform had promised in the 1850s to eradicate what it termed the "twin relics of barbarism"—slavery and polygamy. In response, Mormons formed the anti-Republican People's Party, and applications for statehood were denied as increasingly punitive measures were passed against Mormons by the Republican-controlled national government. But by 1891 church leaders had become convinced it must disband the Mormon party to avoid "carpetbaggers," Republican appointees from Washington who, as they did in the devastated South, exercised insensitive, tyrannous control that essentially disenfranchised the local people. Church leaders knew that if things were left to chance, most Mormons would become Democrats and in reaction gentiles would become Republicans, perpetuating the bitter political/religious division that had plagued Utah territory since the formation of the anti-Mormon Liberal party in 1870.

The insight and intentions of the First Presidency are revealed in a letter written in May 1891 to John W. Young, who had long served as unofficial liaison to national Democratic party leaders. President Wilford Woodruff and his counselors George Q. Cannon and Joseph F. Smith informed Young that the political field in Utah was "ripe ready to harvest," but that Mormons were anti-Republican in their sympathies and thus likely to "rush into the Democratic ranks." They believed it was "of the highest importance that this not be the case." Consider their reason, which helps explain their controversial and still sometimes maligned actions in directing people who naturally would be Democrats to become Republicans: "The more evenly balanced the parties become the safer it will be for us [Mormons] in the security of our liberties; and . . . our influence for good will be far greater than it possibly could be were either party overwhelmingly in the majority."[3]

That statement shows remarkable foresight. It demonstrates, I believe, greater understanding of the basic strength of our political system than that of anti-Mormons of that time, mostly Republicans, who were willing to use any means, however unconstitutional, to destroy Mormonism as supposedly un-American. And it shows better insight into the nature and value of political parties than that of many Mormons today, mostly Republicans, who believe that Truth resides with their party and who therefore seek overwhelming supremacy.

I believe things have come to such a pass that many Utah Mormons should choose to become Democrats—not because the Democratic platform is "truer," certainly not because its leaders and candidates are "better." Utah Mormons should become Democrats because for about twenty-five years Democrats have been a steadily dwindling minority in Utah, and thus Republicans are developing the attitudes and practices of one-party rule. Those attitudes and practices are more dangerous than the actual beliefs or programs of *either* party.

I believe some Utah Mormons should become Democrats for precisely the same reason the First Presidency encouraged some to become Republicans in 1891, which is well worth reading again: "The more evenly balanced the parties become the safer it will be for us in the security of our liberties; and . . . our influence for good will be far greater than it possibly could be were either party overwhelmingly in the majority."

Some may think this is simply a partisan plea by a disgruntled Democrat. Not so! I am a lifelong Republican, a descendant of Willkie and Dewey supporters. I voted twice for Nixon and twice for Reagan. I grew up hearing how my grandfather was kept in near starvation through the latter part of the Depression by anti-Mormon Democrats in Idaho. They swept in with Franklin D. Roosevelt and gave all the work painting state buildings to their incompetent cronies, who, as my grandfather said, besides depriving him of a living, "couldn't paint worth a tinker's dam." I often heard my father, a hard-pressed farmer in southeast Idaho, fulminate about Roosevelt's federal farm agents, many the sons of pork-barrel politicians. With no knowledge of local people and land conditions, they wasted money and tried to impose useless and destructive controls.

Despite all this I sincerely believe that I and other Utah Mormons should become Democrats—at least until the parties are nearly equal in strength again in the state. In fact, it might be good for church leaders to encourage some shifting. This would make clear to Mormons the fundamental Constitutional principle that American freedoms are based on: separation of powers and prescribed checks and balances, strongly aided by the development of the two-party system. If those checks and the party system are kept strong and balanced, they create a *process* of government that is the surest guarantee of our liberties and of civil peace, much more sure than the particular content of any person's or party's ideas about what our government should do.

Political parties have generally had the opposite effect of that anticipated by the framers, who deplored partisan politics as too polarizing to society. Instead parties have reduced partisan polarization; they have helped keep politics in the United States mainly non-ideological, forcing partisans to compromise their demands, trade favors, unite with strange bedfellows to get *part* of what they wanted, and in turn help opponents get part of what they wanted. This has provided a basis for cooperation among people of different religions, races, and sectional interests; it has tended to shrink volatile dogmatisms into manageable issues and has effectively translated what I think was the most profound and inspired insight of James Madison into reality.

In August 1786, just ten years after the Declaration of Independence and only five after the Articles of Confederation had been ratified, America's great experiment in creating a "new order of the ages" was failing so completely that George Washington wrote to John Jay, "What a triumph for the advocates of despotism to find that we are incapable of governing ourselves."[4] But at about this same time Madison, an intellectual and political leader from Virginia, set out to do something. He had been engaged in six months of intense study of books on history and government sent him from Paris by Thomas Jefferson. He now took time off from his studies to attend a convention at Annapolis on regulating trade among the states. There, together with two friends, the strong federalist Alexander Hamilton of New York and Governor Edmund Randolph of Virginia, he successfully led the delegates in making a unanimous call for another convention. It was to be held the next May in Philadelphia and to have a greatly expanded agenda, essentially to amend the Articles of Confederation.

In the meantime Madison wrote two papers and shared them with Washington, Randolph, and the rest of the Virginia delegation. When the new convention began on May 28, 1787, Randolph rose with a prepared sketch for a new Constitution. It was what became known as the Virginia Plan and was based on the papers by Madison. It moved the convention beyond its announced purpose and gave the edge to those favoring a strong national government.

By the second week, in a reconsideration of the means of selecting members to the proposed two-house Congress, a basic roadblock became visible. Some worried that states with small populations like Rhode Island would be "subject to faction," rent by the passions of large minorities, while others suspected that the large states like Massachusetts were so unwieldy as to be impervious to effective democratic government but inclined to anarchy and misrule. Madison turned these apparently mutually supportive arguments against each other. Drawing on his long study of republics and confederacies, he pointed out in an argument he later developed fully in *The Federalist*, letter 10, that all civilized societies are divided into numerous sects, factions, and interests; that whenever a majority is united by a common interest or passion, the rights of the minority are in danger; and that neither honesty, respect for character, nor conscience had succeeded in restraining the majority in past societies from infringing on the rights of the minority. In fact, he reminded his colleagues in a sentence that should burn with memory and caution for every Mormon, "Religion itself may become a motive to persecution and oppression."

What remedy then? It was brilliantly simple, original, and crucial in removing the roadblock to an acceptable Constitution: To *enlarge* the political sphere and thereby create a community with so *many* interests and parties that, in the first place, a majority would not be likely at the same moment to have a common interest different from that of the whole people, including minorities, and that, in the second place, in cases where the majority did have such an interest, they would not be able to unite in the pursuit of it.[5]

Madison thus provided delegates a way to believe that the evils they had seen flowing from an excess of democracy, rather than being increased in a national government and growing country, would actually be decreased as they counteracted each other. And as delegates acted on that faith to create our country, Madison became a prophet of how a pluralistic society can in fact work with unique success. The stability and internal peacefulness of our country have resulted from its governmental structure and what noted writer on education and on government Daniel Bell calls America's "constitutional culture," with its many checks and balances, including the two-party system.[6] Our system encourages the formation of shifting coalitions in ways that safeguard the liberties of all citizens, particularly minority groups, whose rights are always most at risk in any democratic society.

Two other moments stand out for me in that four-month process of compromise and shifting coalitions in the summer of 1787 that produced the document we honored much in the years approaching and including its bicentennial in 1987. Those moments are particularly important to my argument for political pluralism as an essential ingredient of national peace. They are the decision to give the war-making power to Congress, not the president, and the decision not to give either Congress or the president the power to impose what were called "sumptuary laws."

I begin with the second: In late August, as the Convention moved into its final stages, George Mason of Virginia moved to enable Congress to enact laws designed to regulate personal behavior on moral and religious grounds. He argued, in a way that sounds reasonable to most Mormons and conservative people generally, "No government can be maintained unless the manners [by which he meant private moral behavior] be *made* consonant to it."[7] After a few speeches in opposition, the Convention voted down the proposal, and, except for the unfortunate fourteen-year experiment with Prohibition of liquor from 1919 to 1933, our system has generally avoided wholesale infringement upon people's private morality.

Why would I, a teetotaling Mormon who believes that substance abuse and sexual promiscuity are among civilization's most destructive evils, want government to stay entirely away from trying to control those things—except as they directly victimize others? For two reasons: First, I want freedom of conscience in areas of personal faith and morality for myself, and I must therefore protect it for others. Second, I do not want to live in a society, like most of those in the world, driven by the conflict and violence that result from attempts to coerce personal faith and morals—conflict and violence such as were clearly produced under Prohibition and by the earlier attempt to control Mormon polygamy and which currently surrounds the abortion issue.

Daniel Bell's twofold explanation for the stability of our government for over 200 years is instructive. First, there is the unexpected stability in pluralism that Madison predicted, built on coalition-forming between interest groups and thus protection of the interests of potentially rebellious minorities. Second, we have reduced conflict by largely avoiding legislation in areas of personal morality. As Bell points out, for most people such areas are non-negotiable. They often involve deep personal convictions which cannot be adjusted or compromised, and when compliance is forced, that compulsion gives rise to deep resentments and eventual rebellion. The arena of law should be reserved for procedural matters and areas where we directly harm others or restrict *their* rights. These matters are generally clear and acceptable, or are at least negotiable, meaning we can compromise and live with the compromises. When we cannot compromise our consciences or we feel personally infringed upon, conflict is often the result.

Apostle Brigham Young, Jr., reflecting, I am confident, his father's view, confessed during the polygamy persecutions of 1884, "I am willing, in political matters, to . . . let the majority rule. . . . But in the things pertaining to conscience no man, no set of men . . . can control me before my God. . . . I am a free man in relation to these matters, not bowing to any majority nor to any party."[8]

Majority control over conscience was precisely what happened in polygamy, and Mormons should remember it well. As Daniel Bell pointed out to a BYU audience in the fall of 1986, "Cultural conservatives should be political liberals."[9] In other words, those, like Mormons, who want the freedom to practice their strong and unusual personal religious beliefs and ethics should be among the most active in promoting a system where *all* are free to do so, even those whose beliefs and actions are repugnant to them, as long as those beliefs and actions do not unavoidably and significantly infringe on the rights of others.

Mormons should also be among the most active opponents to anything like George Mason's sumptuary laws, such as Prohibition, to "blue laws" such as Sunday closing, etc.—that is, laws that try to control private morality or activities between consciously consenting adults, no matter how perverse. We should be against any governmental coercion upon teachers or curriculum, especially in areas of religious views, organic evolution, human sexuality, and partisan politics. We should even be against prescribed school prayer, including so-called "moments of silence," whenever, however subtly, those publicly mandated forms act to coerce young minds. Spiritual and moral coercion not only violate the most central value of the Constitution but the central values of the Mormon religion, the very ones that lead us to revere the Constitution.

Mormons belong to one of the few remaining religious bodies which still believes the U.S. Constitution was inspired by God. The crucial scriptural passage is Doctrine and Covenants 101:77-80, a revelation to Joseph Smith in 1833. That was only forty years after ratification of the Constitution and not long before Madison died, the last surviving framer and certainly one of those to whom God refers in saying to the Prophet, "I established the Constitution of this land by the hands of wise men whom I raised up unto this very purpose" (v. 80).

Knowledgeable people may laugh at such a description of those fifty-five mortal men, most of them quite secular, very few of them pious, some dissolute. But after reading the story of their accomplishment in William Peters's excellent history, *A More Perfect Union* (1987), I cannot laugh. By devising the first government in history which allowed a group of people consciously to place themselves under the rule of law, these men proved to be extremely courageous and wise. At the same time they achieved a structure that promotes the most fundamental goal of many prophets through the ages, that individuals be able to assume moral responsibility for their own actions.

The revelation I have quoted says that the American Constitution and laws are acceptable to God *only* as they are "established and . . . maintained for the rights and protection of all flesh, according to just and holy principles" (D&C 101:77). These principles, as BYU professor Noel Reynolds points out,[10] are precisely what is meant by the rule of law. In the Lord's own words, "That every man may act in doctrine and principle pertaining to futurity, according to the moral agency which I have given unto him, that every man may be *accountable for his own sins in the day of judgment*" (v. 78; my emphasis). The framers wanted people to be free to pursue wealth and happiness and personal salvation in whatever form they chose and to do so with confidence that laws would apply consistently and equally to all, whatever their private goals. They could make both moral choices and legal contracts with reasonable ability to predict future consequences, confident there would be no intervention by the whims and arbitrary commands of rulers.

This system guarantees that all can be held morally responsible, both before the law where appropriate and always before their consciences and God; they are accountable for their actions and choices since they are free from compulsion. As Hugh Nibley has written: "The best of human laws leaves every man free to engage in his own pursuit of happiness, without presuming for a moment to tell him where that happiness lies; that is the very thing the laws of God can guarantee. At *best*, the political prize is negative."[11]

Mormons have trouble with this. Natural utopians, we tend to want more from the political system than it can give. We want a *positive* prize. Republicans in particular seem to want to legislate private morality, to use law to make people good, to force them not just to refrain from harming each other but to *be* good. Any such effort to do God's work, to use the power of the state to do what only churches and non-coercive social and cultural forces should do, once led the Republican party into one of the most outrageous intrusions upon human rights in American history, one that ranks with Jim Crow laws and our internment in concentration camps of U.S. citizens of Japanese ancestry during World War II.

I mean, of course the anti-polygamy crusade against Mormons. That crusade was doubly pernicious in that it not only violated a fundamental principle that government should not intrude into personal belief and morality, but it adopted unconstitutional means to serve that unconstitutional end. Perhaps most repugnant is that it employed two ancient enemies of the rule of law that the framers explicitly renounced: *ex post facto* laws, which make past actions criminal and thus remove predictability and moral responsibility,[12] and bills of attainder. The latter are declarations of guilt of specifically targeted individuals by legislative bodies rather than by fair trial in court.

Led by Republicans, the government passed, declared constitutional, and then brutally enforced a series of laws designed to coerce Mormons into conformity with Victorian America. The Morrill Act of 1862 forbade people from cohabitation in plural marriage; the Edmunds Act of 1882 imposed five-year sentences on polygamists and deprived them forever of the right to vote and hold office; and the infamous Utah Commission, appointed by Republican president Chester Arthur to enforce the Edmunds Act, imposed a religious test oath by requiring that voters and office-seekers swear they had never practiced polygamy. In Idaho mere membership in the church was used as a test to disenfranchise *all* Mormons, polygamous or not.

In 1887 the Republican Congress moved directly to attack the organization behind the practice of polygamy. The Edmunds-Tucker Act disincorporated the church, confiscated most of its properties, disenfranchised all polygamists and all Utah women (Mormon or not), abolished the Perpetual Emigrating Fund that subsidized immigration from Europe, and took over the Mormon-dominated public school system. No wonder that James Henry Moyle, who witnessed this period as a young man, could write that reading the Republican-controlled *Salt Lake Tribune* for that time demonstrated that

> there was no fundamentally American political principle that [the crusaders] would not have sacrificed to achieve their ambition and determination to secure the political control of the Utah Territory and the destruction of Mormonism. . . . Not a few of them placed no limit on the executive and judicial action which they would take to secure for the minority control of the majority and to deprive the majority of its most fundamental political rights.[13]

Moyle was an ardent, lifelong Democrat and devout Mormon. Though he eventually served as a mission president for the church, he suffered much humiliation under the cloud of anti-Democrat feeling that strangely developed among Mormons after the partitions of 1891. Mormons soon forgot their former evil treatment at the hands of Republicans, and Moyle was amazed and sorrowful that church leaders, in trying to prevent people from going overwhelmingly Democrat (which, in a moving passage of devotion to his leaders, Moyle says they were *right* to do), unintentionally made Utah Mormons overwhelmingly Republican. He regrets mainly the great confusions and personal tragedies these efforts produced, especially the tragedies that befell Mormon Democratic Party leaders B. H. Roberts and Moses Thatcher. He feels deeply the "great injustice to the Democratic Party that was perpetuated in the ingratitude and partisan excesses that followed." He concludes, in a lesson for Mormons and non-Mormons today, that it is futile for even great men "to be both political and ecclesiastical leaders at the same time in a government where political parties are controlling and voters divide on political lines. . . . In America politics and religion should never be entangled."[14]

My concern is that religion and politics are being entangled again in Mormonism, not among high-ranking leaders so much as among local leaders and in Mormon popular culture. It is no longer merely a joke that a good Mormon cannot be a Democrat, and Mormon Democrats are constantly on the defensive, seeming to feel a need to apologize for even *being* Democrats, whatever their particular views. The response church leaders feared in 1891 is also occurring, though now in the opposite direction: Non-Mormons and disaffected Mormons are gravitating to the Democratic Party, so that the political division is becoming a religious one.

One of the most troubling elements of this polarization is the growing Mormon tendency to find absolute or at least superior, even divine, truth in the Republican Party platform. At the practical level our system depends, I believe, on a difficult skill suited to that quality the framers called "the genius of our people." It is the ability to energetically pursue a program or idea in the political marketplace and then calmly to accept its defeat or modification through compromise and even to lend support to the "winners" in a genuinely united community. It is a skill based on recognition that the finest truth or law or program is never the creation of one person or partisan group but rather the result of the passionate conflict and combining of ideas and proposals in a democratic context.

I was somewhat pleased to see the Republican victories nationally in November 1994, because it seemed to me that many Democrats in

Congress, like the Republicans in much of Utah, had during forty years of control begun to adopt the dangerous habits of one-party rule—cronyism, disregard of opposing points of view, failure to pursue new ideas—and I thought a shake-up and new lines of debate and coalition might help us find new solutions. But when the leader of House Republicans, Newt Gingrich, after the election announced he would "never compromise" with President Clinton, he revealed an ignorance of the basic strength of our political system that was breathtaking. When both Republicans and Democrats belittled Clinton's State of the Union address as too full of compromise, too much a combination of left and right, liberal and conservative ideas, I despaired that our political discourse had descended permanently into small-minded partisanship and resentment.

The kind of political skill and virtue I am trying to advocate is based on the notion articulated by Milton in *Areopagitica*, his great defense of freedom of the press and of expression. Milton's surprising idea is that virtue and truth are made pure and whole not by being cloistered and protected from exposure to contrary, even "evil," actions and ideas, but by the opposite: full engagement in a tempting world and a full marketplace of ideas to which we respond with reasoned criticism and rethinking and, yes, even changing our mind and compromising.

Three hundred years after Milton's essay, Walter Lippmann, writing in August 1939, just as liberty was under worldwide assault at the beginning of World War II, reminded us that our vaunted ideal of freedom of speech and political expression is not merely an abstract virtue or matter of simple neighborly toleration but an absolute practical necessity: "We must protect the right of our opponents to speak because we must hear what they have to say. . . . because freedom of discussion improves our own opinions."[15] He points out that in our system we pay the opposition salaries out of the public treasury because like a good doctor who tells us unpleasant truths, an opponent can help us be more healthy.

Lippmann shows how dictatorships defeat themselves by liquidating or terrifying into silence the very voices that would help them avoid or correct inevitable errors. It is precisely such opposition and debate, especially concerning such a crucial matter as making war, which our Founding Fathers placed firmly in an open, contentious body like Congress, because they knew that there, rather than in the patriotic but narrow, cloistered vision of a single person like Oliver North or H. R. Haldeman, the best decisions would be made and most effectively changed if they needed to be. It is there where what Lippmann calls "the indispensable opposition" most effectively operates and where Reagan, as well as Nixon, should have turned to tell and hear the truth. As Lippmann concludes, "A good statesman, like any other sensible human being, always learns more from his opponents than from his fervent supporters. For his supporters will push him to disaster unless his opponents show him where the dangers lie."[16]

Good Democrats or good Republicans are not those who believe their party has all truth and who yearn for complete victory and one-party government control. They are rather those who seek the engagement, compromise, enlightening debate, checks on natural aggrandizement of power, etc., that the process of interparty dialogue makes possible. They are like Todd Britsch, who, while he was Dean of Humanities at BYU, said to me, "I do not feel good when I have power to implement my ideas without argument and opposition. I've learned that without strong rebuttal and rethinking they are likely not to be very good ideas—and may be very bad ones." Good Democrats and Republicans are those who realize that the political process is strongest when the parties are nearly equal in strength—and good Mormons, believers in our inspired Constitution and desirous of political peace and effectiveness, would work, or even change affiliations, to bring that about.

Let me illustrate the danger I feel in devotion to supposed one-party truth. In the spring 1987 run-off election for Brigham Young University student body officers, two students who had had some experience in negative campaigning in statewide elections used such methods to defeat a student they found objectionable simply because he was a "liberal Democrat." The candidate, who had led strongly in the primary and thus was likely to win, had been president of Response, a club that sponsored the Peace and Human Rights symposium held at

BYU each year. He had participated in an on-campus anti-Contra demonstration and had signed a petition published in the *Daily Universe* calling for U.S.-Soviet arms reduction.

The two students, according to a report in BYU's independent *Student Review*, "were committed to the perpetuation of a conservative political philosophy at BYU through the perpetuation of politically conservative [student] leaders."[17] Their campaign consisted of allegations about the candidate's financial management and criticism of his bringing to campus "leftist speakers." The candidate, and others, responded in a *Daily Universe* article with statements such as Yes, he brought liberal speakers to campus—along with conservative and moderate speakers—as part of the function of the symposia to educate people to a range of views, and Yes, there was an $800 deficit listed on the Response account, but it was an accounting error and had been removed.

The two students printed a flyer which quoted only the admissions but not the explanations. When asked why they did this, they responded that to print the explanations as well would have limited the "rhetorical effectiveness" of their flyers.[18] These actions were probably the reason the candidate lost, and they reveal a profound and dangerous misunderstanding of our political process as well as Christian morality by some young Mormons.

Lest anyone think that such intolerance and misunderstanding of our system occurs only at BYU or among conservatives, let me tell about my alma mater, the University of Utah. Because the U was founded by Mormons and remained predominantly Mormon until well into this century, there was much church influence, and the increasing non-Mormon faculty at times felt somewhat beleaguered. In some departments there is probably still a Mormon clique that sometimes controls things unfairly. But when I was a student in the 1950s, I found in all the humanities and most of the social science departments an almost complete swing to the opposite condition. Nearly all teachers were non-Mormons or had left the faith, and I found in many classes and on most public occasions a subtle but unmistakable disdain for things Mormon.

Sometimes the disdain wasn't so subtle. Religiously pious themes and term papers by Mormon students were belittled among the faculty and graduate students. The "local culture" was openly stereotyped as ignorant, repressive, and prejudiced. A faculty member asserted at a public forum that it was inconsistent for a Mormon bishop to be a university professor because commitment to any particular set of beliefs precluded the necessary scholarly skepticism and objectivity. Which left unspoken the interesting question of what professors were to profess—apparently only criticism of religious or conservative beliefs or fostering of particular political and moral crusades. And that professing was done under what I believe is the most dangerous cloak for unexamined beliefs and assumptions, the aura of "objectivity."

In 1975 I found that things were getting worse. My visits to the U, and a stint teaching a class in the extension division, revealed that many professors thought of the university as a small island of light in the great darkness of Mormon country. Their mission was to disabuse the Mormon students of their conditioned naivete and to belittle their church and culture—if in no other way than by simply not taking it seriously. Even though 70 percent of students were LDS, many professors and graduate assistants seemed to feel no obligation to respond to that reality in their teaching, the way their liberal convictions would have led them to respond in any university with predominantly black or Jewish students—by learning about and engaging in respectful dialogue with the ideas and art and literature and institutions and people of the local culture.

One of my former professors, in genuine sorrow, admitted that his department simply would not hire an active Mormon into a tenure-track position. It was extremely hard for me to believe that such blatant and illegal prejudice was possible at a modern state university, but as I looked more closely I could see he was right. They hadn't hired an active Mormon, despite excellent candidates, in twenty-five years and still haven't twenty years later. I also found that friends had similar experiences with other departments, one finding that he had been mistaken for a non-Mormon and invited to the separate non-Mormon party for candidates, where he was told frankly about their determination not to hire such intrinsically handicapped creatures.

Since anything a Mormon president or academic vice-president would do about this embarrassing and costly blot on Utah's fine higher education system would be immediately suspect, it seems to me that it is high time for non-Mormon leaders of stature in the administration and faculty to approach the question as an educational rather than a religious issue. They could set the example, showing respect for their Mormon colleagues and students by engaging openly in serious dialogue with them and their faith and culture. They could act on and vigorously promote the assumption that undergirds our Constitution, that all individuals and groups, ethnic or religious or whatever, are potentially equal in the value of their ideas and feelings and must be accorded equal opportunity to work and learn and teach, without being impeded by anything irrelevant to the matter at hand, whether race, sex, or their religion or lack of it.

There may be some still not convinced. Let me return to one of the two actions by the Constitutional Convention that I said were important to my argument that Mormons should become Democrats. Republicans have recently led the way in the massive erosion of a central constitutional principle, the restriction of war-making to Congress. They need some principled, even religiously passionate, opposition.

On August 6, 1787, the Committee on Detail distributed a printed draft of the proposed Constitution to the Convention which provided, "The legislature of the United States shall have the power . . . to make war." Pierce Butler of South Carolina suggested that the war power be given to the president, who, he said, "will not make war [except] when the Nation will support it." But he was the only delegate, then or ever, to suggest that the executive branch be given power to initiate war.

In fact, the danger of a powerful executive was perhaps the chief concern in forming a strong federal government in the first place. "It has been observed that in all countries," one delegate warned, when they were first deciding in May whether to have a one-person or three-person executive, "the executive power is in a constant course of increase."[19] John Rutledge of South Carolina said, "I am for vesting the executive power in a single person, though I am not for giving him the power of war and peace."[20]

During the August 6 review of the document, Madison moved to replace "make war" with "declare war" in the provision giving Congress that power, "leaving to the Executive the power to repel sudden attacks." And the discussion that followed makes clear that the general concern of the delegates was not to thus *narrow* the power of the Legislature but only to allow the Executive to respond quickly to direct invasion. George Mason of Virginia, the records of the Convention tell us, "was against giving the power of war to the Executive, because [he was] not [safely] to be trusted with it. . . . He was for clogging rather than facilitating war; but he was for facilitating peace."[21]

We have come to a condition, some 200 years later, where the president has effectively taken over the power of initiating war, with almost no opposition from Congress. This encroachment has reached such arrogance that President Johnson intentionally lied to the country and Congress in order to carry on the war in Vietnam, and President Reagan and his executive branch supporters continued the war they began in Nicaragua by secret and illegal means, even when polls consistently showed that a majority of Americans were against it and Congress had expressly forbidden such actions.

Congress is far from faultless. For forty years it has abrogated its Constitutional and morally sensible responsibility to debate carefully, decide cautiously, and then announce clearly to the world a declaration of war. Many Congressmen have violated the Constitution, it seems, out of a misguided loyalty to their president when he is of their same party. Such partisans fail to understand the basic constitutional principle of separation of powers, which means that to fulfill their oath of office they must oppose improper, unconstitutional actions by the president, especially infringement on the separation of powers, even when he is of their own party.

The fault is certainly shared equally by both parties, just as they share about equally the number of Imperial Presidents, beginning with Franklin Delano Roosevelt, who improperly took to themselves the war power. But right now Republicans seem most guilty, which is another reason I think more Mormons, who have particular reason to respect the Constitution and oppose war, should be Democrats.

Mormon Democrats might have had enough independence, as Republican presidents in recent years rushed us into wars, to point out that this country has not been subjected to "sudden attack," in the sense clearly intended by the framers, since Pearl Harbor. They might have asked why, given this fact, we have had a series of horribly costly wars in which tens of thousands of American soldiers and millions of our opponents have been killed and trillions of dollars wasted on massive destruction of both lives and the environment. They might have found impeachable offense in President Reagan's condoning of assassination, preemptive strikes, secret building of permanent bases in Honduras in violation of law and treaties, and his continued, arrogant disregard of the judgment of the World Court that we were to stop our unlawful interference in Nicaragua, a legitimate government which had committed no illegal or aggressive act against the United States.

Too many Mormon Congressmen have apparently become more Republican than legislators or Mormons. They seem more committed to the obsessive hawkishness of their party, which has allowed them to endorse violent efforts to overthrow governments we do not like, than to the teachings of Mormon prophets who categorically reject such acts. The Book of Mormon is quite clear on this, condemning all violence except defense against attacks within our borders (see Alma 24:17-19; 25:32-33; and 43:45-46). David O. McKay, speaking for the First Presidency at the beginning of World War II, outlined for modern nations the conditions under which such purely defensive war is justified, emphasizing carefully the limitations, especially this one: "Nor is war justified in an attempt to enforce a new order of government . . . however better the government . . . may be."[22]

The United States directly violated that prophetic principle in Vietnam, Grenada, Angola, Nicaragua, and the Gulf War. Yet most Mormons approved, apparently willing to accept this kind of argument from government and party leaders: "We're for peace in Nicaragua [or Angola or wherever], but you can't have peace without democracy." That is simply a way of saying we will use force to make other governments do as we want. Such an argument could have been used, just as rationally and probably more morally, to support intervention in South Africa for the disenfranchised black majority, but was not. Nor should it have been—in that case or in the others, where our intervention only led to escalation and perpetuation of violence. In the meantime South

Africa is achieving peace and reconciliation because of the self-sacrificing commitment of both white and black leaders to non-violence.

You can see how important it is for some Utah Mormons to become Democrats. First, it might produce some national leaders who could help stop the executive branch usurpation of power over war that right now most threatens our Constitution and our honor as a nation, our economy, and our lives. Second, it would produce a vital two-party system in Utah, one that could prevent a destructive Mormon/non-Mormon split and lead, through constructive dialogue and compromise rather than lazy ideology, to more innovative solutions to pressing state problems. Third, it might help us all to learn the basic lesson of our Constitution, that virtue and truth are the province of no single person or party—in fact, are best found in the process of civil debate, which includes listening because we want to, adjustment, compromise, and then honest and honorable acceptance of the results until new ones are created in the process.

The *principle* I am arguing for suggests that while Mormons in Utah should become Democrats, those in Democratic strongholds like Massachusetts and Chicago should become Republicans. Not only should qualified Mormons be hired in the humanities and social sciences at the University of Utah, more non-Mormons should be hired at BYU and invited to speak about challenging, controversial, "non-Mormon" subjects. I am suggesting that all military interference in other governments and lands should be renounced, even at the risk of communist or Islamic fundamentalist subversion there. That we should not only switch parties easily to help keep things balanced and the dialogue vital, but we should work against passage of laws about what are clearly private matters, even Sunday closing laws and imposed school prayer.

Is he saying (you might be asking yourself) that we should be less certain about the truth or virtue of our political positions, that we should be more willing to listen to opponents and change our minds, more passionate about the process of give and take in developing new truths than about which side we are on? Is he saying that anti-religious partisanship is as dangerous as religious partisanship, especially when mixed with politics or education?

And is he even saying that what he has said in this essay, despite his very best efforts to speak the truth, is surely a little and might be a lot wrong, that it ought to be argued with and modified?

Yes, you've got it. That's exactly what I'm saying.

NOTES

1. J. D. Williams, "Separation of Church and state in Mormon Theory and Practice," *Dialogue: A Journal of Mormon Thought* 1 (Summer 1966): 37. See also Thomas G. Alexander, *Mormonism in Transition, A History of the Latter-day Saints, 1890-1930* (Urbana: University of Illinois Press, 1986); Gustive O. Larson, *The "Americanization" of Utah for Statehood* (San Marino, CA: Huntington Library, 1971); and Edward Leo Lyman, *Political Deliverance: The Mormon Quest for Utah Statehood* (Urbana: University of Illinois Press, 1986).

2. Williams.

3. First Presidency to Joseph W. Young, 29 May 1891, archives, Historical Department, Church of Jesus Christ of Latter-day Saints, Salt Lake City, Utah.

4. Quoted in William Peters, *A More Perfect Union* (New York: Crown Publishers, Inc., 1987), 1.

5. See ibid., 63.

6. See Daniel Bell, "The End of American Exceptionalism," in *The Winding Passage: Essays and Sociological Journeys, 1960-80* (New York: Basic Books, Inc., 1980), esp. 264-71.

7. Quoted in ibid., 160, my emphasis.

8. Brigham Young, Jr., address given 22 June 1884, in *Journal of Discourses*, 26 vols. (Liverpool, Eng.: F. D. Richards, 1854-86), 25:191 (hereafter *JD*).

9. Daniel Bell, "The Principles of Pluralism and Toleration," Brigham Young University Forum Assembly, 7 Oct. 1986.

10. Noel B. Reynolds, "The Doctrine of an Inspired Constitution," in *"By the Hands of Wise Men": Essays on the U.S. Constitution*, ed. Ray Hillam (Provo, UT: Brigham Young University Press, 1979), 1-28.

11. Quoted in ibid., 15.

12. See *JD* 4:39 for Brigham Young's denouncement of this.

13. James Henry Moyle, *Mormon Democrat: The Religious and Political Memoirs*, ed. Gene A. Sessions (Salt Lake City: LDS Church Historical Department, 1975), 185-86.

14. Ibid., 209.

15. Walter Lippman, "The Indispensable Opposition," *The Atlantic Monthly*, Aug. 1939, 221.

16. Ibid.

17. James Cromar, "When One Man Made a Difference," *Student Review*, May 1987, 1, 16.

18. Ibid., 16.

19. Peters, 57.

20. Ibid., 47.

21. Quoted in Edwin B. Firmage and Francis D. Wormuth, *To Chain the Dogs of War* (Dallas: Southern Methodist University Press, 1986), 18.

22. David O. McKay, in *One Hundred and Twelfth Annual Conference of the Church of Jesus Christ of Latter-day Saints* (Salt Lake City: Deseret Book, 1942), 72.

six

JACARANDA

Coming down into the Los Angeles basin, through Cajon pass from the Mojave Desert, has always seemed like a descent into hell. The continuing desert heat that simply takes on humidity, the whiskey-colored sky, the ambience, almost an odor, of fleshly sin and cultural corruption, have remained in my mind since 1959, when, as a new first lieutenant stationed at George Air Force Base in Victorville, I first drove down the pass, taking Charlotte on an excursion to see the sights of Hollywood and L.A.

In May 1991 we made the trip from Provo, Utah, down Interstate-15, to help our daughter Katherine, who lives in Fullerton, southeast of L.A., with the birth of her fourth baby. As we passed Victorville, we talked of our two years there, about Jennifer, our own fourth child, who was born on the base and almost died because of a diaphragmatic hernia and collapsed lung that went undetected too long. We had heard the base was about to be closed and wondered if we should go and take photos of the cinderblock government housing where we lived and the barracks hospital where Jennifer was born. We could take them right to her, now that she was living near Kathy. But we pushed on through the noon sun, down through the pass into the grey-yellow haze, anxious to reach Fullerton in time to greet Jordan, Katherine's oldest, arriving home on the bus from kindergarten.

From I-15 we turned west along Highway 60, then south on 57 to east Fullerton, west on 91 to Euclid Avenue and north to Wilshire. As we turned back east on Wilshire, we saw masses of blue-violet foliage standing out against the grey sky ahead of us, dominating the skyline with color that shimmered, as we approached, with an electric inten-

107

sity that I later found would not register on the photos we took. Coming along Wilshire towards Woods Avenue, to the corner where Kathy lives, we could gradually see that that street was lined with blossoming trees. Dr. Seuss trees, Katherine called them, when I asked what they were.

After unpacking, as I walked under the trees, I could see her whim in the playful, absurd way they branch, like badly drawn elms, and the storybook profusion of the flowers, covering the grey trees before leaves come, dropping constantly into huge violet pools at their feet, until the whole street was a purple river. I walked around the pools where they washed up onto the sidewalks and lawns; it was wrong, too profligate, to crush the blossoms. I thought of the southern Idaho dryfarm where I was raised, the sparse blossoms of spring, brief apple and plums in April, and in May wild honeysuckle and sweetpea. A few homes had flower gardens, with snapdragons and bleeding hearts, and some had hollyhocks—and lilac bushes, violet like this but spare and brief.

Each bloom I picked up was identical—fluted into a three-inch trumpet, washed almost pink outside but deep violet within, like a snapdragon from my youth but more rich, exotic, and open, without the trap we could see the bees push open and then pull open ourselves and let snap back. The blossoms fell constantly.

Jordan, six, and Jacob, four, alternately shy and rowdy, showed us their new bedroom upstairs and its bathroom, made from the old attic furnaceroom, with an entryway left big enough for a bed for Charlotte and me. Katherine had decorated everything in her unique version of California funky: hand-painted dressers and closets in the boys' room, some with parts of clowns' bodies just coming onto the scene, some mottled black and white like a Holstein cow; vintage Batman and Beatles posters on the walls, with an original 1920s "Watch for the Children" roadsign over the stairway down, the running boy in knickers; a few single glass bricks scattered in the walls between rooms, and the bathroom and guest-room/entry painted pink with sponged on swatches of peach. Hannah, two, woke up from her nap and gazed at us from Katherine's arms for awhile, her head pushed so deep into Kathy's neck she could only peer out of one eye sideways at us.

Katherine had been having pains for a few days, more regular the day we arrived, and she had tried to reach her doctor, thinking she might deliver that night or in the morning. Just as I was taking the boys off to bike over to Euclid Avenue for ice cream, the doctor called back and said he had a meeting that would run late and she'd better come in now. Kathy rolled her eyes at me, mouthing "Men!" but after she hung up, she said, "He's probably worried about a repeat of Hannah. She came ten minutes after I went into the hospital, while he was still trying to get his gown on."

Charlotte took Kathy, with Hannah, over to St. Jude-Fullerton, left Kathy, and came back just as we returned with ice cream. Charlotte and I were immediately full-time parents again for three: dinner, fights, TV and arguments about stopping, bed-time stories, prayers. Paul, Kathy's husband and a dentist, went straight from his office to the hospital at 5:30 and was able to stay with her through the birth at 11:00 and on through most of the night. He told this story:

"I'd had five one hundred dollar bills in my wallet since last week when a patient paid me in cash. Kathy had been talking about having an epidural for the first time. With Hannah the pain was so bad the last ten minutes she thought something had gone wrong and that she would die. It was pure terror. I stood there watching her give out these killer screams. I'd never seen anything like that and couldn't even move. Anyway, this time she started talking about getting the epidural and paying the anesthesiologist with that cash—and, if she could talk down the price, having something to buy some post-pregnancy clothes at the Nordstrom sale.

"So when they put her on oxytoxin around 7:00 and the pains started to get stronger, she found out from the nurse an epidural usually costs around $800. But she had me go get the anesthetist who was on call and she began talking with him. I'd found out he gets a regular $600 a night fee for just being there—the word is these guys live out of their suitcases—even if he's not needed. He gets a percentage of the hospital's bill for the first two cases, enough to cover the $600, and then gets a higher percentage of anything else.

"Kathy told him, 'Look, I've never had an epidural, and I don't have to get one. If we pay cash so you don't have to bill us, how much will you charge?' He began telling us—he still had quite an accent—how he had trained in Taiwan and had immigrated and worked in hospitals all over and never been paid enough. He said (after awhile) that he'd have to have $450. He might have been thinking that he wouldn't even have to report this one and could get the entire fee.

"Kathy told him she had three one hundred dollar bills that were his right now if he did the job. Otherwise, she'd go without and he'd get nothing. He continued talking about his history and troubles—it seemed like maybe half an hour—and then mumbled that he had to get his money, that he'd just spent two hours with an epidural patient across the hall. He'd do it for $375. Kathy said, 'I'm quick, forty-five minutes at most,' and stuck to $300 or nothing. He said $325, and Kathy shook her head. He walked out.

"Five minutes later he came back in with his equipment. He had her kneel on the bed and bend over to expose her spine better, and then put in the needle—which Kathy told me later hurt like hell. She flinched and he yelled, 'Don't do that!' and proceeded to tape on the needle and its tube and package of anesthesia and the flow-metering equipment. Later the woman across the hall said hers didn't hurt a bit. Maybe he was thinking, 'Cheap job,' when he stuck Kathy. Two hours later, the baby came, and he took his equipment and the $300 we'd placed in an envelope. The next week Kathy took a big box of See's chocolates to him at the hospital and thanked him. I can't believe it. She hasn't mentioned that sale again, but she's got the 200 bucks."

Paul brought Katherine and the baby home the next day. Such a short time still seems strange, even wrong, to me, even after watching my daughters and daughter-in-law come home in a day or two with all our eleven grandchildren. After each of our own six children Charlotte stayed in the hospital four or five days—and my mother was gone at least a week with my baby sister in 1938. Katherine seemed more fragile than I had ever seen her, sitting and moving slowly and cautiously, walking with obvious pain. I could feel a sharp shadow between my own legs that made me flinch.

The baby was well-formed, looking a lot like her brother Jacob

but with dark hair. And she seems caught in my memory with the jacaranda—blue eyes and pink skin tinged with violet color. All during the
three weeks we stayed, the blossoms fell, the pools formed and were
crushed by cars or swept away and formed again by morning. Wherever
we went in Fullerton the trees stood out against the grey sky, and
whenever we returned to Kathy's they formed our horizon. Each day,
sometimes twice, I would take two-year-old Hannah for a walk, holding
her hand or sometimes facing her forward in the stroller. As we went
out the front, turned right, and headed south along Woods, I avoided
the pools of violet, going up on the harsh lawns of hard bentgrass,
which had been designed for the desert. All around the block were
strange California flowers in dry earth. In about every second yard a few
agapanthus, which came originally from South Africa, were just coming
into bloom, simple iris-like foliage near the ground, with a three-foot
stem at a slight angle and then the six-inch ball of small blue flowers,
like the first image of a fireworks burst. Two homes had callistemon,
from Australia—"bottle-brush trees" Kathy called them, and I found
that is one common name, for the obvious reason that the flower-clus-
ters, hanging profusely in all directions from the tall, central shrub,
look exactly like pinkish-orange baby-bottle brushes.

Jennifer, who lives with her husband Mark (a lawyer) about a mile
away in a restored early twentieth-century California bungalo that was
moved to make way for a downtown Fullerton parking lot, calls her callistemon "the hummingbird tree." All the homes I saw had trees or
shrubs or flowers strange and attractive to me, rich in color or profusion
(like the massed red bouganvillea vines spilling over trellisses and
porches and white-flowered hedges)—or just unbelievably shaped, like
the strelitzia, bird of paradise, its blossoms just starting to appear,
among its banana leaves, like open-mouth green cranes' heads (upper
beak missing), with spiked orange crests and blue tongues—or with or-
ange-winged, blue-billed hummingbirds launching out of their
mouths. When I turned from the jacaranda pools on Woods west onto
Amerige Street, we were under rows of magnolia, with dark shiny
leaves and huge nests of pure white lotus-like blossoms. Then, on both
other legs of the block, there were palm trees, 100 foot Washingtonias,
each with a huge thatch of dead fronds circling the trunk right under

the new fronds, short, straight, wine and date palms with deeply stri-
ated trunks, and a few leaning smooth-trunked coconut palms and an
occasional small coco polomosa.

Along the side of Kathy's house, next to Wilshire, she has planted
scarlet canna (from the West Indies), which have banana leaves like the
bird of paradise, but then profuse stalks of blood-red blossoms, somewhat like huge lilies in shape but much more heavily massed. When we
turned back on Woods to the front of the house, I stood under the jacaranda until it seemed my own eyes had been colored.

Jacaranda blossoms usually come before the fern-like, compound
leaves that started to appear soon after we got there, but the blossoming is staggered so some trees have both—as well as empty seed-pods
from last season, still hanging like open grey castanets. *Jacaranda mi-
mosaefolia* is one of fifty varities, most of them native to the high deserts
of South America. "Jacaranda" is from the language of the tupi-guarani
peoples, in which it refers to the richly colored, hard, dark wood; these
native people use it to make bows, its boiled bark as a cure for fever,
and its leaves to make a fish poison.

Now it is cultivated in most sub-tropical areas, from northern
Australia to Florida. If it is watered too much the leaves come first,
spoiling the dramatic appearance of bright mauve flowers against grey
branches, so the recent dry spell had much increased the effect of our
first vision of them. The blossoms last into fall and give way to the rich
masses of pale-green leaves, like ostrich plumes, which gradually turn
yellow and drop in late winter, leaving the seed-pods to burst open just
before the blossoms come out again. The tree grows fifty feet high and
arches out fifty feet to easily cover streets and front yards. In South
America it is known as Brazilian rosewood and was long used, until
used up, for cabinet-making, because it is beautifully colored in rich
browns, very hard, and does not weather even if left in the rain. Urban
Brazilians tell me that they have never seen such a tree, except in bo-
tanical gardens. Furniture made from the wood, mostly in the nineteenth century, is extremely rare and expensive.

Kathy had painted her house a bright mauve blue that picks up
the agapanthus and jacaranda, as well as contrasting with the stucco

bungalows along Wilshire. It is an older neighborhood, with small, inexpensive homes built in the 1930s and 1940s, and not only the mature jacaranda and magnolia line some streets but large pepper trees and palms. The homes, of course, are much more expensive now, like all real estate in California cities, but even so the neighborhood seems quite middle class, though unusually diverse, with a large number of hispanics. The neighbors seemed close and at ease with each other, especially a family across Wilshire that rents a small wooden cottage that Kathy bought and fixed up. Even while Kathy was recovering from her delivery, Maxine would call and ask to send her children over while she ran an errand—but then Kathy sent Hannah over for whole afternoons when I made a couple of trips to see friends. And one man from down the street would simply appear at the back door and ask to borrow things. Kathy complained to me that he kept bringing her bike back with a flat tire, but I didn't notice that she stopped lending it.

So I was surprised at an article in the *Orange Country Register* that she had saved for me from back in January, right after the Gulf War started. It led with a color picture of Kathy and reported on the antiwar banners she had nailed to her front porch, which sticks out prominently, close to the busy intersection of Wilshire and Woods. The article reports that the banner she had put out in December, "War . . . Everybody Loses," had disappeared three days after the air war began on January 16. The next one, painted on a white sheet, "War: $500 million/day, Can Our Children Afford It?" had also been torn down and taken. The reporter quotes Kathy as saying, "It makes me sad to think people believe I'm unpatriotic. My neighbors and I have always looked out for one another in the past. . . . I'm an American. I love this country because people can say whatever they believe." The reporter talked to some neighbors who disagree with that idea. One said, "These men are sacrificing their lives to make sure all goes well for us. To put up a sheet like that is disgusting." Another, who had noticed that Kathy put out a Dukakis sign amidst all the Bush placards on her neighbors' lawns and that she had an unusual flag flying on holidays, told the reporter, "They've always been different than everyone else," and that she hadn't minded until the war began: "It offends me. It's like putting up a sign to say you support a rapist and a murderer."

The reporter, giving Kathy's background and apparently quoting her, says she "was raised in a politically liberal family in Palo Alto." I think of those days when I was a graduate student at Stanford. I had been raised in a politically conservative family in rural Idaho, served in the Air Force, ready to fight in Vietnam, voted for Nixon in 1960. But at Stanford I experienced something that shifted my spirit. I had access, through the Stanford graduate library, to translated news accounts from the foreign press—and so I was exposed to a greater variety of views and information than ever before. I had grown up believing not only, as a Mormon, that the U. S. Constitution was God-inspired, but that U. S. Presidents were inspired also—at least that they were noble and honest men. Then, reading various accounts of the Tonkin Gulf incident that President Johnson used to justify bombing Hanoi and to get Congressional approval to escalate the war, I became convinced he was lying, that, in fact, the "incident" was created not by a North Vietnamese attack but by our government's easy recourse to violence and arrogant willingness to mislead its own people.

Years later the lie was proven and admitted, but in the meantime we proceeded with a war that killed tens of thousands of Americans and millions of Vietnamese and desperately wounded our nation. In 1964 I was heartbroken at first, then angry. I joined the anti-war movement and many other causes and spent much time, away from my family, pursuing them. One day I came home very tired and impatient. It may have been while I was spending afternoons after class going door-to-door in south Palo Alto, using my Mormon missionary training to keep up a cheery, articulate patter as I tried to convince people to vote for fair-housing legislation and hearing again and again the argument that they weren't prejudiced but just thought apartment owners ought to be free to set their own rules—it was more American: "The rules are the same for everyone. Negroes and Mexicans can go get their own apartment buildings and keep *us* out." Anyway, I came home late and angry, and getting ready for bed Kathy sassed me over something. And the only time ever, I struck her—slapped her across the face. "Oh, Daddy," she said, and refused to cry.

I looked again at the full color picture at the beginning of the newspaper report. It showed Kathy—clear violet-blue eyes serious and aimed straight at the camera, lovely hair, chin held high, a little too high—in front of the special flag she made to display from her porch on holidays and patriotic occasions. It has the regular field of blue with fifty white stars, and the seven white stripes, but in place of the red stripes are yellow and orange and blue and brown and black and green—for all the rainbow of peoples and ideas in our country and for Mother Earth. The end of the report tells of another sheet Kathy had painted and was about to hang on the porch: "Support Our Troops. Hate the War."

On Kathy's family bulletin board in her sewing room I saw another clipping. It is from the *Fullerton Daily Star-Progress*, March 7, and is a quarter-page picture of Jordan and a girl about his size, in front of a window, apparently of their school, on which has been painted "K-2 Salutes the Troops" above a huge bow tie. The caption reads, "Golden Hill School kindergartners Kelly Brady and Jordan Nelson rest brushes after painting a yellow bow tie on the media center's window to show support for Operation Desert Storm troops."

While Kathy was still at the hospital, I got some messages for her and for Jacquelin, the El Salvadoran Kathy has been helping get naturalized. She used to live in the small upstairs bedroom, with board and room for babysitting, until she got married to Carlos. Now she is pregnant and Kathy pays her to come by once a week, between other jobs, to help clean and watch the kids while Kathy takes a break. But mainly they are friends. They speak in Spanish, which Kathy learned on a mission in El Salvador during the worst of the civil war fighting in 1977-78, and they talk about her family there and the continuing troubles and about making it in America. Carlos, who is a trained machinist, works 60 hours a week at $4.50 an hour, trying to save up for the baby and a better apartment. Jackie takes whatever tending or cleaning jobs she can. Neither can get regular, well-paying work until they qualify for green cards.

One woman who called for Jackie asked me to take the number and have her call back. I said I didn't know when Jackie would be by and she should call Kathy and find out, and then I forgot to tell Kathy when she came home with the baby or Jackie when she visited later in the week. On Friday I heard Kathy's voice rising, then pleading, as she talked with someone. As she hung up and turned away toward the back door, I could see she was crying. "That witch," she said, as she walked out. A few minutes later she came back in and dialed and I could hear the pleading again: "But they're counting on this weekend. They've planned to be there." After a minute she went on, "They didn't know you'd called. Please don't blame them because the message didn't get through." She ended politely but then sat down at the table, shaking with anger as she told Charlotte and me what had happened.

"These people from Brea hired Jackie and Carlos to tend their house this weekend. They demanded a reference, which of course meant someone white to vouch for hispanics who they were willing to pay only half the going rate and who will put up with that but who they don't trust because they are brown. So Jackie gave my name, and the woman's husband—he's behind all this but makes his wife do the dirty work—had her demand I bring them out to the house to meet them. You know how sharp Jackie and Carlos are. They dress great and look great together, and even the woman was impressed. That's probably why she decided to ask them to tend the house the whole next month while they go to Tahoe. But when she couldn't get through, he must have decided he was right the first time, that 'Mexicans' are undependable. So now she's called the whole thing off, not just the month but this weekend too. It's not fair." She teared up again. "And Jackie and Carlos were counting on the money and a chance to move out of their apartment for a month and save even more."

I asked her if this was usual, this much prejudice still.

"Oh, yes. And I have it, too. I resent it that I have to pay everything to have my baby and Jackie gets the whole thing free on welfare. Everyone I've known who served a mission in a third world country is prejudiced against the people of that country." She glanced up sideways and smiled. "I hate El Salvadorans—but these people with the cabin at Tahoe. What scum! And that shop where Carlos works. They know he's worth twice as much but that he won't make any trouble for fear he'll lose the job."

On Friday Charlotte and Kathy took the baby and went shopping, which left me with Jacob and Hannah. Carlos and Jackie came by just before Jordan got home from school at 1:30. They didn't seem as bothered by the loss of their month's job as Kathy was. Carlos had the afternoon off and took the boys to the park while Jackie started doing wash and vacuuming. When Hannah woke up about 2:00, a crew had just arrived to do the yard work, and I took her out on the front porch swing to watch. The first to come was a young hispanic, who drove up in a rusted red '76 Camaro on the Wilshire side of the house about ten to two and sat there eating a hamburger. Two others, older hispanic men, came at 2:00 in an ancient black truck. When I described them to Kathy later, she told me their names. The young man is Jesus Manzo, the other two Pascuala Mendez and Leonardo Nava. "Leonardo is the oldest," she said, "a sweet man."

When the truck pulled up, Jesus took out a gas-powered blower, strapped the motor to his back, and began blowing the jacaranda blossoms into piles along Woods Avenue. Pascuala took out a weed-eater and hoe and began working through the flowerbeds against the front of the house and in the narrow flowergarden, full of the scarlet cannas, that runs between the fence on the Wilshire side and the kitchen and family room windows. Leonardo did the mowing, first the parking along Wilshire and then Woods and then Kathy's front lawn. Hannah and I were facing front and didn't see him take out the mower, but Paul later told me he is the only man he has ever known who is strong enough to hold the large powermower at arm's length when he lifts if out of a truck or puts it back in.

Leonardo mowed with steady concentration, never once glancing at us. As Leonardo finished each section, Pascuala would leave the flowers and trim the edges of the sidewalk with the powered whirling vertical blade that showered sparks when he occasionally touched the cement. Then Jesus would come over and blow the grass and sticks and blossoms from the lawn and sidewalks along to a dirty canvas square, which he would use to gather them for dumping in the truck. But mainly Jesus swept the pools of jacaranda. The crew did the smaller yard across Wilshire, too, the house Kathy had bought and rented out, which also fronted on Woods. So Jesus swept the violet blossoms in growing waves along Woods from the north to the intersection, then across to the front of the truck for gathering. Then he swept back from the south along Woods, in front of Kathy's, and around the corner to the truck. Hannah and I, keeping silent against the buzzing motors, watched the mounds of color build and then saw the blossoms mashed into the sheet and poured into the truck. As the crew left there were already more jacaranda blossoms spotting the manicured lawn and clean sidewalk and forming the dim outlines of pools on the street as the truck turned and made a track of crushed blossoms through the pools as it left.

That night Kathy told me the crew came twice a month and did essentially all the yard work on both lots—no planting—for $120 a month. It took the three of them about an hour, which works out to about $20 apiece per hour, but they must buy and maintain all their own equipment. Over the three weeks I could see that most of the homes along Wilshire had yard service and that the crews were all his-panics or orientals.

On Sunday we visited the singles ward where Robert Rees is bishop. It was the first Sunday, testimony meeting, and after the sacra-ment a young man in levis and a full linen shirt and white cap to match walked up to the pulpit and thanked the ward members for accepting him as a homosexual. He related how he had struggled to combine his faith in the gospel with his conviction that his sexual preference was an undeniable part of him, not a sin but something to live with. He felt it was working out, that he could live a faithful, chaste life, that he was acceptable to God. He quoted the passage from Isaiah 56 about eunuchs: "Thus saith the Lord unto the eunuchs that keep my sab-baths . . . and take hold of my covenant; even unto them will I give in mine house and within my walls a place and a name . . . I will give them an everlasting name, that shall not be cut off," and said he saw there God's acceptance of faithful people with sexual differences and be-lieved the general authorities would become more accepting eventu-ally.

Rachel Jacobs gave her name and talked about learning to accept herself as a unique, worthwhile woman. She wore a dark dress and black tights, hair simply brushed back, no lipstick. She spoke somewhat haltingly about finding that in this ward that she didn't have to be a Molly Mormon to be loved, that she didn't have to punish herself anymore. Later Karyn Pate picked up this theme. She talked about the ward as a place where there were indeed "no more strangers and foreigners" and said how much Bishop Rees had contributed to that spirit, especially for women. "I'm so grateful," she said, "to know that I don't have to be a Stepford Wife—a submissive robot, a thoughtless pleasure-machine—to a man to be a real Mormon woman." She half turned back towards Bob, gesturing, and laughed: "I'm grateful Bishop Rees isn't a Stepford Bishop."

The last speaker approached the pulpit tentatively and announced he was Keith Fitzgerald, used to seeing this building only from above—as a traffic reporter flying daily over the freeways. Though he was trying to use the forms and phrases he had first heard that day, it was soon clear that he was not a Mormon, but had stood up simply because he wanted to join in this interesting form of personal sharing. He told how he had wished to know more about what made his Mormon friends tick, of being invited, of finally coming today, of liking the informal confessing and wanting to join in. He told a little about his life, busy but lonely, his yearnings for meaning. He hoped he would be able to come back.

We went from sacrament meeting to Sunday school, where Sue Bergin taught about the parables of lost sheep and coin and prodigal son, and then to priesthood meeting, where, because the instructor had called in sick that morning, Bob had me teach the elders. They were all in their twenties and thinking, in fear and trembling some of them said, about marriage. I had them turn to 2 Nephi 26:33, and we talked about what it could possibly mean that "both male and female . . . are alike unto God."

After the meetings the ward gathered on a patio for what had been announced as a "mingle and munch" to break their fast—sliced vegetables and dip, punch and cookies, and much lively conversation that continued for an hour or so, well after we left. An older, deadly serious man came up to me as I was trying to find a place to sit along the patio wall and thanked me for the priesthood lesson. He had been quite defensive in class ("Why are we talking about this, when the

Prophets will be the ones to decide what it means and to give women the priesthood") until I had reminded him no one had mentioned priesthood and had reassured him we were not trying to decide official doctrine but to explore what this obviously important but little discussed scripture could mean in everyday courtship and marriage. Now he seemed at peace and genuinely grateful.

I had seen the youth in the linen hat in a quiet corner talking with Bob, and now he came over and asked me to go someplace private with him. He said, "I know you're a friend of Bob, and I want to know what you think of what he just told me. He said I was not to speak in his meetings about what the general authorities might decide in the future about homosexuality, that it could seem disrespectful. Isn't testimony meeting a place to tell the truth, honestly and openly?"

I said, "It certainly is. And you did. And Bishop Rees has helped create a ward where you can feel free to do so and to ask for and get the love and understanding and help you need. But he is also bishop to all the rest, including some who may have been offended by what you said today. To keep this a ward where *all*, not just you, can come and be helped and keep coming back to be helped and to help others, he needs to give some direction, like he's just given you, according to the inspiration he has the special right to receive as bishop. I'd listen to him carefully, as I think you have in the past about other things where he helped you." He tightened up at first when it looked like I was giving him a sermon. But then I stopped and we talked about my own outspokenness and how being a bishop had cramped my style as a general gadfly. He laughed with me and relaxed and we were able to talk about his own cross for a while.

Late in the afternoon we went to the Reeses' to have dinner with a visiting poet at UCLA, Alice Fulton, and her husband, Hank DeLeo, a fine artist who had provided the cover for her latest book, *Powers of Congress*. The home is a rather simple, English-style cottage that Bob and Ruth bought when he began teaching at UCLA in the 1960s—and that he added some bedrooms to as their children came, redecorated, including hand carving all the doors and window frames to look like English hammerbeam. Bob sent me out into the yard to pick some huge, luscious lemons to make slices for the ice water for dinner. I spent some time looking at Ruth's flowers, perhaps spruced up for the sale, but gorgeously lush—roses in full bloom along a low ornamental front fence under a huge Monterey pine and, along the front walk and around the doorstep, clumps of deep purple, and a stunning bush I had never seen before. It was formed into a large circle at the top of a single thin trunk and was completely covered with purple and white flowers, shaped like honeysuckle but much larger. Ruth called it "yesterday, today, and tomorrow."

Bob had become good friends with the Fultons when he planned and directed a tour of China by a group of noted American writers and their spouses in an exchange series he had set up through his work as director of the Arts Division of UCLA Extension. Bob and the Fultons began reminiscing about the trip, especially the pervasive sexism they encountered in the attitudes even of the avant garde Chinese writers and scholars traveling with them. In that politically sensitive situation, they had felt some need to restrain their opinions, even their questions. Alice said she had felt especially constrained as a woman and a guest, but then she turned to Bob's sons, Matt and Bobby, whom he had taken with them, and told them how much she had admired and appreciated them on the trip: "Your innocent dignity and good hearts were soon clear to our hosts. They could accept from you better than anyone the lesson of your treatment of all women you met and the challenge of your guileless questions."

I had been reading from Bob's copy of Alice's poems before she came, with its cover by Hank, to whom the book is dedicated—a violet and blue, yellow and black swirl of abstract, bird-like forms. The poems are crowded with ideas as well as images, intricate and dense in their rhetoric, even when using vernacular. Many are religious, some ironically so, like "The Gilt Cymbal Behind Saints"—or "The New Old Testament" (which is spoken by God): "Least Little Ones, / gnash your teeth till Kingdom Come, I won't be there / to intervene, who would have let the South secede, / Hitler kill six million more."

One evening I took the Amtrak to L.A. Jennifer had ordered tickets for the Joffrey Ballet, performing in its last-ever appearance at the Civic Center. She and Charlotte drove up to the city to visit museums

121

in the afternoon and were to pick up Mark at his office, then meet me at the station. The train, I had learned from Mark, who rides it each day to his law office, comes up from San Diego, passing through the affluent beach towns and the edge of Irvine and past Disneyland before stopping at the small Spanish-style station in Fullerton where I got on—and then plunges into what Mark calls the underbelly of Orange County and Los Angeles. The next town is La Habra, where hispanics have extended their houses with added-on rooms and lean-tos for extra relatives until the houses nearly fill the yards—just like what he saw in Brazil on his mission, Mark claims. As I went through I did not see the man Mark said often comes out to flip the bird at the train.

Not long after La Habra the train began to pass through miles of industrial plants and warehousing yards. The Lever Brothers factory is a tangle of huge tanks and flumes, pipes and spouts that I could imagine filling tanker trucks with liquid Palmolive soap. The distribution yard for the Ralph's grocery chain, at least ten acres, was stacked with what looked like dry goods being loaded onto trucks, keeping maybe fifteen forklifts busy. Further on were acres of Toyotas and Nissans, fresh off the ships at L.A. Harbor I supposed. The reds and metallic greens shown bright and still dust-free in the setting sun.

Then the train crossed the L.A. River, really a huge concrete storm drain now, perhaps thirty feet deep and about two hundred feet wide, with a channel, six to eight feet across, flowing down the center. The slides slope up at maybe thirty degrees, so people and even cars can get down into the bottom. I could see a few trickles of liquid flowing from pipes along the sides, and the water in the channel, though it seemed fairly clear, was edged by froth and made phospate bubbles in the eddies. Some of the concrete on the sides and especially the buttresses that supported the trestle we crossed on—and others I could see on up the river for each crossing street or set of tracks—were all covered with graffitti and paintings, layers of patterns upon patterns. The paintings were garish—mainly, it seemed, symbolic—but I couldn't make out the slogans, except near a large glass with a line painted across the middle and words to the side, "HALF EMPTY OR HALF FULL?"

As we slowed and turned north along the riverbed, I could see the shining towers of downtown L.A. and just to our left the huge Amtrak switching yard and then a long wall which I learned from Mark is part of the L.A. County jail and an adjacent police station. I could see just outside the wall what looked like a moat, perhaps seven feet wide and six feet deep. A few men were putting sheets of plywood across this. Although the evening was warm, they were dressed in layers of clothing, including winter coats. One wore a Raiders jacket over a long dress coat. Most had on scarves or hats, a few had Lakers caps. I looked out to the right and could see a man and woman and three children bathing naked in the channel and then, just under the next trestle, a group of boxed lean-tos, with clutter all around, shopping carts and paper and clothes and cans and plastic toys and junked cars. In what seemed a clearing in the middle were two couches and some chairs with people in them and a fire circle.

That night, driving home after the ballet, Mark told me that occasionally the city bulldozes these shanty-towns for the homeless that develop under the trestles along the river by the jail and on public property and even on sidewalks right next to city hall. The people start to rebuild the next day. He thinks some choose the quarter-mile long area by the river because it's close to the police station in case they are attacked. They organize themselves into "families" for security. The people seem to be mostly hispanics, some anglos, but he has seen no African-Americans. He sees almost no one in the morning; they seem to be already out on their business by 7:15 when he passes. In the evening, returning home about the time I rode up to the city, he sees more people, often getting shelters ready for the night. Sometimes he sees people in the city pushing their shopping carts. He says they often seem very intent, each grasping their cart with clenched hands and moving quickly and directly, their eyes fixed ahead. They seem to be going someplace terribly important.

Mark told me he had seen a news report about the arrest and imprisonment of one of the graffitti artists. Apparently some take great pride in their work, especially in getting it widely spread around and onto many inaccessible surfaces. This artist, whose name is Chaka, had put his works in 200,000 places in L.A., many high on granite and marble walls of buildings, which cost thousands of dollars to remove. While he was in jail, others continued to copy his style and sign his name to their work.

After a week Kathy and the baby seemed to be doing well and the other kids getting into a schedule, so my help wasn't much needed. I called Jim McMichael, a friend from Stanford graduate school in the 1960s and now a poet and teacher at the University of California at Irvine, to see when we could get together. He mentioned he had been invited to read a poem at a service honoring the war dead on Memorial Day, the next Monday, and I invited myself down to hear him and have a visit.

Kathy had planned a family outing, along with Jennifer and Mark, for Memorial Day morning at Irvine Regional Park, so we went a little early and took an extra car so I could drive on down from the park to Jim's. We drove east on highway 91, then south on 57 past Disneyland to Chapman Avenue and followed it east through Anaheim and northern Irvine into the first hills of the Santa Ana mountains, then turned left on Orange and into the huge park that had been formed around the outlet of Irvine Lake. We wound through large, mowed fields and cultivated shrubs and trees, to the fountains and ponds and large trees just under the lake, where there are tables and swings and asphalt paths that lead up and down the wooded hills, around the ponds, and across bridges.

Charlotte noticed that everyone we saw was black or hispanic, and Kathy, who can't resist taking a little advantage of her mother's innocence, told her that the park was reserved for non-white races—which she believed for a few minutes until she saw Jennifer's grin. Along the road back of where we parked and laid out our food in front of the car, a large group of African-Americans, apparently from a church congregation, were gathered, sometimes singing, occasionally moving in a group up and down the road, almost in formation. An older man seemed to be their leader, exhorting the group from time to time about something I couldn't hear, then walking off with one or two of the young men in intent conversation, then helping one of the children with their bike-riding or frisbee-throwing.

Jordan took off along the paths on his bike and Jacob tried to follow him, sitting inside his red plastic tricycle-car. But he couldn't pump up the hills, so I got him to let me push him up a small hill and coast down—again and again, screaming with frantic joy as he barely steered away from the pond at the bottom. Kathy seemed worried about Jordan being gone alone, so I walked around the ponds until I found him and brought him back. I pushed him and Jacob in side-by-side swings for awhile, keeping them out of phase so I could push Jordan with a strong right and follow through and then step back and push the lighter Jacob with a strong left. Kathy got in her van and watched us awhile, intently, while she nursed the baby. She is thinking of naming her Bronte, after the English sisters who wrote novels.

I had planned to leave at 12:30 but Jacob turned up missing, and I did a fast run through all the paths until I could hear Kathy calling that he had been found. I drove fast back along Chapman to highway 55 and south to where it meets I-405 right by the new John Wayne Airport. I turned left onto I-405, immediately left again on Jamboree, then, after a few blocks through the new Irvine business district, right on Alton Parkway and a few more blocks to where I could see the Civic Center on the left. I was late and worried about missing Jim if I didn't go right to the Plaza where he had told me he was speaking. I made a lucky guess and turned into a driveway that took me around the back, where I could see people gathered at the crook of the L-shaped building. I parked and slipped along a covered walk that took me close to the stand, where Jim had just stood up. I moved behind a pillar and watched him from the side as he read what turned out not to be a standard poem but a short prose meditation:

> As I understand them, Memorial Day services are for the living. They offer the living a chance to offset at least a little of their immeasurable debt to men and women who died in war. I confess that I don't like to think about the nature of that debt. For what Memoral Day obliges me not to forget is the difference between a living person and a dead one. . . .

It had been eighteen years since I had seen Jim, the handsome face with eyes that crinkled deeply even in a shy smile—and the perfect body that our friends from New York, Robert Pinsky and David Thorburn, had mocked affectionately as making him a caricature of the California jock. Now his hair had greyed and receded, making his fine tan even more dramatic. I noticed the skin was loosening along his jaw.

> Because it was each one of their bodies and not my own that was undone by war, the judgment about what they died for is a judgment each of them alone had to make and not I. While it is tempting to believe that each willingly gave up his or her body for reasons each judged worthy, I am not sentimental enough to believe there wasn't one among them who judged otherwise.

I watched the crowd, seated on folding chairs in the sun, many with American Legion caps, and wondered what they could make of this effort by my friend to be fully true both to his ritual public responsibility to the war dead (and these patriotic mourners) and also to his private hatred of what had killed them—his rhetoric stretched to the breaking point:

> Memorial Day obliges me to remember *all* the persons who died in war, not just those who found reasons worth dying for. And as it obliges me not to speak *for* any one of these dead, Memorial Day obliges me as well not to speak *to* them by saying thanks. Just as they are not pretending to be dead, I must not pretend that even my simplest words can reach them. Memorial day obliges me to pay my respects not to what I wish with all my heart these dead could be but rather to the irreplaceable persons each of them once was.

There was polite applause, a few remarks from the mayor, a Souza march from the band, and the service was over. I stayed back while a reporter talked with Jim, then I embraced him, noticing he was taller than I had remembered, met Amy, and then followed them to their new home in faculty housing: From Alton we took Harvard, lined with immaculate lawns in front of Spanish-style double condos, back south across the 405, through an older section with interesting-looking shops and a theatre, shaded by two jacaranda, then forked left onto Berkeley and began to rise into hills covered with more condos, forking again and again until we came out into a driveway where I could see beyond their

immaculately white, very modern new house into open fields stretch-
ing to the south and east. The front room angled up two stories, huge
windows opening to the fields. While Amy fixed us some cool drinks,
Jim talked about the burrowing owl that lives just across the dry ditch
between the back yard and the field. He told me how that morning,
when he had gone running, the owl had stood above the burrow without moving when he passed just a few feet away.

As we sat in white chairs on the white rug, with clear glasses of ice
and Sprite, I talked about what I had been doing, about the book on
Shakespeare's avengers and healers that I now felt I was ready to write
after reading René Girard on violence and especially the post-modernist philosopher Emmanuel Levinas, who put ethics before theory, our
encounter with each other in mercy as the basis for any justice. At the
mention of Levinas he turned and smiled at Amy: "I told you he would
probably have been reading Levinas." To me he said, "It's uncanny how
our work has brought us to such a similar place. I was turned on to
Levinas by my colleague Francois Lyotard. But perhaps it isn't surprising. Our minds came together at Stanford." We talked about Pinsky,
now a foremost American poet, and Thorburn, who teaches at M.I.T., a
leading critic—appreciator—of popular culture. Jim spoke of the writing program he directs at Irvine, how the young poets are chosen. I
thought of a line from one of his poems that always stays with me,
about how trout "measure the pool" with their shadows, a line I had
stolen for one of my essays.

After a while, Amy left to pick up her twelve-year-old daughter
Jessica. Jim told of the immense struggle of his second marriage and divorce—and finding Amy. He said, "I am writing a long poem about the
divorce." Before I left, I walked over to an alcove off the living room
where, as I stood looking out the high, angled windows, I could see
fresh pages with penned lines of poetry, alone on the antique desk.

Going back, I turned left off Berkeley across the broad flood plain
of the San Diego river. Two white egrets flew along the small strip of
green rushes near the center. Then I turned right on Jamboree and
back to the 405 and made it from Irvine to Kathy's in a half hour. Later
that week I noticed that her copy of *Lear's* magazine for May had an es-

say by Robert Scheer, the UCLA sociologist, called "Withering on the Irvine," a wry deconstruction of the place where he—and my friend Jim—live. Scheer calls it "white-flight country," known as the "most successful planned community in the nation," the newest and already perhaps supreme model of the American dream: "booming, green-belted checker-board of high-tech, low-rise production centers, discreet high-rent shopping malls, and hierarchically niched villages." I thought of the new downtown I had passed through just before the Civic Center, all tan brick and glass, perfectly clean, strangely deserted now that I thought about it. And the condo villages along Harvard we had passed, also deserted, no garage doors open. Scheer tells how the villages, each with its shopping mall and lake and bike paths, are controlled by homeowners' associations, which even set the height of fences and geraniums, so that "grass roots democracy has come down to fierce meetings . . .about the spacing of speed bumps and the approved colors for awnings."

The new Irvine has been built in the past two decades, on half of the old Irvine ranch, to combat "suburban sprawl" from L.A.—and modeled on the Disneyland notion of "maximizing collective freedom by sharply restricting individual prerogatives." The population of fiercely free market Republicans submit because the system is good for home equity (average price $256,000), for which the mainly two-income families are hanging on by their fingernails to meet payments. This "planning for profit" Scheer claims has produced docile kids (who "go nuts only when they are old enough to drive" and then wreak havoc in other places) and has left a city devoid of variety. Not even the university makes a difference. When students set fire to a Bank of America as part of the spreading post-Cambodia bombing reaction in 1970, town planners decided to separate the zoned villages and malls two miles to the northwest of town and control them with armies of security guards, though Scheer writes that the no-man's-land, which I passed going along Harvard and Berkeley, is filling up with small shops and apartments and "has become known locally as a poor-man's West-wood."

Scheer worries that we can see in Irvine the future of our highest affluent vision, the "citadel of the good life" for our brave new world of international business, but where the planners in their very drive for perfection, "particularly in the security and the cleanlinesss . . . may have created a legacy of godliness and boredom." Fundamentalist religion and materialism "permit essentially absentee parents who are born again to reunite with their children each Sunday for fast embrace of God's plan, faithfully implemented during the work week by hustling in the marketplace." Irvine was the base for the Lincoln Savings & Loan Federation run by Charles Keating, who, before the S&L scandal broke, "found time to crusade against a local X-rated movie theater while tending to the financial needs of widows and U.S. senators." Scheer admits, "We never have any gardening chores. An army of Mexicans moves in each morning to clip, cut, and blow away the errant leaf; they steal away at night-fall to the barrios of Santa Ana in the other Orange County."

The teenagers have the same high level of drug and alcohol abuse and society as other such communities. They call Irvine "The Bubble": One says, "You rarely see poor people, and you come to think all of America is just like this place."

The last day before we were to leave, I spent the afternoon with Jordan at "rock park" (his name for Richman Park because of its pile of huge rocks to play on), doing hide the ball and plain old hide and seek and "baseball" (with an oversized plastic bat and a tennis ball and trees for bases). When we got back Charlotte was rocking the baby and Kathy was resting on the couch, reading. Jennifer was there, playing with Hannah. I noticed some chili in a pan on the stove and turned it on to heat while I got some bread and a plate. Charlotte had just started reading Robert Fulghum's new book, *It Was on Fire When I Lay Down on It*, and when she commented how good it was, Kathy said, "Let me read you my favorite part," and got the copy Charlotte had left by the couch.

I took my food to the table that divides the kitchen from the small, carpeted "family room." Kathy read the section that describes three occasions in the relationship of a father and son. The first ("This is 1963") is about a disaster at the supermarket. The boy is three and tips over their shopping cart and a pickle shelf and leaves the father calmly thinking about running away from home—but of course he doesn't. The second episode, in 1976, tells of the father, standing in Fulghum's living room, crumpling and uncrumpling a letter from the now sixteen-year-old son, a scene during which the father tells Fulghum "he hates [the son] and never wants to see him. The son is going to run away from home. Because of his terrible father. The son thinks the father is a failure as a parent. The son thinks the father is a jerk."

During this section, I finished my chili and carried my dishes a few steps to the sink, wondering just what might have brought father and son to such a pass. Suddenly I heard Kathy's voice change: "And Dad wonders why we don't listen to things he tries to read to us." I hurried back to my seat as she continued into Fulghum's third episode:

> This is 1988. Same man and same son. The son is twenty-eight now, married, with his own three-year-old son, home, career, and all the rest. The father is fifty.
>
> Three mornings a week I see them out jogging together around 6:00 A.M. As they cross a busy street, I see the son look both ways. . . .

I heard a small catch in Kathy's voice and looked up to see tears edging both eyes as she pushed on:

> . . . with a hand on his father's elbow to hold him back from the danger of oncoming cars, protecting him from harm. [Here she paused again but didn't look up. No one else seemed to notice.] And when they sprint toward home, the son doesn't run ahead but runs alongside his father at his pace.

She continued, in full control now, to read Fulghum's sermonizing on this narrative ("sometimes they come back in their own time and take their own fathers in their arms"). I thought that it might be my death I could see in her violet eyes.

WHY NEPHI KILLED LABAN: REFLECTIONS ON THE TRUTH OF THE BOOK OF MORMON

There is a glass-walled classroom that extends behind the BYU Study Abroad Center in Baden, near Vienna, Austria. On a windy spring afternoon in 1985 Charlotte and I, with a few students, sat in that room, watching apple blossoms and forsythia toss and lean over the fence from a neighbor's yard. Still weary after a late arrival by train, we were helping to provide an audience for a missionary "concert" we had just heard about at lunch. A few members from the local branch of the church were able to get transportation, and there were some investigators and the mission president and some elders. We weren't expecting much.

Elder Kevin Kenner, tall, a bit awkward in his double-breasted grey pinstripe suit, announced that Cynthia Lang, a recent convert, would play Mozart's "Violin Sonata." He unbuttoned his coat, sat down on the piano bench, and placed his large hands on the center's brightly-polished black Yamaha. Cynthia, with a serious, generous face and strong body that moved with her bowing, began to develop Mozart's strange, delightful patterns with that rare skill that convinces you the instrument is under full control. We realized we were in for an unusual hour and began to forget the apple blossoms. Elder Kenner next played a Gershwin piece, then announced that Lun Liang, a young man investigating Mormonism, would perform on a Chinese violin. We lost all sense of duty, even of self, in the presence of continual grace—from Kreisler to Rachmaninoff then back to the Chinese violin and on to more Kreisler and some Chopin for encores.

How strange the connection of these three superficially very different people—a young missionary from San Diego, a woman of Eastern Europe's great tradition studying with Professor Ernst Kuchel, and a shy Asian playing his delicate, two-stringed instrument with its drum-like box. Though they divided the world in thirds by their geographical and cultural differences, they became absolutely united in this human obsession, raptly making and raptly listening to organized, patterned sounds.

Five days before that concert we had felt and witnessed a similar and equally strong human obsession as we listened raptly to Malcolm Miller "read" the windows at Chartres cathedral. For thirty years he has been learning to read the "book," actually the library, that the miraculous preservation of a large proportion of the stained glass of one—and only one—of the medieval cathedrals has made available to a nearly uncomprehending modern world. His one-hour lecture could only open the first few pages of the first book there at Chartres, but what a fascinating, strange, but satisfying vision began to appear. He read the third window from the right along the north wall of the transept—the story of Joseph seen in terms of his being a type, a pattern for the future Christ. He read the three great western windows, recently cleaned, whose brilliant clarity suggests how the whole cathedral looked inside when it was young, and how it could again look if funds for cleaning the other 170 windows could be found. The central window on the west gives the greatest story in human history: God becomes like us to save us. On the right is the pattern of preparation for that event, Christ's descent through the loins of Jesse, and on the left are the details of Christ's life and death after the incarnation.

We then went to the nave to read the great rose windows. The north one depicts part of the pattern of Old Testament preparations; the south one is focussed on Mary, continuing the story of patterns in Christ's life that corresponds to the typological preparations. Everywhere I saw an obsession with order, pattern, types, and parallels, prophecies and fulfillments in literal but meaningfully similar structures: the "soldiers" who went before Christ—the Old Testament prophets who foretold him—marshalled on the north; Christ and his "soldiers" that followed him, the martyrs and confessors, along the south; the four major prophets of the Old Testament with the New Testament evangelists literally on their shoulders; the Garden of Eden as Old Salem, "lost Peace," to be completed in the New Jerusalem; and, giving a shock of recognition to Book of Mormon students, a deep green cross based on the medieval legend that the tree Christ was hung upon was made from Eden's Tree of Life.

The Book of Mormon? Yes, because that most typologically structured book—the only one that uses biblical patterns with intensity and consistency and ultimate significance—has as its central pattern what Bruce Jorgensen has called "The Dark Way to the Tree," an archetypal journey to a tree which is multiple in form. With that image the Book of Mormon unites, to create greater understanding and power, four patterns of the human pilgrimage: (1) Adam and Eve as Everyman and Everywoman, who find their dark but necessary way to the tree of life through partaking of the tree of knowledge; (2) Jesus Christ, who provides the essential means for all from Adam and Eve onward to make that dark journey personally to the tree where death on a cross makes possible eternal life; (3) Lehi's dream, a personal drama of searching through darkness for the fruit of a tree that represents God's love (1 Ne. 8 and 11); and (4) Alma's explication, uniquely appropriate for modern, science-oriented skeptics, of the central crux of the pilgrimage—how to know the truth and act upon it—best symbolized as planting a seed, growing a tree, and partaking of the fruit (Alma 32:28-43). Lehi's dream, which begins the Book of Mormon narrative, becomes the type for all its main stories. As Jorgensen has shown, the conversions of Enos and Alma the Younger are told in ways that highlight similarities to the dream pilgrimage, and even the overall structure of the book appears to be shaped as a version of such a journey for humankind. This typological structuring invites all to participate in the journey of salvation, even as God leads the whole earth through such an epic in order to make our own journeys possible.[1]

Patterns, and the process of patterning, are clearly central to both the Bible and Book of Mormon. They seem to be central to basic human interests and needs. But mere pattern is not enough. We seem to yearn not only for pattern but for *meaningful, saving* patterns, ones that involve what Lehi called "things to act"—living agents, mortals and gods. Patterns obsess us because they emphasize what is most fundamental in the universe, what is repeated, necessary, irresistible, final. But there is one particularly deep-set pattern, the source and goal of all our searching for order, what Northrop Frye in his book of the same title calls "The Great Code." It is the great scriptural pattern which, beyond what the universe is and has been, also images for us what life *can be* at its most satisfying, fulfilling, and enduring. That is the pattern Frye finds unique to the Bible. He traces the way patterns ultimately shape our mythology, our metaphors, and our rhetoric itself—in a word, *all* our literature, not just what directly alludes to the Bible. I believe Frye's most important claims for the Bible can also be demonstrated for the Book of Mormon.

Actually, the Book of Mormon seems to me even more amenable than the Bible to Frye's analysis. It is mainly the product of a single mind, that of Mormon, and the resulting unity is remarkably similar to patterns only now being explicated in the Bible by critics such as Frye. Mormon, and other Book of Mormon writers, understood Christ's role in human history, perhaps more so than biblical writers, and are thus more responsive to typological patterns. I believe that, given adequate attention by sympathetic critics, the Book of Mormon will provide an even deeper, more intellectually consistent and powerful, witness than the Bible for the *Logos*—both for Jesus Christ as our divine and only Savior and also for the Word, for language imbued with divine power.

Frye has long been intrigued by the Bible's unusual potential for "polysemous" interpretation—that is, for being understood and having enormous influence not only at the literal, historical level but even more so at various metaphorical levels. He has examined particularly the typological level, which connects events and people throughout history in a cohesive pattern of images and imitations of the process of salvation through Christ. He has pointed to the success of medieval and subsequent commentators with the "moral" and "anagogical" levels of interpretation (at the moral level each passage is understood as teaching us, in addition to the literal story, how to imitate Christ's life in the practical world, at the anagogical level how to see our lives in the context of life in eternity with him).

Frye finally concluded, and set out in *The Great Code* to demonstrate, that "polysemous meaning is a feature of all deeply serious writing, and the Bible is the model for serious writing."[2] He argues that the influence of biblical language is so powerful on all other uses of language that it alone has guaranteed the possibility of retaining polysemous meaning in modern culture despite powerful influences to the contrary.

Such claims, of course, imply a particular history of language. Frye makes a crucial distinction, not provided in the single English word "language," between sound patterns that make up a language, which of course cannot be adequately translated, and the essential sense or force of dramatic patterns, which can. This latter is the French *langage*, as opposed to *langue*. *Langage* is "a sequence of modes of more or less translatable structures in words, cutting across the variety of *langues* employed, affected and conditioned but not wholly determined by them."[3] This is a valuable distinction; it turns us from exclusive attention to the formal elements of literature (such as sound patterns, multiple meanings, prose rhythms, concision, texture, and puns) that have preoccupied much literary criticism in this century. Such preoccupation has diverted us from other, perhaps weightier, patterns of stories and repeated events that reveal the nature of sin and salvation. In the process we have been kept from full appreciation of the literary merit of the Book of Mormon. With few exceptions, such as Steven Walker's defense of the quality of language in the Book of Mormon,[4] it has been criticized as dull, flat, even awkward, while the extraordinary beauty of its concepts has been neglected (for example, the philosophical sophistication of 2 Nephi 2 and Alma 32, the full and moving understanding of the Atonement in Mosiah 3-5 and Alma 7, 34, and 42). We have focused on *langue* (which might have been beautiful in the original but—except for chiasmus, which we are learning to appreciate more fully—is largely untranslatable), and we have negelected *langage*, the meanings that survive translation, such as the typologies of the tree of life.

According to Frye, the Bible is unique in its consistent power to preserve and to re-create in each new reader the reality of metaphorical language and typological patterns because of the force with which it brings those two elements of *langage* through the translations and into the modern world. It does this because, surprisingly, myth and metaphor provide the answer to the question: What is the "literal" meaning of the Bible? Frye also argues that the Bible invokes "a historical presence 'behind' [its language], as [French literary critic Jacques] Derrida would say, and that the background presence gradually shifts to a foreground, the re-creation of that reality in the reader's mind."[5] That historical reality is, of course, the typological keystone—Christ's involvement with the world, and it is a reality that I think Frye senses, though he never quite admits, is uniquely saving.

Frye is essentially right about the nature and importance of the Bible's contribution. He is certainly wrong in his defense of its uniqueness.[6] The Book of Mormon also preserves the full power of metaphorical language, typological structure, and Christ-centered moral and eschatological meaning for our secular, literalistic world. It is a second witness to Christ not only as the Savior of each individual and all the world but also to him as the *Logos*, the Word. It witnesses that Christ is the one who used language, both as God and as a man, in ways that provide the most important clues to our nature and potential as his children, and it reminds us that we are inheritors of that same crucial gift of language.

Bruce Jorgensen has already cut a deep swath into the rich harvest of typological interpretation awaiting us in the Book of Mormon. In "The Dark Way to the Tree," he has demonstrated the book's potential with definitive examples and a persuasive overall typological reading and at the same time has developed a theory of the value of such a reading. The following passages give an example, summarize the theory, and suggest the quality of the Book of Mormon as a typological work to stand with the Bible:

> Having eaten the fruit and rejoiced, Lehi immediately "began to be desirous that [his] family should partake of it also" (1 Nephi 8:12); similarly, the forgiven Enos immediately "began to feel a desire for the welfare of [his estranged] brethren, the Lamanites" (Enos 1:9-11). As later with the two Almas, the converted man is moved centrifugally outward from private partaking of grace

to communal sharing—from conversion to covenant or, if you will, from the sacrament of baptism to the sacrament of the Lord's supper. What drives the larger and more inclusive narrative of the Book of Mormon is a hunger for sanctified community. . . .
For [the Book of Mormon prophets], typing or figuring or likening, guided by revelation, is simply the one way to make sense of the universe, time, and all the dimensions of individual and communal human experience. [Their work] may suggest a theology of the Word, which in turn might suggest a philosophy of history and of language.

History may well be . . . a sequence without story. Yet to write history is to compose it . . . , to figure it, to order it by concept and metaphor. The minds that made the Book of Mormon clearly believed that this was not only possible but essential, even crucial, if humanity was to continue. Further, those minds believed that the master-figures [in the typology] were both immanent and transcendent: that God could and would reveal them to human minds, and that once received, [they] would be seen (and could be used) to order all experience. . . . Likening, then, . . . might be seen as the root-act of language itself, logically prior to the utterance of any word even if temporally simultaneous with it. . . . The dynamics of the Word in the Book of Mormon entail a view of language deeply at variance with the post-modernist view that we dwell amid infinitely self-referential and nontranscendent signs. . . . The Book of Mormon seems . . . to say that signs point beyond themselves not finally to other signs but ultimately toward God. Our trouble . . . is to read them.[7]

Besides Jorgensen, R. Dilworth Rust and George Tate[8] have made important contributions to typological analysis of the Book of Mormon. Stephen Sondrup and Noel Reynolds[9] have built on John Welch's discovery of Hebraic poetic patterns, particularly chiasmus, in the Book of Mormon.[10] What is needed is for one of these perceptive analysts to explore the relation between poetic chiasmas and typology.[11] Chiasmas is the small-scale use of repetition, with inversion, of words, concepts, and other language units, focused on a central turning point (such as abc-cba); typology is a large-scale repetition of events, persons, images, etc., all focused on the central event of Christ's mortal life. Both of

these formal devices seem to be natural expressions of a way of thinking and experiencing life that we need to understand and recover in order to approach the formal beauty and powerful message of scripture
and understand and experience how the beauty and message are inte-
grated.

I am convinced that a typological understanding of the Book of
Mormon can help us to understand the Bible itself in new ways. Such
reflection can help us see, better than we do now, I believe, that both
books provide, in their unique *langage*, the most powerful way to do the
most important thing words can do—which is, in the Book of Mormon
prophet Jacob's words, to "persuade all men not to rebel against God,
. . . but that all men would believe in Christ, and view his death, and
suffer his cross and bear the shame of the world" (Jacob 1:8). That
possibility for language—to access the meaning and the experience of
Christ's atoning sacrifice—brings us directly to René Girard.

While Frye's work on the Bible has provided us with new insights
to help us appreciate the *formal* elements of the Book of Mormon, Girard, another ground-breaking and influential contemporary literary
critic, has developed theoretical tools by which we can explore the
powerful *content* of the Book of Mormon, content which is comparable
to that of the Bible. Girard's work in anthropology led him to see similarities between various mythologies and the Bible that have led modern scholars and many others into a dogmatic religious relativism—but
also helped him see crucial differences that powerfully "make manifest
the uniqueness and truthfulness of biblical perspective."[12]

In *Deceit, Desire, and the Novel* and in *Violence and the Sacred*, Girard
presented convincing evidence from a variety of disciplines that human conflict derives from desire which is imitative; that is, we desire
what others desire.[13] Competing desires focused on the same objects
inevitably lead to envy, rivalry, blaming others and making them scapegoats even as we imitate them, as well as to various forms of cruelty and
violence. Girard has demonstrated with numerous examples that societies develop a remarkably universal mechanism to survive this process,
without which antagonisms spread like a plague as people naturally respond to disappointment by hurting others and to opposition to their

desires with revenge. Groups of people, sensing the threat of expanding imitative violence, collectively choose scapegoats to blame rather than acknowledging that their own imitative desires and revenge spirit are the true sources of the plague. Masking the scapegoating process in ritual and rationalization, even using religious and literary forms to authenticate this mechanism, people justify their violence against the scapegoats.

In *Things Hidden since the Foundation of the World*,[14] Girard argues that one effective alternative to the plague of spiritual destruction is to face and overcome imitative desire. Girard claims that the ideas and power necessary to do that are found uniquely in the central Judeo-Christian theology and ethics recorded in the Bible and epitomized and given ultimate, divine sanction and victory in the life and death of Christ. He reads Hebrew history and scriptures as a progressive effort to reveal the roots of violence and to renounce scapegoating by taking the side of the victim. He finds in Christ's persistent identification of the violence mechanism and his refusal to participate in it the superhuman victory over violence that potentially redeems all humans and all human history.

Christ's answer is to renounce false desire and to eliminate the category of enemy—thus removing rivalry, blame, jealousy, revenge, and scapegoating. For Girard, the Bible is our greatest and truest book because it refuses to participate in the illusory suppression of evil through scapegoating. Instead, it reveals the innocence of the victims and offers examples, notably in the stories of Joseph in Egypt and Christ, of how to stop the cycle of self-perpetuating violence permanently by refusing to participate in it. The Bible, particularly in the Gospels, offers forgiveness and love—in imitation of Christ and empowered by Christ's pure love expressed in the atonement—as the only solution to hatred, scapegoating, and violence and thus the only source of ultimate human salvation.

A growing body of evidence demonstrates the power of Girard's ideas to stimulate new thinking about myths, classical literature, and the scriptures. For instance, a Girardian reading of *Oedipus Rex* offers the view that the Theban community conspires, and gets Oedipus to submit, in a kind of ritual sacrifice when he in fact had *not* been guilty of patricide.[15]

Gordon Thomasson builds on Girard's insights in reading the Genesis account of Joseph and his brothers, detailing the processes of mimetic violence and scapegoating there. He relates that story to the version recalled in the Book of Mormon (2 Nephi 3) and to the striking parallel between the stories of Joseph and those of Nephi and *his* brothers. Thomasson traces the way commentaries on the Joseph story from ancient rabbinic to post-Holocaust times display "an amazing willingness to explain away or modify crucial details" so that Joseph "becomes less admirable, less of a threat to our own consciences, and consequently a more justifiable victim." In particular, many commentaries "neuter the Joseph story as it might apply to us, and undermine the significance of his refusing to retaliate against his truly guilty brothers."[16]

In Mormon commentary (including, I regret, some of my own teaching), there has been a similar tendency to see Nephi, like Joseph, as a favored son who somewhat insensitively and self-righteously intrudes on his brothers' feelings. I have often heard people say of Nephi, as they do of Joseph, "With a younger brother like that, no wonder the older ones got mad." We thus unwittingly conspire in the victimization and cloud the ethical issues of violence versus self-sacrificing reconciliation. Girard's perspective can help us appreciate Nephi's efforts to stay out of the cycle of rivalry, reciprocal violence, and self-justification. But Girard can also perhaps help us penetrate one of the most troubling cruxes in Nephi's account, his killing of Laban.

Thomasson reminds us of the interesting parallels between events in 1 Nephi and details of the scapegoat tradition from Leviticus 16. Girard claims that the Leviticus account is a *product* of the violence mechanism operating in Hebrew society, as well as a description of religious ritual. Part of the Hebrew tradition was the choosing of two scapegoats by lot—one to be sent away and one to be killed. In the Book of Mormon Lehi and his family are scapegoats for Jerusalem's troubles. Rather than face those troubles, the community focuses its growing anger on Lehi, "even as with the prophets of old, whom they had cast out, and stoned, and slain" (1 Ne. 1:20). They thus force Lehi to take his family and flee for their lives. When Lehi's sons return for the brass plates, the oldest, chosen by lot to approach the plates' keeper, Laban, is scapegoated by Laban in classic Girardian terms (that is, accused of a crime, robbery, to justify Laban in his envious desire to obtain *their* treasure) and is cast out and nearly killed. But then Laban himself is made into a second scapegoat, and the punishment of death he had decreed for Laman is meted to him by Nephi.

The problem with this interesting parallel to Leviticus lies in the justification offered for killing Laban, "It is better that one man should perish than that a nation should dwindle and perish in unbelief" (1 Ne. 4:13). This is a classic statement of the scapegoat rationale, and Girard claims that such a rationale is the foundation of human violence and is absolutely repudiated by Christ—a repudiation Girard argues is evidence that the Gospels are inspired.[17] But Nephi tells us that the rationale has here been expressed *by the Spirit of the Lord!* Furthermore, he claims that Spirit also makes the ethically troubling claim that God not only uses his divine ends to justify violence by himself but also as the rationale for a demand that one of his children, Nephi, should also use such violent means: "The Lord slayeth the wicked to bring forth his righteous purposes" (v. 13).

Girard goes to great lengths to show that the Old Testament passages seeming to implicate God in violence are records of people gradually working their way beyond an understanding of God that all other cultures retained. Though "in the Old Testament we never arrive at a conception of the deity that is entirely foreign to violence," in the later prophetic books, Girard notes, God is "increasingly divested of the violence characteristic of primitive deities."[18] Girard's analysis is persuasive, focused on a close look at the "suffering servant" passages of Isaiah, where humans wrongly ascribe responsibility for violence to God (Isa. 53:4). Girard also points out explicit rejections of violence, even God's "righteous" vengeance, that emerge in the Old Testament: "I have no pleasure in the death of the wicked; but that the wicked turn from his way and live" (Ezek. 33:11). This rejection of hatred becomes completely clear in the Gospels, where Christ rejects all notion of justified violence: "Ye have heard that it hath been said, Thou shalt love thy neighbour, and hate thine enemy. But I say unto you, Love your enemies, . . . and pray for them which despitefully use you, and persecute you; That ye may be the children of your Father which is in heaven: for he maketh his sun to rise on the evil and on the good" (Matt. 5:43-45).

Girard does not ignore the few passages in the New Testament that seem to contradict this demand by Christ, such as the cleansing of the temple and Christ's claim that he came not to send peace but a sword (Matt. 10:34). As with similarly troubling passages in the Old Testament, he deals with each in detail, persuasively showing some to be descriptive of the culture rather than prescriptive of what Jesus intends and some to be interpretations we impose from our own *still* violence-prone culture. In a few cases Girard claims a passage or its translation is simply inconsistent with Christ's overwhelmingly central and oft-repeated nonviolence and thus probably a later interpolation.

It is important to recognize that Nephi, probably recounting the killing of Laban many years after it happened, quotes God's spirit in almost exactly the same words as the Jewish priest Caiaphas later used in an ends-justifies-means argument to the Sanhedrin in order to condemn Christ: "It is expedient for us, that one man should die for the people, and that the whole nation perish not" (John 11:50). John, the recording evangelist, shows the dramatic shift from the Old Testament to the Gospel perspective when he writes that Caiaphas thus accurately, though unknowingly, "prophesied that Jesus should die for that nation" and also for all "the children of God" (vv. 51-52)—thus *not* be sacrificed or scapegoated in the usual manner. This raises the interesting but rather troubling image of Laban as a type for Christ, since the deaths of both figures bring salvation to all nations: Laban's death made possible the obtaining of the brass plates, the literal "word" that brought salvation to the Nephites and a redemptive second witness of Christ to all the world, and Christ's death fulfilled his mission as *Logos*, the "Word" that saves all peoples, including the Jews.

But even more troubling is the evidence, not only from the Bible but from the Book of Mormon itself, that Nephi's account directly contradicts the full revelation of God's nature as the One revealed in Christ who utterly rejects violence—and who demands that we do the same. Fred Essig and Dan Fuller have written an exhaustive but inconclusive study of the legal status, in the religious and moral code of the Israelites, of Nephi's rationalization for killing the unconscious, drunk Laban with his own sword. They remind us, "Few passages of the Book of Mormon have inspired more criticism. . . . Many point to this episode as evidence against the Book of Mormon being an inspired document."[19]

Though Essig and Fuller wish to counter such criticism and offer several reasons for exonerating Nephi, they finally admit, "Until we more thoroughly understand the role of Deity in the daily affairs of ancient Israel and how that role was perceived by the Israelites, we may neither condemn nor extol the acts of Nephi."[20] It is difficult to wait for such understanding (which at any rate may be completely beyond scholarship), when this passage is used by critics to dismiss the Book of Mormon. Some Mormons themselves continue to use the passage to justify troubling, violent rhetoric and even violent action—by assuming that the Spirit indeed teaches that the end justifies the means. (The fundamentalist Lafferty brothers, for example, used the passage in court to defend their "inspired" slaying of their sister-in-law and her baby in American Fork, Utah, in 1984.) For those of us troubled by such rhetoric and actions, no other passage has seemed more contradictory to New Testament and other Book of Mormon teachings about the impartiality and absolute goodness of the Lord—and about the central role pacifism plays in Christ's mission.

This is not the place for a full analysis of the Laban story, but I offer some questions and reflections, based on Girard's insights, to illustrate how his work can help us approach the Book of Mormon: First, is it possible that Nephi's decision—or at least his rationalization—was simply wrong and that he had deluded himself about God's approval? This very young man, already a victim of life-threatening jealousy, knew of Laban's murderous intent for him and his brothers. When he found Laban temporarily vulnerable but still a threat to himself and his goals, which he believed were divinely inspired, he may have very naturally been tempted to take revenge. Years of reflection before he actually wrote the account may have gradually convinced him that the Lord directed him to kill Laban to obtain the plates and thus make possible the preservation of his people, which he had indeed subsequently witnessed. The text lends some support to this possibility: Nephi is still, thirty years later, troubled by the experience and its moral meaning. His account contains a remarkable combination of unsparing completeness and honesty with what seems like rationalization, even obsessive focusing on unnecessary but psychologically revealing details (see 1 Ne. 4, esp. v. 9, where Nephi notices the sword before anything else and examines its hilt and blade in detail, and v. 18, where, after lengthy rationalization, he confesses, in what seem to be unneeded specifics, "[I] took Laban by the hair of the head, and I smote off his head with his own sword"). It seems, as one might expect of a highly religious and moral young man, that he had frequently reflected on his killing of Laban and with some ambivalence.

There are other indications that throughout his life Nephi continued to be deeply troubled by something that may have consisted of—or included—this killing of Laban: In his remarkable psalm of self-reflection, in 2 Nephi 4:27, Nephi asks, "Why should I give way to temptations, that the evil one have place in my heart to destroy my peace and afflict my soul? Why am I angry because of mine enemy?" There is no explicit evidence that he was angry with his brothers or even the Lamanites as a whole. Was he angry enough with Laban to kill him and then feel continuing remorse, which led to eventual self-justification?

On the other hand, Nephi's psalm speaks of his enemies "quaking" (2 Ne. 4:22), which seems to refer to his brothers in 1 Nephi 17. In addition, the very details Nephi includes in his account of Laban, though to us they seem strangely irrelevant—that he entered the city not knowing where he would go and that the Lord delivered Laban into his hand—are details that would establish under Mosaic law that the killing was not premeditated and thus not murder (Ex. 21:12-14; Num. 35:22).

Any reading that sees Nephi as making a mistake certainly challenges conventional thinking. We want to believe that a prophet of God, even before he is called, should be above such self-delusion and that scripture should tell us only what is best to do rather than merely describing what was actually done. We do this despite the book's own warning on its title page that "if there are faults they are the mistakes of men." Whatever the case, even an interpretation such as I have postulated, one that finds a fault in Nephi or a mistake in his account, actually increases my own conviction of the account's psychological richness and sophistication, particularly given Girard's insights. It is hard to imagine Joseph Smith concocting such an account. Even a reading that blames Nephi provides interesting and unusual evidence that the Book of Mormon is what it claims to be, an account of real experiences by a real person from the Israelite world.

However, there is another possible reading of this event, the one I believe is best. Though it avoids the problems I have reviewed, it raises what I find to be even more profoundly troubling questions, questions that Girard has also been troubled by in his work on the Bible and has clearly not yet resolved. What if God truly did command Nephi to slay Laban, but not for the very questionable reasons most often offered by Latter-day Saints—reasons that God himself has denied often in other scriptures? What if it was a test, like the command to Abraham to kill Isaac? What if it was designed to push Nephi to the limits of the human dilemma of obedience versus integrity and to teach him and all readers of the Book of Mormon something very troubling but still very true about the universe and the natural requirements of a saving relationship with God? What if it is to show that genuine faith ultimately requires us to go beyond what is rationally moral, even as it has been defined by God—but only when God himself requires it directly of us? And what if each reader is intentionally left to solve the dilemma on their own through a vicarious experience with the text?

Elder Jeffrey R. Holland, in an address to the student body in 1989 when he was president of BYU, suggested that the Laban account is given prominently and in such personal detail at the beginning of the Book of Mormon in order to force readers to deal with it and to focus "on the absolutely fundamental gospel issue of obedience and submission to the communicated will of the Lord. If Nephi cannot yield to this terribly painful command, if he cannot bring himself to obey, then it is entirely probable that he can never succeed or survive in the tasks that lie just ahead."[21] I think Elder Holland is right, but most of us need a little more help with why God would ask us to turn directly against our greatest values, the very commands God has given us. The paradox is that Nephi is asked by God to violate Christ's demand that we reject all violence, even against those who "deserve" it, and that we never again try to justify our violence by blaming God ("If ye do good to them which do good to you, what thank have ye? for sinners also do even the same. . . . But love ye your enemies, and do good, . . . and ye shall be the children of the Highest: for he is kind unto the unthankful and to the evil" [Luke 6:33, 35]).

Girard recognizes, with seeming anguish, that much of the Bible, especially the Old Testament, describes a natural order in which God seems to compromise to bring about ultimate change. Perhaps we can come to Girard's aid a bit here. Joseph Smith's revision of the Bible and the clear statement in Doctrine and Covenants 1:24 that God's revelations are given to prophets "in their weakness, after the manner of their language," indicate that scripture is at least partly limited to the perspectives of the writers, not simply expressive of God's perspective. It is natural that those writers, though prophets, would be limited in their perceptions of reciprocal violence and scapegoating in ways Girard documents as occurring in all cultures and literature. They could also be inspired to describe, accurately and fully, real human dilemmas of the kind Nephi experienced in ways that open up, with rich and educational moral complexity, the full challenge of human violence.

Girardian analysis of Shakespeare shows the dramatist pushing the scapegoat mechanism to tragic extremes—not because he accepts it, but in order to reveal it more fully and make us abhor it.[22] Thus Shakespeare becomes a kind of therapist, creating fictive dramas that imitate and reveal mechanisms we otherwise try to hide. Shakespeare's plays demonstrate how such insight must sometimes be achieved through dramatic shock, as when heroic characters such as Prospero and Cordelia tell obvious half-truths to bring about healing. Could it be that God, having similarly to deal with human limitations, could create a dramatic action for Nephi as both a test and a therapy that reveals to him *in extremis*—and also to us—that *anyone* can become a scapegoater capable of imitative violence? Or could it be that, as Elder Holland and others have suggested, God was both teaching and helping Nephi to develop obedience—while perhaps also teaching Nephi (and us) the costs and limits of such obedience?

Like Adam and Eve, Nephi had to choose which of God's commands to violate, either of which would exact a toll of anguish. His psalm of repentance and harrowing, complex memory of the event years later demonstrate this. The experience, of course, profoundly changed him and indeed prepared him for future tasks and further learning. Soon afterwards he was blessed to be the first among the Nephites to receive a full vision of the life and mission of the still far-future Christ and to understand Christ's atonement, symbolized in the tree of Lehi's dream ("It is the love of God, which sheddeth itself abroad in the hearts of the children of men" [1 Ne. 11:22]). Based on that understanding, he later states unequivocally the true nature of God as revealed in Christ, who was the absolute *opponent* of all imitative desire, all violence, all scapegoating, in a way that seems to contradict directly his own earlier report of what an angel had told him about God:

> The Lord God hath commanded that men should not murder; that they should not lie; . . . that they should not envy; that they should not have malice; that they should not contend one with another; . . . and that they should do none of these things; for whoso doeth them shall perish. For none of these iniquities come of the Lord; for he doeth that which is good among the children of men . . . and all are alike unto God (2 Ne. 26:32-33).

While in London years ago, just before the trip to Chartres, I saw, at the National Theatre, a version (based on the York cycle) of the medieval "Mystery Plays." These are the cycles of connected dramatic stories, generally taken from the Bible, once performed all over Europe annually at the feast of Corpus Christi (the medieval Catholic celebration, each June, of Christ's atonement), each segment performed by one of the town's guilds of workers. Much like the great cathedral windows, the plays taught the scriptural story of salvation to a mainly illiterate populace. In addition, much like the Mormon temple drama, the plays served remarkably well to involve actors and audience in reconfirming their own literal place in the ongoing divine drama, in patterns of grace that would save each of them, as well as Adam and Eve; Noah and his wife; Mary and Joseph; and Peter, James, and John.

The somewhat modernized script enacted by sympathetic and skilled actors in the National Theatre production engaged the contemporary, secular audience to a surprising degree. One of the most powerful scenes was the sacrifice of Isaac, prolonged by an imagined dialogue between the son on the altar and his father holding a knife, that stretched our pain at this potential violence by God upon his own children and upon his own teachings against violence—and heightened our relief at God's intervention. The medieval authors, in their genius, cut immediately from this scene to the annunciation of the birth of the Savior.

The significance of this connection is intensified by Abraham's anomalous plea to the yet unborn Jesus, as he sees Isaac's increasing anguish and knows he must act: "Jesu, on me thou have pity/ That I have most in mind." This anguish is echoed in God's words to Abraham, after intervening, that make the connection to Christ explicit: "Like thine Isaac, my loved lad/ Shall do full heartily his Father's will,/ But not be spared strokes sore and sad,/ But done to death upon a hill."[23]

In the London production the effect was heightened even more when a group of actors representing the butchers' guild, traditionally assigned (with macabre appropriateness) to play the sacrifice of Isaac, came forward. After a complex, ritual dance of controlled violence at the completion of the sacrifice, they ended by interweaving their long sword-like butcher knives into a Star of David and carried it up to the balcony where it became the star of annunciation of Christ's birth.

The typology is certainly clear and has been recognized by many (see Jacob 4:5, where Abraham and Isaac are called a "similitude" of God and Christ), but the connections between God's apparent endorsement of violence and the violent victimization of his own son, which saves us, have not been very adequately explored. I think the Book of Mormon can help here, mainly because it provides the basis for an understanding of the Atonement that can complement but also go beyond Girard's fruitful ideas.

The Book of Mormon suggests connections between such things

as Nephi's killing of Laban and his remarkable visions soon after of Christ and the "condescension" of God (literally, the one who does not look down in judgment upon us from a physical and moral distance but who "descends with" us into mortal pain and suffering and sickness [1 Ne. 11:26]). Subsequent Book of Mormon scriptures explore the idea that God accomplishes the Atonement by transcending the paradox of justice and mercy, and in doing so these scriptures use the same image of condescension: He is the "Lord Omnipotent" who gives us the law and will ultimately judge us, but he is also the suffering servant who will "come down from heaven . . . and shall dwell in a tabernacle of clay" (Mosiah 3:5) and thus learn how to save us by literally taking upon himself our "pains and . . . sicknesses" and "infirmities, that his bowels may be filled with mercy" (Alma 7:11-12).

The Book of Mormon is consistent, I believe, with Girard's helpful focus on the Atonement as achieved through love rather than through traditional sacrifice, through reconciliation rather than through payment. The Book of Mormon also makes clear that Christ's atonement was centered in the Garden of Gethsemane, not on the cross. As King Benjamin teaches and as Doctrine and Covenants 19 powerfully reconfirms in Christ's own words, it was in the garden, when Christ momentarily shrank from what he knew was necessary and then fully joined all humankind as he experienced the most terrible sense of alienation and pain we can know—descended below all and the worst of our experience in order to raise us to accept our acceptance by him. It was there that "blood [came] from every pore, so great [was] his anguish for . . . his people" (Mosiah 3:7; see also D&C 19:18).

Perhaps most startling is the unique Book of Mormon witness that many people, such as King Benjamin's audience, who lived 125 years before Christ, were able to experience the Atonement fully and be completely changed into new creatures long before the Atonement actually occurred in history. This fact shows that, contrary to traditional Christian teaching, the Atonement was not a sacrificial event that changed people only from that moment on, but an expression of unconditional love from God that freed all people throughout history to repent and become like God simply by knowing about it, by hearing the prophetic witness, whether expressed before Christ lived or after.

In addition, the Book of Mormon gives perhaps the most direct affirmation in scripture of Girard's claim that Christ's atonement put an end to all claims for the legitimacy of sacrifice and scapegoating (indeed of *any* kind of violence):

> [The Atonement will not be] a sacrifice of man, neither of beast, neither of any manner of fowl; for it shall not be a human sacrifice. . . . [But] *then shall there be*, or it is expedient there should be, *a stop to the shedding of blood*; then shall the law of Moses be fulfilled. . . . And thus he shall bring salvation to all those who shall believe on his name; this being the intent of this last sacrifice, to bring about the bowels of mercy, which overpowereth justice, and bringeth about means unto men that they may have faith unto repentance (Alma 34:10, 13, 15; my emphasis).

Besides confirming some of Girard's insights, the Book of Mormon illustrates the proper role of justice, of punishment, even of God's own participation in processes that involve or threaten violence. Amulek's discourse on the Atonement in Alma 34 and Alma's in Alma 42 make much clearer than anything available to Girard in the Bible the crucial part justice plays in God's plan for our redemption.

The Bible's well-known accounts of what seem like divinely directed or justified violence may result from imperfect attempts to express that principle of God's justice. The Book of Mormon more clearly shows why God must use justice to establish conscience in us before his forgiving love, which ends the cycle of violence, can effectively operate. For instance, Alma teaches his son Corianton that God affixed laws and punishments, "which brought remorse of conscience unto man"; if he had not done so, "men would not be afraid to sin . . . [and] the works of justice would be destroyed, and God would cease to be God" (Alma 42:18, 20, 22). Alma also teaches Corianton that such a condition has the inevitable, unfortunate result of placing man "in the grasp of justice." It is therefore necessary, to counter that result, that "God himself [atone] for the sins of the world, to bring about the plan of mercy, to appease the demands of justice, that God might be a perfect, just God, and a merciful God also" (vv. 14-15).

A major problem for many of Girard's readers is his explanation of how original violence lies at the foundation of society and religion and then how that original violence is continually obscured over time, even in God-directed biblical cultures. The Book of Mormon may be able to help us understand how the constraints of human nature and agency require God, in working out a possible plan of salvation for us, to cooperate in—or at least allow—that natural obscuring process. Perhaps it is only in such a way, in which the processes of *quid-pro-quo* justice and thus imitative violence work with full force for a while, that our consciences can be adequately formed by justice. Then, as the Book of Mormon uniquely explains, such demands of justice in our own minds can be appeased by our knowing certainly, through prophetic witness, the plan of God's mercy (Alma 42:15). Thus our consciences, which remain too self-critical to accept Christ's forgiveness and acceptance of us, can be overpowered by the bowels of his mercy (Alma 34:15). Our difficulty with apparently contradictory scriptures may be a matter of understanding how God's justice and his mercy work *together* to bring us to self-knowledge and guilt, but also to self-acceptance and repentance.

In addition to all this, the Book of Mormon provides an example of a group actually practicing Girard's implied unique solution to imitative violence, with precisely the results he predicts. A group of people converted to the Christian gospel in 80 B.C. makes a covenant with God "that rather than shed the blood of their brethren they would give up their own lives" (Alma 24:18). In keeping with that covenant, they ritually bury their weapons. When attacked by vengeful enemies, they respond with astonishing courage in a way directly *contrary* to the universal tendency to reciprocal violence that Girard has described: They "would not flee from the sword, neither would they turn aside to the right hand or to the left, but . . . would lie down and perish, and praised God even in the very act of perishing under the sword" (v. 23). When their enemies see this, the reverse pattern, what Girard calls the "benign reciprocity of love," takes over: "There were many whose hearts had swollen in them for those of their brethren who had fallen," and they too "threw down their weapons of war, and they would not take them again" (vv. 24-25). Speaking from the perspective of four hundred years of Nephite history, Mormon draws a pointed lesson: "And now behold I say unto you, has there been so great love in all the land? Behold, I say unto you, Nay, there has not" (26:32-33).

It would be hard to imagine a better complement to Girard's analysis of the Joseph and Judah story. When Joseph threatens to keep his brother Benjamin in Egypt as a suspected thief, Judah, archetypal head of the Jews, offers—in an exact reversal of his previous treatment of Joseph—to take Benjamin's place. Joseph is moved to tears and reconciliation with his brothers. As Girard writes, "This dedication of Judah stands in symmetrical opposition to the original deed of collective violence which it cancels out and reveals."[24]

The central question still remains how to cope with the imitative desire that leads to envy and rivalry and sets in motion all the problems that produce violence and our consciences' demands for reciprocal justice. For Christians, including Girard, the question is how Christ's atonement makes it possible for us to stop the cycle even before it starts—or at least to make repentance and forgiveness possible so it can end.

In the Book of Mormon King Benjamin teaches how this redemptive process can be initiated and then maintained. First, he proclaims the essential and primary reality of the Atonement, by which Christ extends unconditional love to us, even in our sins. Consistent with Amulek and Alma, he teaches that Christ's love can move us to overcome demands within ourselves, placed there by our God-given consciences, to punish ourselves and others. This breaking of the bands of justice, he claims, enables us to accept Christ's mercy and forgiveness and to become new creatures. Intensely moved by learning of Christ's love, the group of Nephites taught by King Benjamin loses all "disposition to do evil" (Mosiah 5:2). King Benjamin also reveals that the only way to maintain this change of heart is to seek "a remission of your sins from day to day" (4:26). The key is humility, the abdication of imitative desire through recognizing that we are "all beggars" (v. 19). Just as God does not reject us, does not refuse to love us or to extend his healing grace and continual blessings because we sin, we must not reject those who beg help from us though they do not "deserve" it. We must never judge their desires or condition; we must never think that "the man has brought upon himself his misery; therefore . . . his punishments are just" (v. 17). If we do so we have "great cause to repent," and if we fail to repent we have "no interest in the kingdom of God" (v. 18). Instead, we must constantly recognize our weakness and dependence on God, judging no one but engaging constantly in specific acts of sacrificial love: "feeding the hungry, clothing the naked, visiting the sick and administering to their relief, both spiritually and temporally, according to their wants" (v. 26).

The point is this: After receiving grace, we must extend grace to others. If we judge others, we unconsciously judge ourselves and thus reject the mercy that can change us. We must constantly give mercy in order to accept it. We cannot exact revenge, even in the name of perfect justice, without taking vengeance upon ourselves, the sinners we inwardly know most certainly deserve it.

These two passages from the Book of Mormon, the account of the pacifist People of Ammon and King Benjamin's address, provide a basis for meeting one of the main criticisms made of Girard's work. Even those who find that his hypotheses fit the available facts better than any others are troubled that despite the claim that his work can help us cope with violence in our lives and in relations between nations, neither he nor his disciples have offered concrete, practical steps toward that goal.[25] Active, self-sacrificing love, even of our enemies, and nonjudgmental, merciful feeding of the hungry are seldom recommended and even less seldom practiced in our world. The Book of Mormon provides powerful evidence, in theory and example, that they could work—and in fact are essential for *our* salvation.[26]

What do these reflections on recent literary criticism and Nephi's killing of Laban suggest about the Book of Mormon? That no one has mastered or explained or exhausted it. It not only stands up to the most sophisticated modern thought about literature; it also challenges our most sophisticated ethical, theological, and political concepts. I am encouraged by my study so far to find that what Frye and Girard claim for the Bible can also be claimed, point by point and often more clearly and usefully, for the Book of Mormon. But more important, their insights deepen my understanding and appreciation of a book I already believe is both as historically true and as spiritually valuable as the Bible. As I approach difficult parts of the book, such as the Laban story, with these new tools, I find the book responding with truth and richness.

Girard focuses on content, Frye on form. Girard reminds us of the central ethic at the heart of the *Logos*, mercy transcending justice. Frye reminds us of the best way to get to that heart: pattern transcending reason. The Book of Mormon, if we will work—and open ourselves—to find it so, is a restored second witness to both the ethic and the pattern, to Christ as Redeemer and to Christ as the *Logos*.

NOTES

1. Bruce W. Jorgensen, "The Dark Way to the Tree," in Neal A. Lambert, ed., *The Literature of Belief* (Salt Lake City: Bookcraft and BYU Religious Studies Center, 1979), 218-30.

2. Northrop Frye, *The Great Code: The Bible and Literature* (London: Routledge & Kegan Paul, 1982), 221.

3. Ibid., 5.

4. Steven C. Walker, "More Than Meets the Eye: Concentration of the Book of Mormon," *Brigham Young University Studies* 20 (Winter 1980): 199-205.

5. Frye, xx.

6. Ibid., 80.

7. Jorgensen, "The Dark Way to the Tree," 222-29.

8. Richard D. Rust, "All Things Which Have Been Given of God . . . Are the Typifying of Him: Typology in the Book of Mormon," 233-44, and George S. Tate, "The Typology of the Exodus Pattern in the Book of Mormon," 245-62, both in Lambert, ed., *Literature of Belief*. More recently, Avraham Gileadi and Alan Goff have built on this work with detailed book-length studies of passages and themes, including explicit connections to biblical typology: Avraham Gileadi, *The Last Days: Types and Shadows from the Bible and the Book of Mormon* (Salt Lake City: Deseret Book, 1990), and Alan Goff, "A Hermeneutic of Sacred Texts: Revisionism and Positivism, and the Bible and the Book of Mormon," M.A. thesis, Brigham Young University, 1989.

9. Stephen Sondrup, "The Psalm of Nephi: A Lyric Reading," *Brigham Young University Studies* 21 (Summer 1981): 357-72, and Noel B. Reynolds, "Nephi's Outline," in Noel B. Reynolds, ed., *Book of Mormon Authorship* (Salt Lake City: Bookcraft and BYU Religious Studies Center, 1982), 53-74.

10. John W. Welch, "Chiasmas in the Book of Mormon," in Reynolds, *Book of Mormon Authorship*, 33-52.

11. An initial step has been taken by John W. Welch in his "Chiasmas in Biblical Law: An Approach to the Structure of Legal Texts in the Hebrew Bible," *Jewish Law Association Studies* 4 (Boston Conference volume, 1990), connecting the balancing features of chiasmas with the reciprocal and proportional typologies of talionic justice.

12. René Girard, "The Bible Is Not a Myth," *Literature and Belief* 4 (1984): 8.

13. René Girard, *Deceit, Desire, and the Novel* (Baltimore: Johns Hopkins University Press, 1965), and Girard, *Violence and the Sacred* (Baltimore: Johns Hopkins University Press, 1977).

14. René Girard, *Things Hidden since the Foundation of the World* (Stanford, CA: Stanford University Press, 1987).

15. Sandor Goodhart, "*Leskas Ephaske*: Oedipus and Laius's Many Murderers," *Diacritics* 8 (Spring 1978): 55-71.

16. Gordon Thomasson, "Madness, Differentiation, and Sacrifice, or Reconciliation: Humanity's Options as Seen in 2 Maccabees and Genesis," unpublished paper presented 15 November 1984 at the Eighth Annual BYU College of Humanities Symposium, "Myth, Literature, and the Bible," 17; copy in my possession.

17. Girard, *Things Hidden*, 141-79.

18. Ibid., 157.

19. Fred Essig and Dan Fuller, "Nephi's Slaying of Laban: A Legal Perspective," *FARMS Preliminary Report* (Provo, UT: FARMS, 1982), 1.

20. Ibid., 25.

21. Jeffrey R. Holland, *The Will of the Father in All Things* (Provo, UT: Brigham Young University Press, 1989), 6.

22. See, for example, his *A Theater of Envy: William Shakespeare* (Oxford: University of Oxford Press, 1991).

23. Tony Harrison, ed. and tr., *The Mysteries* (London: Faber and Faber, 1985), 48.

24. Girard, "The Bible Is Not a Myth," 15.

25. Robert North, "Violence and the Bible: The Girard Connection," *Catholic Biblical Quarterly* 47, 1 (1985): 10.

26. For additional exploration of this idea, see my "Fasting and Food, Not Weapons: A Mormon Response to Conflict," *Brigham Young University Studies* 25 (Winter 1985): 141-55; reprinted in *The Quality of Mercy* (Salt Lake City: Bookcraft, 1992), 117-38.

eight

"THOU SHALT NOT KILL": AN ETHICS OF NON-VIOLENCE

On April 24, 1898, Apostle Brigham Young, Jr., gave the last in a series of speeches he made against Mormon involvement in the impending Spanish American War. Consistent with the attitude of his father during the Civil War and church leaders generally to that point in Mormon history, he urged the Saints to remain aloof from the nation's violence: "If I knew of any young men who wanted to go to this war," he said, "I would call them on a mission to preach the gospel of peace." The next day Congress declared war, and Elder Young's half-brother, Willard Young, and his nephew, Richard W. Young, both West Point graduates, called on the First Presidency to object to Elder Young's remarks and to report they had volunteered for service and intended to recruit other volunteers in Utah.

In response, President Wilford Woodruff departed from the views of his predecessors and announced that "Utah should stand by the government in the present crisis and that our young men should be ready to serve their country when called upon." Of this crucial juncture in Mormon history, Woodruff's biographer Thomas G. Alexander writes, "Moving in a direction evident at least since the 1887 Constitutional Convention but nevertheless crossing an immense intellectual Rubicon, Woodruff subordinated the ideal of the kingdom of God to the ideal of loyalty to the United States. In order to prove Latter-day Saint patriotism, he proposed to offer the ultimate sacrifice—the blood of Mormon youth—to the nation."[1]

During most of the nineteenth century the church promoted what historian Jan Shipps has called radical restoration, its social, political, and moral institutions and attitudes fundamentally at odds with the world, including the United States. The church generated opposition that by 1890 had nearly destroyed it. Then followed a period of conservative accommodation and preservation, including the end of polygamy, theocratic politics, and isolationist economics. This was apparently necessary not only for survival but to enable the building of a strong base in the United States from which the gospel could be taken to all the world in preparation for Christ's coming. But one of the costs was an accommodation to this world's violence, especially that of a particular nation, the United States.

Now, more than one hundred years later, we are indeed able to send missionaries virtually throughout the world—including twelve new missions in former Soviet-controlled Eastern Bloc. I remember praying in the 1950s—and 1960s and 1970s and 1980s, as our leaders constantly exhorted us to—that God would touch the hearts of the leaders of nations to open their doors to the gospel. Like many Mormons, I suppose, I prayed without much faith, mainly in hope for something far in the future. But God did touch hearts and open the nations—aided by the faith of non-violent Christians who, carrying candles instead of guns, marched out of churches into the streets of East Germany; and by Russians who stood before tanks in Moscow, some to be crushed to death. It is time, I believe, to reaffirm our faith in the God of peace and healing. It is time to take to heart the symbolism—and literal miracle—in the young pair of Mormon elders preaching the gospel of peace together in 1991 in northern England, one the first missionary called from Russia, a former soldier who had served in Afghanistan, the other a former cadet at West Point, where he had been trained to fight Russians.

The scriptures and modern prophets call us to revere life as the most fundamental value, even to sacrifice our own lives to avoid violence as we respond to injustice and evil that threaten us. This is the ethic preached and lived by Christ. Even in the Old Testament the Lord, whom Mormons understand is Christ, commanded, without qualification, "Thou shalt not kill." In the Doctrine and Covenants the resurrected Lord reaffirmed the command, with an important addition: "Thou shalt not . . . kill, *nor do anything like unto it*" (59:6; my emphasis). When he was in mortality, that same Lord admitted that before then, in Old Testament times, his people had not lived up to—or even fully understood—the absolute ethic. But he called his disciples to practice it as a condition of genuinely following him and God the Father: "You have heard that it hath been said, Thou shalt love thy neighbor, and hate thine enemy. But I say unto you, Love your enemies, . . . do good to them that hate you. . . . That ye may be the children of your Father which is in heaven. . . . Be ye therefore perfect, even as your Father which is in heaven is perfect" (Matt. 5:44-5).

Christ completely disassociated himself from society's traditions of violence. Even in his own extreme danger, he rejected Peter's use of a sword to defend him, instead healing his enemy's ear and then stating a pragmatic reason for non-violence: "*All* they that take the sword shall perish with the sword." Generally, however, he simply makes a pure ethical *demand*: "Resist not evil" (Matt. 5:39). His apostle, Paul, adds a positive pragmatic purpose to the ethic: "Be not overcome of evil, but overcome evil with good" (Rom. 12:21).

The Book of Mormon at times reflects the values of a violent Hebraic culture of the kind that Christ called his disciples to rise above. At other times the Book of Mormon clearly advocates a higher non-violent ethic which it makes clear *is* a higher standard. Regarding the Lamanites converted by Ammon who renounced violence, even in self-defense, Mormon writes, "Thus we see that when these Lamanites were brought to know the truth they were firm, and would suffer even unto death rather than commit sin" (Alma 24:19). The sacrifice of these Lamanite pacifists ended violence, while the "just" wars of the Nephites did not and were followed by a decline into apostasy.

When Christ appears in America, he issues the same call to non-violence that he made in the Sermon on the Mount in Galilee, again charging his disciples to rise above the old ethic, even that practiced in God-assisted defensive wars earlier in the Book of Mormon ("It is written, an eye for an eye. . . . But I say unto you, that ye shall not resist evil" [3 Ne. 12:38-39]). This willingness of God to allow one ethic while nursing us toward another has confused many Mormons, but as Hugh Nibley has pointed out, "The contradiction is only apparent, for if one examines the passages on both sides throughout the scriptures, they fall clearly into two categories: general principles and special circumstances. The verses forbidding conflict are of a general universal nature, while those which countenance it all refer to exceptional cases."[2]

Mormons sometimes cite examples of what seems like approval of violence by God, such as his command to the Israelites to slay every living thing in cities they captured or to Nephi to kill Laban, but these can all be explained, I believe, as exceptional cases which are extremely dangerous if used for precedents. Some such scriptural examples, when distilled to their essence, are examples of humans engaging in wish-fulfillment, *imagining* that God condones their "just" vengeance. Some show God doing the best he can with rather intractable people. The most serious problem is the Old Testament, which seems to present a vengeful God of violence—*if* all the passages are taken as literal and of equal authority. Many commentators point out the intellectual and moral inconsistencies in such literal reading of the scriptures or in the failure to see some texts, especially those giving Christ's perspective, as more authoritative than others.

As we learn to distinguish the highest ethic from what may contradict it, I believe the principle of conformity with what is most Christlike and fundamental is crucial. We must constantly ask, "What ethic is most consistently taught throughout the scriptures, especially by Christ, both when he was on the earth and as the resurrected being who speaks in the Doctrine and Covenants and to modern prophets? What is most consistent with other principles, especially those we are regularly taught and feel by our own experience and inspiration are most fundamental, having to do with the nature of human beings and of God?"

In answer I believe the most fundamental thing we can say about humans, confirmed throughout the scriptures, is that they are infinitely and equally precious. Each human by their very existence constitutes an absolute claim on every other human to be treated as an end rather than a means, to have their personhood respected as the most basic of all realities and rights. That is why we must do only good to each other and must make the welfare of each other paramount. That is the way God is portrayed as responding to each of us and the way we are told we must respond if we are to be true to our nature as his children.

For Mormons this understanding is enriched by the conviction that our most essential selves, what we call "intelligences," have existed forever, uncreated and co-eternal with God; that we each have therefore the potential to become genuinely godlike; and that it is God's declared work and glory to help us *all* to do that (Moses 1:39). Joseph Smith declared in his King Follett Discourse: "All the minds and spirits that God ever sent into the world are susceptible of enlargement and improvement."[3]

Versions of this concept have been developed, of course, by such thinkers as Martin Buber, in *I and Thou*, and by Immanuel Kant in his "categorical imperative" always to treat others as ends rather than as means. Emmanuel Levinas, the post-modern Jewish philosopher, claims that such understanding of ourselves is pre-conceptual—based on the most fundamental of life experiences, the confrontations that begin with birth, or even at conception, in which we respond to the "other," to humans and to God. If we reflect, I believe we can sense what Levinas tries to articulate, that each other human constitutes a pre-rational demand on us, a demand to respond to them as ends in themselves and do them good according to their needs and our ability to respond—but at least never to dehumanize them, never to define them ("totalize" them in Levinas's word) in ways that limit them to a category or a static judgment and thus limit our infinite responsibility to them.

Think of the unique call upon us that the face of another human makes, whether represented by little black dots in a news photo of a grieving mother in Somalia or the glance of a loved one or the sound of a human voice crying in the dark—or the presence of a face in the womb implied by a baby's kick. If I am right that this notion of what it means to be human makes being treated as human, as a person, the most fundamental right of all humans, then there is no other right, or claim of justice or ethics, that could justify violating that basic right—not even a so-called just war. But before I consider war, let me try to apply the principle I have just discussed to abortion and capital punishment.

The questions abortion raises seem to be tearing our nation apart and could similarly polarize church and family because questions about the nature and control of unborn life inevitably lead to questions about

161

the nature of moral agency and the control of women by men. The principle I have tried to articulate about the most fundamental right of individuals seems to me to carry some weight from the moment of conception. The obligation to heed the ethical demand of others, perhaps particularly when the other is produced within one's own body and lives helpless there, is suggested by Christ's extended modern commandment, "Thou shalt not . . . kill, nor do anything like unto it." The fact is that in the U.S. well over a million embryos are "terminated" each year, at least some quite brutally—many more than was the case twenty years ago. A large percent of these terminations are "elective," that is for reasons other than incest, rape, the mother's health, or defects in the fetus. This widespread and too often unmourned termination of life violates our natures in ways that I believe maim the souls and darken the future lives of many women—and also of consenting or encouraging fathers.

Abortion is connected with a growing unwillingness to take responsibility for the results of promiscuous sexual desires and actions, which are increasingly presented in the movies and media as uncontrollable. It seems to me to constitute an enormous drain on the moral and spiritual health of our nation and world. It expresses and thus tends to increase a disrespect for life and desertion of our responsibility to other beings that is, in the words of the official LDS church statement in 1991, "devastating."[4]

That statement is one important basis for a consistent life ethic for Mormons in the twenty-first century. It clearly reaffirms opposition to "elective abortion" (which seems to mean abortion simply for convenience), but also spells out "rare cases in which abortion may be justified—cases involving pregnancy by incest or rape: when the life or health of the woman is . . . in serious jeopardy; or when the fetus [has] severe defects that will not allow the baby to survive beyond birth." Even these are not automatically approved but require a careful decision made together by the parents, with their bishop's counsel and "divine confirmation."

However, on the vexing question of what role civil law should play in controlling abortion, of defining when the fetus becomes a "person" which the state must protect against "murder" and for religious people is related to the question of when the spirit enters the body, the LDS church is neutral and undogmatic. It "has not favored or opposed specific legislative proposals." The church's *Handbook of Instructions* states clearly that abortion is *not* murder.[5] Although the First Presidency in 1909 said that the spirit enters the body "at a certain stage," leaders have disagreed about what that means. Significantly, the church does not record miscarriages or stillbirths on its records, does not seal them to parents, or teach they will be resurrected and raised by the parents—which may imply that the spirit has not yet entered the body or that the spirits of all who die before birth are simply sent into other bodies to have their opportunity for mortal life.

The absolutism of much pro-life rhetoric, which calls abortion murder, is rejected both by the LDS church's position and by common sense. It can also be tragically dangerous, as was clear in the killing on March 10, 1992, of a doctor at an abortion clinic in Florida by a "pro-life" activist. He claimed the Bible justified his killing a "murderer."

Many who call themselves pro-life seem to be remarkably insensitive to the rights of others in a pluralistic society that profoundly disagrees about when, during pregnancy, abortion becomes an attack on a person and thus a matter for governmental interference. Constitutional experts emphasize that the stability of governments results from the state's general unwillingness to legislate in matters of personal morals and conscience. When we *force* people's compliance in matters that in their view (and the view of a large proportion of the citizenry) do not clearly harm others, they feel personally infringed upon. The difference between passing laws against abortion and those against murder, as George J. Church points out in a remarkably sensible essay in *Time* (6 Mar. 1995, 108), is that in the case of murder there is overwhelming consensus that it is an attack on a person and the conduct clearly is a serious threat to public order—whereas neither of these crucial conditions is met for abortion. Some commentators, like Charles Krauthammer, express dismay at the "inconsistency" revealed in poll after poll that reports that a large majority of Americans opposes abortion—and just as high a majority opposes stringent laws against it. But this seems perfectly consistent to me. We value *both* life and moral agency. We are uneasy about intruding, with the force or law and sanctions, in such a difficult case where there is no consensus about when something like murder occurs.

This distinction about when law may appropriately try to proscribe action is crucial. We came to earth to learn moral agency—as Brigham Young said, to learn "to be righteous in the dark."[6] Christ tells us in the Doctrine and Covenants that the central principle of our Constitution, to be "maintained for the rights and protection of all flesh," is to foster that agency, so "that every man may be accountable for his own sins in the day of judgment" (101:78). That is, law should protect people from each other but not try to force individual morality. Abortion is a gray area, where the distinction between harming others and making a personal moral choice is difficult and where we must tread carefully between two crucial values, life and freedom.

To contribute to a moral and peaceful society, it seems to me that Mormons can feel free to work passionately but peacefully and non-judgmentally for whatever *legal* restrictions they feel best express their own beliefs about when that point of legally protected personhood begins, from nearly total restrictions to very little. But Mormons must also be willing to accept compromise arrived at in our political process without condemning gentiles who disagree as murderers or branding their brothers and sisters who disagree as heretics in areas where the church has not given official direction.

There is much violence in our culture against women and children, violence that in turn produces the violence of abortion, and pro-life rhetoric often fails to address this. Traditionally men have exercised a great deal of control over women, and the struggle about abortion is in part a struggle to end that control—which many believe is itself a main cause for abortion.

On the other hand, much pro-choice rhetoric exalts romantic individualism over social responsibility and trivializes the serious life-and-death questions of abortion. Use of such phrases as "elective abortion" and flippant slogans like "Abortion on demand and without apology" or "Choosy mothers choose choice" reveal an appalling insensitivity to what is going on in abortion clinics and to the feelings of those who oppose it. Even if some pro-choice arguments make political and moral sense, the coarseness of language and general unwillingness even to mourn the millions of deaths seem part of a general decline in respect for life that is transferred to other areas as well, such as euthanasia.

More seriously perhaps, much pro-choice rhetoric reveals a personal unwillingness to honor the demands of life and of the "other," to deal with the hard moral issues involved in increasing the autonomy of women without destroying life. Pro-choice activists generally give too little attention to the continuing sorrow and guilt felt by women who abort—and also by fathers—or to the tide of irresponsible sexuality and the general depreciation of respect for life, including women's lives, that the wholesale aborting inevitably brings.

I believe Mormons should disassociate themselves from both "pro-life" and "pro-choice" labels and movements. Both movements sometimes employ activities and rhetoric that are inconsistent with the gospel of Christ. Both have proven, in the main, ineffective at either improving the status of women or reducing abortions. I suggest instead that Mormons unite under some such banner as "Mormons for life and choice" and work through a variety of means to reduce the forces, including male domination, that produce unchosen pregnancies, to improve choice through education, and to reduce poverty, bad health care, and other social conditions that discourage women from wanting to bear children.

I believe that moral persuasion (along with the social improvements of the kind I have mentioned) as opposed to reliance on legal sanctions is the morally superior and more effective means to attack the evil of abortion. We can work together to formulate laws that could protect the unborn without victimizing mothers—for instance, family leave laws and laws that combat unsafe and exploitive abortion clinics. We can work—with laws, financial benefits, and information—to increase the attractiveness of parenthood as an option. We can teach equal male-female parenting responsibilities and combat the pernicious and debasing idea that women need abortion rights so they can compete equally with men in our economy. We can reveal and condemn sexist assumptions that pregnancy is a kind of handicap or cosmetic blemish that should be cured by surgery. We can teach the value of restricting sexuality to marriage and greater sensitivity to the meaning of genuine consent in marriage. We can help young people value their sexuality in relation to *life*. Such an approach, aimed at building a national consensus that abortion is an evil except in rare cases and always a tragedy, and finding pragmatic rather that coercive ways to make it rare, is outlined by George McKenna in "On Abortion: A Lincolnian Position" in the September 1995 *Atlantic Monthly*.

The church has set an example of what McKenna calls for with its morally empowering official position, with talks like that of Elder Russell M. Nelson in April 1985 general conference entitled "Reverence for Life,"and with its series of public service advertisements which, without identifying church sponsorship, simply present vignettes of the great variety of human lives and the message, "Life, what a beautiful choice." Elder Nelson's is the kind of powerful voice of persuasion that we could all energetically emulate throughout our society:

> For years I have labored with other doctors here and abroad, struggling to prolong life. It is impossible to describe the grief a physician feels when the life of a patient is lost. Can anyone imagine how we feel when life is destroyed at its roots, as though it were a thing of naught? If one is to be deprived of life because of potential for developing physical problems, consistency would dictate that those who already have such deficiencies should likewise be terminated; continuing, then, those who are either infirm, incompetent, or inconvenient should be eliminated by those in power. Such irreverence for life is unthinkable.[7]

A number of other Mormon voices are now speaking with this kind of intelligent and charitable moral power. Though I dislike the labels they have assumed and disagree with them about the degree of legal control, I recommend their work as beginning points for conversations about a consistent Mormon life ethic. Some "pro-choice feminists" in BYU's *Student Review* and in *Network*, a Utah women's journal, have explored ways to increase women's autonomy so there will be no unchosen pregnancies and thus no abortion. Camille Williams and Anne Eberhardt Clark, "pro-life feminists," in the *Mormon Women's Fo-*

rum and *Network*, make strong cases that the emphasis on abortion rights, besides increasing violence and insensitivity to violence in our society, has undermined the cause of women. Here is a sample from Clark, from the *Deseret News* in July 1992, approving in part a recent Supreme Court decision about requiring informed consent:

> [The court] has taken a small step toward empowering women to make better-informed abortion decisions—a victory for the unborn. . . . with more complete and accurate information about the child growing within her body, if the woman then chooses not to abort, everyone should be happy—those who are pro-life because she did not destroy her child, and those who are pro-choice because her decision was freely made.

One reason I admire Anne Clark is that she is consistent in her defense of life, which I find not always true of Mormons. Two weeks after she published the editorial quoted above she joined a group of us in front of the Governor's Mansion in Salt Lake City in a protest against the execution of William Andrews, who had participated in the infamous Ogden "hi-fi" robbery and tortures but not the killing. Announcing that she was the Utah chair for Feminists for Life in America, she called on Mormons to be consistent and apply their pro-life ethic to Andrews.

A Mormon theology of life seems to me to require that kind of consistency, a full recognition of the ethical demand for mercy placed on us by every human being. Capital punishment is, in every case, a denial of mercy, which LDS president Gordon B. Hinckley has called "the very essence of the gospel of Jesus Christ," the best "expression of the reality of our discipleship under Him."[8] Lowell Bennion, speaking at the rally in July 1992, pointed out that, especially in the case of Andrews, who had not taken a life and had become a model prisoner, capital punishment could only be intended as revenge, for which there is no place in the gospel of Christ.

The majority of countries in western Europe and North and South America have abandoned capital punishment. Its application has been grossly unfair, heavily weighted by race, sex, and income, even by where the trial occurs. In this century alone nearly 400 people in our country have been convicted of capital crimes and later proven innocent, but not before about thirty were executed. There is no conclusive evidence that capital punishment deters crime—possibly because many such crimes are committed under great emotional stress or the influence of drugs or alcohol. As Andrei Sakharov, Nobel Peace Prize-winning physicist who lived under a regime that relied on executions, wrote, "Savagery only begets savagery." Far from being a deterrent to others, highly publicized executions are known to be followed by an increase in violent crime; in order to deter the confessed murderer from killing again, life imprisonment without parole is a more humane option.

In the Andrews case, his accomplice Dale Selby, who committed the murders, had already been executed. The original jury was presented with only the options of death or life imprisonment with the possibility of parole for both Selby and Andrews. The board of pardons and the governor refused a retrial which would have made life without parole an option. One of the Lafferty brothers and Mark Hofmann, both white Mormons who committed multiple and brutal murders, received life sentences with possible parole, while Selby, a black, was executed for similar killings and Andrews, a black, was executed without having killed at all.

Herman Melville's *Billy Budd* contains one of the most anguishing scenes in literature. A young seaman, innocent and naive, is falsely accused of a crime by a jealous minor officer who hates his very goodness. Desperate to try to defend himself and somewhat tongue-tied, Billy strikes out at the lying officer and kills him with one blow. The remarkable Captain Vere immediately perceives both the lad's innocence and his own duty to hang Billy in order to uphold civilized law in a time of threatened mutiny in the English Navy. At the execution scene no one, none of the crew or officers or Billy—or the readers, wants the ritual of execution to proceed, but it does, inexorably, as if law had some force of its own superior to the people administering it.

When Andrews was executed, many of us had the same feeling of helpless horror. Everyone in authority expressed regret, but the trial had been reviewed and found proper. There were petitions from various groups, including ours, plus a letter from the Pope, but the governor felt he could not override the board of pardons. The state proceeded with the execution immediately after midnight on the appointed day in order to forestall further appeals. Outside some conducted a prayer vigil, while others with signs yelled slogans celebrating Andrews's death. A reporter appointed to witness the execution-by-lethal-injection wept as he tried to describe the experience.

I believe that execution by the state sends a message that problems can be solved with violence, that the state itself, our highest civil authority, in fact approves of such methods—or at least is in the grip of impersonal forces that deny individual mercy. As Anne Clark said at the rally, "Capital punishment encourages the upward spiral of brutality in an already brutal society." I am aware that capital punishment has been defended on the grounds that it satisfies victims' families' need for closure, for some sense of justice and satisfaction that can help end their grief—and that society itself needs such a strong witness that crime has been punished and justice satisfied. I share that grief and concern for confidence in a just society, but I believe that the desire for punishment, however understandable, is itself unethical and cannot be satisfied in ways that do not further undermine personal and social morality—especially if we are willing to execute even one innocent person to meet that desire.

The church issued a statement of neutrality concerning Andrews's execution, saying, "We regard the question of whether and in what circumstances the state should impose capital punishment as a matter to be decided by the prescribed processes of criminal law." I believe Mormons, consistent with our understanding of the value of each life and the tendency of violence to encourage further violence, should work to encourage legal alternatives to capital punishment, such as life imprisonment without parole, and encourage all judges and governors to exercise all the merciful and healing options that our modern legal system provides.

Melville, in *Billy Budd*, faults the Mutiny Act, which allowed Captain Vere no option for mercy, but he also raises one of my main objections to the thing from which that Act derives: war. Vere tells his officers, in the summary court martial, that they are not free to act as their hearts or consciences dictate concerning Billy—because they all "wear the buttons of the King." That is, when anyone puts on a military uniform, their conscience is placed in hostage to an impersonal force. They no longer act, and are not acted upon, in terms of that most basic ethical principle I have described—individual response to the other in terms of their need and right to be treated as a person.

Any action intended to hurt or kill, including abortion and capital punishment, is such a serious violation of our nature, and our given ethical relationship to each other, that, to numb our consciences and enable us to do it at all, we mentally dehumanize our victims (calling embryos mere tissue, "like fingernails," or turning state executions into cloaked, depersonalized rituals)—but that of course is itself a violation of our nature and given ethical relationship. War in particular requires that we immediately totalize a whole group or nation. What had recently been individuals, ends in themselves, each with a unique and infinite claim on our response to them as humans, suddenly become mere means to our supposedly higher and more just ends, even obstacles to be destroyed in pursuit of those ends. Enemy soldiers, by putting on a uniform, lose all individual claim on us, or to such moral imperatives as the ten commandments, and become mere targets to deceive, maim, and kill. In modern warfare this is extended beyond those in uniform to include the civilian population—all of whom also become dehumanized targets or at least acceptable victims of "collateral damage." This is perhaps most horribly apparent in the mass bombings of civilian populations in World War II, as at Coventry and London, or Dresden and Hiroshima, and our willingness to do so again expressed in the targeting of missiles at Moscow and Beijing and Baghdad. Just because a nation leader, an Adolf Hitler or a Saddam Hussein, has declared war does not mean the people of that nation give up that most basic, truly inalienable right I have discussed, the right to be treated as persons. Indeed they *cannot* give up that right, and we cannot be excused from our *responsibility* to treat them as persons, ends in themselves, which is also infinite, inalienable.

In this connection let me suggest another ethical principle, introduced by Christ, that ought to enter seriously into our conversations about violence. In Matthew 5:27, 28, Christ defines what might be called "thought sin": "You have heard it was said by them of old time, Thou shalt not commit adultery; but I say unto you, That whosoever looketh on a woman to lust after her hath committed adultery with her already in his heart." This could be paraphrased, "You have heard it was said, 'You shall not commit murder'; but I say to you, that every one who looks on a person to murder him has committed murder already in his heart."

This concept of sin through intent suggests that, though absolute non-violence may not be clearly required by the scriptures, opposition to nuclear deterrence may well be. The ethical demands by Christ in the Sermon on the Mount imply that planning and organizing to kill millions with nuclear missiles may be the same as *actually doing it*. It may be the ultimate dehumanization, targeting for destruction whole cities of people whom we will never face, and our silence on this issue may well qualify as "thought sin."

How does this principle apply to abortion and capital punishment? Do the ethical demands of Christ suggest that, even if one is morally anti-abortion, consenting to laws that allow millions of abortions to be performed may also be a kind of "thought sin"? Perhaps not, since our government, though it represents us, is only *allowing* a choice for abortion, not making it for us—though this principle might suggest we oppose all funding of abortion and work for laws that help provide alternatives, regulate unsafe clinics, etc. But with capital punishment, our government is doing the killing—in a sense *for* us—and in a certain number of cases killing innocent people, and assenting to that I believe *is* a form of thought sin.

We are confronted, in scripture and experience, with a God who is completely without violence precisely because he treats all humans as infinitely precious, as persons, ends in themselves. The God revealed in Jesus is able to feel the mere touch of a woman in the press of the crowd. He sends rain and sunshine on the just and unjust alike and therefore, as Luke testifies, commands us: "Love ye your enemies, and do good, and lend, hoping for nothing again; and your reward shall be great, and ye shall be the children of the Highest; for he is kind unto the unthankful and to the evil" (Luke 6:23). In this passage Christ goes on to state the ultimate *pragmatic*, as opposed to the fundamental, purely ethical, reason, for pacifism: "Give, and it shall be given unto you; good measure, pressed down, and shaken together, and running over, shall men give into your bosom. For with the same measure that ye mete withal it shall be measured to you again" (v. 38).

A Christian ethic of non-violence in its practical aspect is complete faith in that law of return, the law of the harvest: "Whatsoever ye sow, that shall ye also reap." We benefit directly from energetic, even sacrifical, but non-violent efforts to help others, to right their wrongs and bring them justice as well as give them mercy. Consider the stunning success of Gandhi's non-violent liberation of India, the Marshall Plan that rebuilt Europe, Anwar Sadat's creation of peace with Israel, and Martin Luther King's peaceful civil rights revolution. Only peaceful ways bring lasting peace. The only way effectively to do away with enemies is not by dehumanizing and killing them but by converting them into friends.

Pragmatic Christian non-violence is also, of course, based on an understanding of the *negative* law of the harvest. That law is made clear in Christ's rebuke to Peter's violent effort to protect him—surely as justified a violence as we could imagine, protecting the purely guiltless son of God. The First Presidency of the LDS church, after citing that example, put the case this way, in 1942 as WWII began: "There is an eternal law that rules war and those who engage in it. . . . The Savior laid down a universal principle ["all they that take the sword shall perish with the sword"] upon which He placed no limitations as to time, place, cause, or people involved [whether righteous or wicked]. . . . [T]his is a universal law, for force always begets force."

Despite that unequivocal statement of the consequences of *any* violence, even that engaged in by people who are "righteous," the First Presidency, in the same statement, lent grudging support to World War II as just, even extending to combatants on both sides assurance that if they were forced by their leaders to participate, the leaders and not they would be culpable. This position, which I agree with, makes clear the inevitably tragic nature of a Mormon theology of life: It cannot dictate an absolutely non-violent national policy or even a personal one, but it does dictate an absolute ethic which stands in judgment over all compromises we make with it. That ethic thus should act as a brake and reminder even after we have temporarily, in extremity, chosen violence.

Yes, there are circumstances—such as when my wife or children are threatened—when I might use violence. But the highest ethic would call me to do everything possible, long before the attack, to avert the threat of attack (including building a less violent and sexist society where attacks on my wife and children would be less likely), to use an absolute minimum of violence, and to follow up with doing good to the victimizer as well as the intended victim.

I agree with the First Presidency that, in World Ward II, when everything else we seemed capable of doing could not bring peace, a force so irrational and powerful as to threaten destruction of the Judeo-Christian civilization, of wiping out some of the main sources of the very ethic I have been describing, had to be stopped, even with violence. But the ethic I have outlined would force me to recognize such decisions as tragic, as being forced into a dilemma where all courses available bring evil. The highest ethic would also serve as a constant reminder that I must try constantly not to dehumanize my enemy, to draw back as soon as possible, and to mourn rather than rejoice at my necessity.

Such a view of the tragic consequences of compromising with the fundamental ethic, even when constrained by tragic choices, would help us be unified in mourning the violence: Even if women continue to abort their babies, through ignorance, in response to a violent and still sexist society, or simply in the absence of legal constraint, we should mourn the loss, including that to the women themselves. If sincere people continue to believe that capital punishment prevents murder and governments continue to execute, we should mourn that compromise with fundamental respect for life, mourn the death of innocents, the ritualized waste—and never rejoice in revenge. If a war is judged necessary, after our best efforts at peacemaking, we should mourn—even in victory—rather than brag or celebrate, as many did after the Gulf War. Remember what the angel in the movie, *It's a Wonderful Life*, approvingly reminded us about how most people responded at the end of World War II: "On VE day they wept and prayed. On VJ day they wept and prayed."

A Mormon theology of life then is based, I believe, on an absolute ethic, grounded in the right and need of all humans to treat and be treated as humans. War, violence of any kind, including torture, physical punishment, abortion for convenience, and capital punishment, violate that right and consequently dehumanize the objects, the perpetrators, and the society that condones that violence. Even when we are pushed to the ultimate dilemma of seemingly having to violate that ethic in order to keep others from violating it or to choose between conflicting values, the ethic stands as witness to the inevitable costs of our tragic choice, a constant reminder to minimize the violence and dehumanization and to return quickly to our full humanity and its obligation to do only good to others.

This ethic may bring us to fearful choices, even the losing of our own and loved ones' lives. But Christ's call is clear, and one we as Latter-day Saints now, perhaps for the first time in 100 years, can have the security to obey fully—to come out of Babylon, which includes the United States, and approach Zion, which is wherever in the world we create it. In the book of Revelation Christ commands, "Come out of her, my people, that ye be not partakers of her sins, and that ye receive not of her plagues" (18:4). In the Doctrine and Covenants he invites us to "renounce war and proclaim peace, and seek diligently to turn the hearts of the children to their [parents], and the hearts of the [parents] to their children" (98:16). Then a time will come, Christ promises, when "there shall be gathered to Zion out of every nation" those who are not "at war one with another" (45:69). After a century of difficult choices and detours, it is time for Mormons to think about returning to that goal.

NOTES

1. Thomas G. Alexander, *Things in Heaven and Earth: The Life and Times of Wilford Woodruff, a Mormon Prophet* (Salt Lake City: Signature Books, 1991), 321.

2. Hugh Nibley, "If There Must Needs Be Offense," *Ensign* 1 (July 1971): 54.

3. "The King Follett Sermon: A Newly Amalgamated Version," ed. Stan Larson, *Brigham Young University Studies* 18 (Winter 1978): 204.

4. LDS Church News Release, 11 Jan. 1991, copy in my possession.

5. In Russell A. Nelson, "Reverence for Life," *Ensign* 15 (May 1985): 65-66.

6. Brigham Young Office Journal, 28 Jan. 1857, archives, Historical Department, Church of Jesus Christ of Latter-day Saints, Salt Lake City, Utah.

7. Nelson, 65-66.

8. *Ensign* 20 (May 1990): 69.

"NO RESPECTER OF PERSONS": AN ETHICS OF DIVERSITY

We are told in the New Testament that the apostle Simon Peter, one day shortly after Christ's ascension, fell into a trance and, as dinner was being prepared, dreamed three times of "all manner of fourfooted beasts of the earth, and wild beasts, and creeping things, and fowls of the air. And there came a voice to him, Rise, Peter; kill, and eat" (Acts 10:9-13). Peter, an orthodox Jew, recoiled at this invitation, having "never eaten anything that is common or unclean. And the voice spake unto him again . . . , What God hath cleansed, that call not thou common" (vv. 14-15). While Peter pondered the meaning of this dream, a messenger arrived from Cornelius, a Roman soldier, inviting Peter to come to his home in Caesarea.

Cornelius was a gentile, and Peter, though he was an apostle, had to be prepared to accept him. Upon arrival, Peter said, "Ye know how that it is an unlawful thing for a man that is a Jew to keep company, or come unto one of another nation" (v. 28). Cornelius responded that an angel had told him to call for the apostle, at which Peter, finally understanding the dream, "opened his mouth, and said, Of a truth I perceive that God is no respecter of persons: But in every nation he that feareth him, and worketh righteousness, is accepted with him" (vv. 34-35). He then preached the crucified Christ to these gentiles, and they were baptized, the first non-Jews in the universal church.

Peter uses a strange expression for what he had learned: "God is no respecter of persons." It means, of course, not that God doesn't respect persons, but that he does not have respect of some over others, that his respect is *equal*, not conditional or partial, and does not vary, as human respect does, according to irrelevant matters: race, gender, creed, intelligence, politics, wealth, sexual orientation. The apostle James, Peter's counselor, makes this clear when he implores early Christians not to forget what Peter has learned—and at the same time implies that some faithful Christians had already forgotten it:

> My brethren, have not the faith of our Lord Jesus Christ, the Lord of glory, with respect of persons. For if there come unto your assembly a man with a gold ring, in goodly apparel, and there come in also a poor man in vile raiment; and ye have respect to him that weareth the gay clothing, and say unto him, Sit thou here in a good place; and say to the poor, Stand thou there, or sit here under my footstool: Are ye not then partial in yourselves? (James 2:1-4)

To have respect of persons is to be partial—in both senses, I believe: to show partiality to others (respecting a part of humanity, not all) and to be only part of one's true self, split apart, less than whole, to lack integrity.

James teaches how serious this is: "If ye fulfill the royal law according to the scripture, Thou shalt love thy neighbour as thyself, ye do well: But if ye have respect to persons, ye commit sin. . . . For whosoever shall keep the whole law, and yet offend in one point, he is guilty of all" (2:8-9). The scriptures use this expression, "respect" or "regard" of persons, to teach us what God is like and also what he expects of us when we understand who he is and try to be like him. In Deuteronomy we are assured that "the Lord your God . . . regardeth not persons, nor taketh reward: He doth execute the judgment of the fatherless and widow, and loveth the stranger. . . . Love ye therefore the stranger: for ye were strangers in the land of Egypt" (10:17-19). In the Book of Mormon, we are given a picture of a Zion society: "In their prosperous circumstances, they did not send away any who were naked, or that were hungry, or that were athirst, or that were sick, or that had not been nourished; and they did not set their hearts upon riches; therefore they were liberal to all, both young and old, both bond and free, both male and female, whether out of the church or in the church, having no respect to persons as to those who stood in need" (Alma 1:30). In other words, when converted fully to Christ, these Nephites responded to others liberally, generously, freely—and only in terms of what was relevant, their need, not what was irrelevant, their class or sex or even church membership.

The language here echoes the other great New Testament affirmation of this principle, by the brash young apostle Paul, who even after Peter's vision had to convince some of the church leaders that the gospel should go even to the uncircumsized beyond Israel (see Acts 15). Paul writes to the Colossian saints, who apparently also needed to be taught that the gospel was for everyone, though some were once excluded gentiles themselves: "[You] have put on the new man, which is renewed in knowledge after the image of him that created [you]; Where there is neither Greek nor Jew, circumcision nor uncircumcision, Barbarian, Scythian, bond nor free: but Christ is all, and in all" (Col. 3:10-11).

Nephi uses similar language in what, for Mormons, is the most straightforward, challenging, and perhaps still not fully understood expression of God's nature and expectation concerning "respect of persons"—what is, in fact, the fundamental Mormon source for a theology of human diversity: "The Lord . . . doeth that which is good among the children of men; . . . and he inviteth them all to come unto him and partake of his goodness; and he denieth none that come unto him, black and white, bond and free, male and female; and he remembereth the heathen; and all are alike unto God, both Jew and Gentile" (2 Ne. 26:33).

The basic principle, consistent throughout scripture and eminently sensible, seems clear enough: God loves us all equally, treats us all equally and liberally, expects and hopes the same for all of us—and asks, *expects*, us to do the same for each other. But of course we have not done so. Human history, including religious history, is perhaps most notable for "respect of persons," for fear and abuse and even terrible violence centered in our rejection of those who are in any way different—our willingness to hurt, exclude, and kill those who are *other*, those not of our color, gender, stratum, beliefs, even those with different culture or customs. Rather than rejoicing in diversity, as God seems to, on the evidence of the marvelous diversity of his creation, the abso-

lute and stunning plenitude of human form and behavior that has flow-
ered from the agency he has given and fostered in us—rather than
praising God and reaching out to that ever-renewing richness, we have
too often recoiled in fear and set up walls of protection.

God constantly calls his children to accept, even love, diversity.
Luke records Paul's sermon before the Court of Areopagus on Mars
Hill, about the God they were worshipping without understanding at
their altar "To an Unknown God" (I use the New English Bible for clarity):

> He created every race of men of one stock, to inhabit the whole
> earth's surface. He fixed the ordered seasons of their history and
> the limits of their territory. They were to seek God, and, it might
> be, touch and find him; though indeed he is not far from each one
> of us, for in him we live and move, in him we exist; as some of your
> own poets have said, "We are also his offspring." As God's offspring,
> then, we ought not to suppose that the deity is like an image in
> gold or silver or stone. . . . As for the times of ignorance, God has
> overlooked them; but now he commands mankind, all men every-
> where, to repent (17:26-31).

We Mormons are among those God has been patient with in the
time of our ignorance but who are now called to repent and join in
God's delight in the diversity of his creation. We are his offspring, part
of the plenitude of his creation, and ought not to suppose he is like an
idol, partial, loving only those who have made and worshipped him. He
created and loves all races—and now commands us to repent. Why?
Claiming to be specially chosen children of God, inheritors of his true
kingdom, we have denied our parenthood and the universal atonement
of our brother, Jesus Christ, by having respect of persons. We have not
only been partial in our response to difference, asking some, by virtue
only of their class or color or gender, to "sit thou here in a good place"
but others to "sit here under my footstool." We have also set limits to
spiritual opportunities and taught spiritual inferiority, based only on
race or gender.

The most obvious example so far, of course, is our denial, from
about 1852 to 1978, of priesthood rights and temple blessings to blacks

of African descent. Despite the announcement giving blacks the priesthood and the new understanding that action supposedly brought to the church, I find that many Mormons at BYU and in Provo still believe that the *reason* blacks did not receive the priesthood before 1978 was that they were unfaithful in the pre-existence—in other words, that people come color-coded into the world, exhibiting in their very flesh that God has differing opportunities and expectations for them, that he is a "respecter of persons."

A worldwide revolution is taking place—not primarily a religious one, though many religious people are involved, but an essentially political and moral one, uniting in common cause people of many different beliefs and backgrounds. The revolution is away from the violent fear of diversity that has plagued all human history and toward a guarantee of equal rights for all and, even more, a rejoicing in the rich diversity of human life. We as Mormons have an unparalleled opportunity to be part of, to benefit from, and to contribute to that revolution, given our theology, our remarkable record of openness in the early church, and the divinely directed and energized reach of our worldwide mission. But we mainly missed participation in the first part of that revolution, the quest for civil rights for American blacks in the 1950s and 1960s, and our fears and uncertainties are thus far keeping many of us from contributing much to the second major phase of that revolution, the quest for equal rights and opportunities for women worldwide.

Why does it matter? After all, the restored church has its own agenda—to take the gospel to all the world and save all the dead. We don't need to be involved in faddish and divisive revolutions for minority rights, do we? It is true that any quest for rights tends to be self-centered and vindictive, that excesses have occurred and will. Minorities have struggled for redress of past grievances and in the process have sometimes taken vengeance, or have gained power only to use it unrighteously. Increased pride in ethnic or religious identity has sometimes brought, not mutual respect and tolerance that builds community but tribalization, re-opening of centuries-old wounds and violent conflict that has destroyed community in the former Yugoslavia and Soviet Union, in Sri Lanka and Rwanda—and increasingly even in our own country. The revolution is not without its failures and setbacks—about which we should not be surprised.

Abraham Lincoln recognized, in his *Second Inaugural Address* in 1865, "If God wills that [this terrible Civil War] continue until all the wealth piled by the bondman's two hundred and fifty years of unrequited toil shall be sunk, and until every drop of blood drawn with the lash shall be paid," we could not question God's justice. We Americans are still paying those costs in the seemingly unbreakable cycles of discrimination, poverty, alienation, and violence in our ghettoes which increasingly affect us all. We are paying similar costs for our wholesale exploitation and destruction of Native Americans and the dehumanization of their descendants. And we have not even begun to recognize the costs we are paying and yet must pay for thousands of years of suppression of women.

Despite the costs and setbacks, we must work our way through, I believe, towards a world where there is no respect of persons—even if for a while we who have benefitted most from past exploitation, whites and especially males, are treated unfairly. Thoreau wrote in *Civil Disobedience*, "If I have unjustly wrested a plank from a drowning man, I must restore it to him though I drown myself," and we must bear the costs of returning those planks we and our ancestors have unjustly taken from minorities and women. For instance, when affirmative action programs work to help break the cycles of discrimination leading to bad education and jobs leading to poverty and differences of opportunity, we whites must, for a time, be willing to receive less than seems "fair." We must do so not because we are *responsible* for others' sins or because some abstract justice must be served, but simply because some of the inequities still remain and many of the effects from past sins have been passed on in families and attitudes and laws and customs and continue to cause damage for which we are *response-able*, about which we *can* do something. Mormons must do something about such past and continuing damages precisely in order to achieve our world-wide mission. We cannot succeed fully in taking the healing and unifying gospel to a world that remains divided by race and sex, by any form of fear of the other—we can't especially if we as Mormons remain divided. I do not believe Christ can come again until, like him, we have no respect of persons, until for *us*, as well as for our God, all are alike, black and white, male and female.

But my main reason for thinking so is not social, but personal. I believe our individual salvation, at the very deepest level, is tied to this principle. Perhaps the greatest paradigm shift of the Old Testament, one very much related to that which came to Peter in his vision of the diversity of meats God had cleansed, was the understanding, recorded most clearly by the literary prophets like Isaiah and Amos, of what has been called "ethical monotheism." This is the new idea that the God of Israel, unlike pagan Gods, cannot be known directly, through personal piety and sacrifice. We can only know God as part of a triangular relationship that includes all other humans, his other children whom he loves as much as he does us. He speaks clearly through the prophets: "I hate, I despise your feast days, and I will not smell in your solemn assemblies. Though ye offer me burnt offerings . . . I will not accept them. . . . Take thou away the noise of thy songs. . . . But let judgment run down as waters, and righteousness as a mighty stream" (Amos 5:21-24). "When ye make many prayers, I will not hear: your hands are full of blood. . . . put away the evil of your doings . . . Learn to do well; seek judgment, relieve the oppressed, judge the fatherless, plead for the widow" (Isa. 1:15-17). In other words, it is *only* through accepting human diversity in unconditional love, as God does, he who is no respecter of persons—only through seeking justice and mercy for all his children and taking delight in them all—that we can know and love and please God our eternal Father. We therefore cannot be partial, cannot have respect of persons, without denying our fundamental nature as children of God or trying to deny the most fundamental claim that others, including God, have upon us. If we have respect of persons, we injure them, ourselves, and God.

How great is that injury? The following passage is from the Lectures on Faith, which were partially written and fully approved by Joseph Smith and included in the Doctrine and Covenants as scripture until 1921:

> It is also necessary that men should have an idea that [God] is no respecter of persons ["but in every nation he that fears God and works righteousness is accepted of him"], for with the idea of all

the other excellencies in his character, and this one wanting, men could not exercise faith in him; because if he were a respecter of persons, they could not tell what their privileges were, nor how far they were authorized to exercise faith in him, or whether they were authorized to do it at all, but all must be confusion; but no sooner are the minds of men made acquainted with the truth on this point, that he is no respecter of persons, than they see they have authority by faith to lay hold on eternal life, the richest boon of heaven, because God is no respecter of persons, and that every man in every nation has an equal privilege.[1]

This is a marvelous argument, though we seem to have missed it in popular Mormon thought: All human beings *must* be alike unto God, with no respect of persons, for him to *be* God, and we *must* understand that that is *true* for the plan of salvation even to be able to *work* for us—for faith unto repentance, the experience of Atonement, and exaltation to be possible. The passage describes precisely how it feels to be a rejected person in a racist or sexist culture, supposedly being punished or limited in some way, purely on the evidence of the bodies they inhabit, for something done by an ancestor or in the pre-existence or inherent in their nature, with no way to repent of that "something" and no certainty about its effects on their future. Joseph Smith provides us here with the most powerful practical reason why we must immediately stop believing or teaching racist and sexist notions in popular Mormon thought and develop an affirmative theology of diversity: We are denying others—and ourselves—full access to Christ and his plan of redemption. In a culture that believes God is a respecter of persons—or simply acts as if he is—neither the victims nor the victimizers can have sufficient faith in God unto salvation.

The root reason for this, I believe, is that the Atonement, as we understand from the Book of Mormon, is only efficacious when we can *accept* the unconditional love Christ gives us, even in our sins. The chief barrier to that acceptance, according to Alma, is "the demands of justice"—the felt need to pay debts fully and condemn ourselves when we haven't, even when full payment is impossible. Those demands can only be appeased by Christ's "plan of mercy," which offers infinite and unconditional love, not as a *payment* for repentance but as a means to *empower* our repentance; it provides "means unto men that they might have faith unto repentance" (Alma 34:15). But, as King Benjamin makes clear, we tend to remain caught up in justice, in deciding what others "deserve," and therefore withhold unconditional love and service to them, *not*, as God requires, "administering to their relief, both spiritually and temporally, according to their *wants*" (Mosiah 4:26; my emphasis). And King Benjamin declares that anyone who has such respect of persons cannot retain "a remission of. . . sins from day to day" (v. 26)—that is, cannot enjoy the continuing blessings of the Atonement, and "except he repenteth of that which he hath done he perisheth forever, and hath no interest in the kingdom of God" (v. 18).

With so much at stake—our personal salvation as well as the salvation of the world in preparation for Christ's coming—it seems to me useful to review the history of diversity as a value and challenge in the restored gospel and church. God revealed to Joseph Smith a remarkable theology of diversity, which seems to have been followed by a sometimes swift, sometimes gradual, decline from that theology in popular Mormon thought and custom, but there are some hopeful signs of recovery in recent years. The Restoration was a stunning rejection of the racism, sexism, and general fear of diversity that had plagued even the great world religions for thousands of years. God revealed to Joseph that most explicit, foundational claim in the Book of Mormon, that "all are alike unto God"; then, through continuing revelation and Joseph's own developing character and insights, came many remarkable specific advances directly contrary to the views and customs of early nineteenth century America: Joseph ordained blacks to the priesthood and contemplated their participation in the Nauvoo temple; he opposed slavery in his U.S. presidential campaign of 1844; at a time when wholesale genocide of American Indians was preached and practiced, he declared them to be of the chosen House of Israel and destined to rise to great power in preparation for the Second Coming; he included women as essential to the building of God's kingdom, organized them and gave them keys of authority after the pattern of the male priesthood, included them as equal participants with men in temple ordinances that bestowed upon them saving gifts and healing authority from God, and taught a doctrine of eternal marriage that exalted the equality of men and women to the very highest level, guaranteed in divinity itself. For Joseph Smith Godhood, the ultimate goal of eternal marriage, required a divine union of the two genders in the future, and thus by implication—and according to Eliza R. Smith, Joseph taught it directly—our present God is actually Heavenly Parents.

In the Book of Mormon and Doctrine and Covenants the prophet Joseph struck directly at the chief theological error that has led to the suppression of women in Judeo-Christian cultures, the idea that Eve was the first to fall and that all women are consequently cursed with child-bearing and subservience to their husbands. In 2 Nephi 2 Nephi makes clear that the fall was necessary and positive, and in Doctrine and Covenants 29:40 God declares it was "Adam" rather than Eve who made that difficult and courageously intelligent choice that cost them dearly but blessed us all. In context God clearly means by "Adam" what President Spencer W. Kimball called "Mr. and Mrs. Adam," the model first couple *together*—which is surely the way such a crucial decision would be made.

Later in the Doctrine and Covenants God condemns the false traditions and "creeds of the fathers" in Western thought. Christian creeds all include that false idea about Eve, and we are told in section 123 that it is our "wives and children, who have been made to bow down with grief, sorrow, and care" as a result of such creeds. In the King Follett Discourse, given just before his death, Joseph Smith declares the fundamental truth that explains why God is no respecter of persons and we must not be—the infinite God-like potential of *every* mortal: "[God] once was a man like one of us and . . . dwelled on an earth . . . like us. All the minds and spirits that God ever sent into the world are susceptible of enlargement and improvement."[2]

With such a clear and dramatically challenging theology of diversity, if we had held true to it, the restored church should by now have radically changed the world—or been destroyed in the attempt. But God has always adjusted his demands to some extent to his people's ability and circumstances; he has given us lower laws to live, such as the Old Testament laws of performance and our present law of tithing, schoolmasters to bring us gradually to Christ. By 1852, for inspired cultural and survival reasons, I believe, but not because of metaphysical realities or eternal doctrinal principles, we were denying blacks the priesthood and practicing polygamy openly. By the late nineteenth century, the person still honored as our most liberal high church leader and outstanding intellectual, B. H. Roberts, felt comfortable opposing women's suffrage and supporting the theories of the time about Negro inferiority.[3] In accommodating to American government power in the 1890s in order to survive, we also increasingly accommodated to American culture, including its military violence, its racism, and its sexism. By the early twentieth century polygamy had ended but by the 1940s women's roles in healing and blessing ordinances were gradually diminishing, and paradoxically the very autonomy and forceful roles in publishing, politics, and professional life that polygamy had provided some Mormon women were declining and have continued to do so almost to the present.

In 1931 Elder Joseph Fielding Smith published, in *The Way to Perfection*, his speculation that the proscription on blacks was reasonably explained by some fault in their pre-existence.[4] That idea gradually achieved doctrinal force in popular Mormon thought and, combined with unexamined notions derived from certain passages in the Book of Mormon and false Christian traditions about God cursing whole races, was generalized to all colored races, including Native Americans and Jews. Skin color was nearly universally seen as an indication of spiritual inheritance—the darker the worse.

By the 1950s, when I was a college student, Utah culture was thoroughly racist and sexist and characterized by popular Mormon notions that uncritically assumed a divine mandate for the culturally assigned roles and limitations for women and colored races. In other words, much Mormon thinking and teaching was founded on the implicit—and sometimes explicit—assumption that God is a respecter of persons and all are *not* alike unto him. The almost totally Mormon Utah legislature passed stringent laws against inter-racial marriage and persistently killed fair housing and employment bills. Good Mormons cheerfully canvassed our neighborhood in eastside Salt Lake City with a petition to keep out a Jewish family. And most Mormons began to accept as the natural order the unusual gender role differentiation (perhaps only widespread before in upper-class Victorian society) that the prosperity after World War II made available to middle-class America—the father as boss but at a job in an office all day and the mother totally absorbed in nurturing her children in isolation in a suburban home.

It is easy to see why, despite our radically liberal theology and early history, we have responded very conservatively to the revolution toward racial equality that began in the late 1950s and the revolution toward gender equality that began a decade later. Very few Mormons got involved in the early stages, some church leaders for a time opposed equal rights laws because they might lead to integration, and the church made only luke-warm statements affirming civil rights in 1963 and again in 1969 in its last official statement about blacks not being allowed the priesthood. That policy, of course, tended to make even liberal Mormons defensive and reluctant participants in civil rights efforts, partly, as I learned at Stanford, because our credentials were automatically tarnished and our motives suspect.

All that seemed to change with the announcement in 1978. There was instantaneous churchwide rejoicing (we all remember what we were doing when we heard), quick expansion into areas missionaries had not been allowed to go before, and, with very few exceptions, loving acceptance of the new black converts and of their participation in the temple and in leadership. But we have never officially renounced the false theology that blacks—and by extension other races—are color-coded as to pre-existent righteousness, and some blacks feel their full acceptance as persons and as leaders is still limited.

One black BYU student told me, in 1990, of sitting in a Pearl of Great Price class where someone asked why blacks had once been denied the priesthood and the instructor and class speculated for fifteen minutes on the various sins blacks might have committed in the pre-existence, with no apparent awareness that he was present—truly "the invisible man." Those two embarrassing books published in the 1960s, John J. Stewart's *Mormonism and the Negro* and John Lewis Lund's *The Church and the Negro*,[5] have not been repudiated, though both try to explain why blacks are denied the priesthood by using a temporary church practice to support a thoroughly racist theology and a concept of God as clearly partial, a respecter of persons. Such teachings directly contradict the central scriptural teaching that all are alike unto God, that he is no respecter of persons, and those teachings must be kindly but firmly rebutted in whatever form they appear, with knowledge and authoritative resources.

Elder John K. Carmack, in his recent book *Tolerance*,[7] provides the most explicit renunciation yet by a church leader of the false ideas about the inferiority of non-white races—because of supposed "degeneration" from the "pure" white race of Adam or "choices in the pre-existence"—that developed in the church prior to 1978 and are still published, taught, and believed by some Latter-day Saints: "We do not believe that any nation, race, or culture is a lesser breed or inferior in God's eyes. Those who believe or teach such doctrine have no authority from either the Lord or his authorized servants."[7]

Elder Bruce R. McConkie, in a remarkable address given shortly after the 1978 revelation, quoted the passage from 2 Nephi 26:33 about all being alike unto God and said, "Many of us never imagined or supposed that these passages had the extensive and broad meaning that they do have,"[8] apparently because we had assumed, until that revelation, that there were essential differences, distinctions "unto God," between the races. Of course, we may still not understand the "extensive and broad meaning" of that scripture as it applies to gender—how all are alike unto God "male and female."

The most challenging—and meaningful—human diversity is, of course, gender diversity. It directly affects us all, touches our deepest joys and insecurities, determines the very survival of human life, and for Mormons is intimately connected to the meaning of exaltation and the very possibility of Godhood. For most of us, in our highest concept of earthly felicity, in our sweetest imagining of heavenly glory, and in our excited anticipations of what makes Godhood desirable and defines the nature of Godly power and creativity, "Neither is the man without the woman or the woman without the man" (1 Cor. 11:11).

The gradual retrenchment from the remarkably liberated gender theology and practices of the early church continued into the 1970s, when there was some disempowering, under Correlation, of the Relief Society, including the ending of its own publications and independent budget, even control over its lesson manuals. The Equal Rights Amendment was defeated, in good part through Mormon opposition. Through determined right-wing political influence, Mormon women were marshalled against even the clearly beneficial proposals put forward during the International Women's Year convention in Utah in 1977, beginning a process of dividing Mormon women and aligning the popular majority with fundamentalist religions which dogmatically oppose all efforts to improve women's rights and opportunities that can be labeled feminist.

Perhaps most indicative of the depth of our present anxieties in the church about women is the process of fearful escalation at local levels that has followed the admonition by President Gordon B. Hinckley in 1991 not to pray publicly to Mother in Heaven.[9] I understand that some local leaders are now telling their people they can't even *talk* about Mother in Heaven, and some students at BYU seem to have accepted that view as orthodox. What is most disturbing about such unauthorized "improvement" on President Hinckley's counsel and the fear it reveals is that the concept of Mother in Heaven is one of the great gifts of the Restoration, a keystone concept in the crucial theology of diversity I have described because it establishes genuine diversity as intrinsic to the very nature of the Godhead. It gives the highest possible guarantee for the perfect equality of men and women, showing that there cannot be respect of persons in God because *two* persons dwell there, in perpetual otherness to each other. If we cannot solve our intrinsic aversion to the other, which places infinite and inescapable demands on us, it isn't simply that we thus cannot be more *like* God, we cannot *be* Gods—which requires a perfect union of male and female.

What are we to do then about what seem increasing divisions in the church centered around the efforts of some Mormons to join in the multicultural and feminist revolution? One frequent response is to quote Christ's command, "I say unto you, be one; and if ye are not one ye are not mine" (D&C 38:27), as a way of condemning those whose otherness and interest in diversity seem to bring division. I don't believe, however, that Christ means "Be all alike in the Church or I won't accept you," but rather "Be like me by accepting each other in the Church, even if you're not all alike." He is asking us to be one in our *acceptance* of diversity, not as a *denial* of diversity.

As evidence for this crucial interpretation, I offer the following: Just before making that command, Christ pleads, "Let every man esteem his brother as himself." He then retells a story of a man who has twelve sons and who *claims* to be no respecter of persons, a just man, but nevertheless "saith unto the one son: Be thou clothed in robes and sit thou here; and to the other: Be thou clothed in rags and sit thou there" (D&C 38:25-26)—a clear parallel to the example I cited earlier that the apostle James uses to teach what "respect of persons" looks like (James 2:1-4). Finally, Christ concludes, "This I have given unto you as a parable, and it is even as I am. I say unto you be one." Clearly, to be like Christ rather than the man in the parable, we need to learn to love unconditionally and treat equally all the members of our church and human families, no matter how different they are.

I believe this is our greatest single challenge as Mormons—and as Americans and human beings—right now. We Mormons are experiencing the inevitable growing pains as we become a genuine world religion, preaching the gospel in nearly every nation and with a membership approaching ten million. As a nation we are trying to cope with our increasing racial diversity and the struggle for women's rights. As a human family we are trying to cope with increasingly deadly prejudices, of which neo-Nazism in Germany, the "ethnic cleansing" in Bosnia, lethal religious intolerance in Northern Ireland and the Middle East, and racial violence in American cities are only the most prominent examples.

There is no room for smugness in this matter. *All* of us are sinners in this regard and need help so that we can be one, even be gratefully accepting of each other, despite our differences, in the Mormon and in the human family. In just the past year I have seen Mormons of all political and intellectual and spiritual varieties guilty of judging and rejecting others on partial and irrelevant grounds. Feminists have been called Nazis—and conservatives have been called Nazis. Conservatives have been stereotyped as stupid, not fit participants in the University community; liberals have been stereotyped as evil, not fit participants in the church community. The very terms "intellectual" and "feminist," which are traditionally neutral words describing certain people's commitment to rational discourse or gender equality—and thus ought to be terms of honor or at least respect for all Mormons—have been perverted into something like swear words.

At the same time, general authorities have been stereotyped as senile, unresponsive, dishonest, sexist, even diabolically conspiratorial. Letters to the church's *Deseret News* and BYU's *Daily Universe* are a constantly embarrassing revelation of the aggressive prejudices of some Mormons, their frank willingness to be respecters of persons and hunker down in fear of diversity. The challenge to Utah high school graduation prayers a few years ago provoked a huge outpouring of letters condemning the American Civil Liberties Union and asserting the right of the Mormon majority in Utah to control public religious life; one letter frankly stated, unaware of the irony, "We were once a persecuted minority who were denied religious freedom and driven out of the United States. Now we're in control, and if minorities don't like what we do they can leave." How easily we chosen people forget, when we get political control, that plea of God to his chosen people in Deuteronomy, "Love ye therefore the stranger: for ye were strangers in the land of Egypt" (10:19).

A letter last year in the *Deseret News* asking for understanding of those who have same-sex preference and challenging people to find any biblical evidence that God condemns the preference brought a huge number of homophobic letters that confirmed my sense that most Mormons do not make any separation between same-sex *preference* and homosexual *acts*, condemning both as sinful—even though the church position *does* make a clear distinction. A speech given by a visiting educator, Dawn Person, in 1993 at BYU during Black Awareness week, titled "Diversity: The Critical Need to Nurture Pluralism in Higher Education," was reprinted in May in the *Brigham Young Magazine* for BYU alumni; the author discussed difficulties posed by the increasing diversity in our colleges and the great opportunities this could bring us all if we would learn to solve the resulting problems: "I challenge you to dream a world of higher education that is caring, just, open and honest, disciplined, civil, and supportive of diversity, multicultural issues, and pluralism." The next issue carried a host of negative letters attacking the article for "advocating a message so opposite to the standards of BYU and its alumni" and attacking the editors for publishing it. A letter in the BYU *Daily Universe* about the same time defended discrimination as merely part of God-given agency and as having scriptural precedent: "With god's help, Abraham discriminated by race, religion, sex, and national origin to choose a wife for his son. [The Book of Mormon] describes God creating race to segregate people."

Such use of authority to justify attitudes and practices that directly contradict our affirmative theology of diversity must be clearly repudiated and thoughtfully rebutted. In doing this, we need to look more carefully at what prophets are saying to us in our own time about the need for change in our cultural limitations. Elder Boyd K. Packer, concerning our entry into third-world nations, has exclaimed, "We can't move *there* with all the baggage we produce and carry *here*! We can't move with a 1947 Utah Church!"[10] President Howard W. Hunter has said:

> The gospel of Jesus Christ transcends nationality and color, crosses cultural lines, and blends distinctiveness into a common brotherhood. . . . *All* men are invited to come unto him and *all* are alike unto him. Race makes no difference; color makes no difference; nationality makes no difference. . . . As members of the Lord's church, we need to lift our vision beyond personal prejudices. We need to discover the supreme truth that indeed our Father is no respecter of persons.[11]

Contemporary philosophy and literary criticism have thoroughly demonstrated, I believe, the truth of the Lord's statement in the Doctrine and Covenants, section 1, about how all language, even scriptural, is *affected by*, though certainly not *determined by*, the cultural constructs of the speaker. This idea does not undermine prophetic authority but rather establishes clearly the need for continuous revelation and continuous individual spiritual confirmation and renewal in our understanding of prophetic discourse. As part of this we must constantly listen and respond as the prophets change. The "supreme truth" President Hunter evokes, that God "is no respecter of persons," must constantly take precedence over earlier statements by seminary teachers, authors of popular books, or anyone else that contradict it.

We need to accept wholeheartedly the enormous, prophesied success of the church worldwide, and change ourselves so we can rejoice in it rather than impede it. Fine models for us are becoming available in both the increasing diversity of the church itself and also in the diverse spokespersons who are telling us their stories and challenging us to move forward with them. Catherine Stokes, whom most Mormons in the Chicago area know well, expressed to a gathering of Mormon women at Nauvoo shortly after the 1978 announcement an insight she had gained through her own sometimes painful diversity that could help us all: "[When I went to the temple for the first time], I took my blackness with me, and that was part of what I consecrated." The woman who assisted her wept openly and apologized: "I never had the privilege of doing this for a black woman before, and I'm so grateful." Cathy reassured her, "That's one of the things I can do for *you*. My blackness is one of the things that the Lord can use if he wants to."[12]

On 26 January 1993, Elder Yoshihiko Kikuchi, our first native Japanese general authority, spoke at BYU's International Week and challenged us:

> We now see great turmoil and anger, pain, hunger, suffering, hate, jealousy, and dishonesty in our society, [which] cause us to lose human dignity and values. . . . We must continue to break down barricades. We must bring down the barriers of cultural misunderstanding and misconception. We must break down the spiritual Berlin walls in us. [To do so] we must understand [that] (1) God made all these nations and is now gathering them under His Wings. (2) The best prescription is to implement the Savior's teachings. (3) The love of God is already in the souls of the human family.[13]

The best teacher of these truths I know is Chieko Okazaki, the first non-Caucasian member of a church general board and now the first in a general presidency. As you may have noticed in any of her recent addresses, she makes diversity a central theme: In her first book, *Lighten Up!*, she begins by announcing,

> Diversity is a strength. I attend a lot of meetings where I'm the only woman. And I attend many, many meetings where I'm the only Oriental woman. . . . Have you ever had the feeling that you're the odd one, the different one? Maybe even too odd or different for this church? The truth is that you're not odd—you're special. When white light falls on a wall, it makes a white wall. But when it passes through a prism, that same light makes a rainbow on the wall. . . . [Like God during creation, I say] "Let there be light" All kinds of light! Red, orange, yellow, green, blue, and violet light. We need our differences.

Sister Okazaki claims her favorite saying is

> In principles, great clarity. In practices, great charity. . . . When it comes to practices, I want kaleidoscopic vision. . . . I want the whole world of options to be at our fingertips so that we can consult our needs and wants when we decide how to apply those principles. I want us to make up our own minds, experiment with one form and abandon it without feeling guilty if we find it doesn't work, listen to what works for other people, find something else.[14]

She summarizes, in personal and practical terms, the heart of any theology of diversity:

> In Hawaii, I was surrounded from babyhood by differences—in language, in physical appearance, in dress, in economic level, in religion, in traditonal men's and women's roles, in education, in race, in life-styles, and in customs. I observed differences, but I did not learn to label them as "good" or "bad.". . . Being different, I internalized, is all right. Heavenly Father wants differences. He does not make two identical blossoms or two snowflakes that are the same.[15]

I thought of these words in March 1993, at the Sunstone Symposium in Washington, D.C., as I listened to a panel of recent converts talk about the difficult new challenges as well as benefits of difference that are coming to the universal church. A young woman told how offensive to the Japanese is our standard Mormon phrase, "I *know* the gospel is true"—too assertive, too prideful; she pled that translation must increasingly recognize such extremely different cultural inheritances. A young Israeli talked of continuing to wear his Jewish skullcap, his yarmulke, for a year after he converted and of attending his family's prayer ritual for the dead—done for *him* as dead to them—while he was standing fifty feet away because he was still a Jew in culture and family. One friend tells me how difficult it is for the Finns to understand or live by our American Mormon concept of "authority," and another tells me the French have such different ideas about visiting others, about the pace of life and family vacations, etc., that our Utah Mormon ways of doing home teaching and burdening bishoprics simply must be reconsidered.

I recently heard that one new Mormon branch in India, before sacrament service on Sunday, gathers to chant for half an hour the name of the church in Hindi—as a mantra. As Sister Okazaki points out in her new book, *Cat's Cradle,*

> If you're a convert in the LDS church, you're aware of two separate religious cultures, but the gospel culture is the one that will ultimately infuse, replace, and transform every human culture on the earth. Are we trying to move into that gospel culture already, or are we putting our energy into preserving one of these old cultural forms like hierarchy and gender and youth and wealth that will be swept away when the Savior comes again?[16]

We are seeing new challenges and new delights—and gradual change, often encouraged by our leaders. In 1979 Elder Carmack, in an article in the *Ensign* entitled "Unity in Diversity," pled with the Saints not to encourage in any way jokes that demean and belittle others "because of religious, cultural, racial, national, or gender differences. All are alike unto God." He warned about stereotyping and judging: "Labeling a fellow Church member an intellectual, a less-active member, a feminist, a South African, an Armenian, a Utah Mormon, or a Mexican, for example, seemingly provides an excuse to mistreat or ignore that person."[17]

In October 1993 general conference, Elder Russell M. Ballard announced that in a recent meeting with the presidencies of the women's auxiliaries he'd been told that "very few women in the church express any interest in wanting to hold the priesthood. But they do want to be heard and valued and want to make meaningful contributions." He then went on to give specific suggestions about how the councils of the church could improve their work through focussing on people, through free and open discussion, and through wide and responsible participation.

We live in difficult times. Many of us who value diversity, who believe the cause of truth is served by dialogue and the quality of our social and political and ethical life by healthy encounters with the other, have ourselves been excluded—labeled intellectuals, feminists, dissidents, heretics. We must not let these exclusions lead us to lose faith that God is no respecter of persons, that he has restored the gospel in part to provide a base and a people to "gather in one" all the lovely diversity—of race and culture and gender and perspective—that he has created and encouraged. We must be part of the gathering—to help it succeed and to save our own souls through the atonement of Christ.

We must not let our resentments about being excluded—or seeing those we love and admire excluded—move us to exclude anyone or to put up walls that will further shut us out. Chieko Okazaki is a great model. She has been excluded often and painfully and bears her witness to us: "Having been excluded ourselves, we've learned to take extraordinary measures to include others. . . . What can you do? If you're waiting to be included, think about some steps you can take to put yourself at the center of a circle, a circle of inclusion."[18] We must keep ourselves included, by staying active, serving gently and creatively, seeking out those we offend to apologize and repent if need be, seeking out those who offend us to seek understanding and reconciliation rather than harboring resentments that easily turn into revenge.

We must act to create circles of inclusion, in our wards, across ward boundaries, throughout the church. We must keep the community of independent Mormon thought and scholarship alive and Christ-centered. To do so lend your voice for peace-making and humility, for gentleness and meekness and love unfeigned. Write directly to church leaders with your concerns—never criticizing them to others. And also write directly with your love and support and specific thanks: write Elder Robert Hales and thank him for his acceptance for the church of the thousand white roses sent at general conference in October 1993 as a gesture of reconciliation; write Elder Ballard with thanks for his talk at that same conference on including women's voices in our church councils; write Sister Okazaki and thank her for her courageous faith in Christ and in God's love of diversity.

The widespread and thorough discussion, during the 1992 "quincentennary," of the nature and consequences of Columbus's voyages to America, raised important questions that we must face as Mormons who are now confronting very similar challenges to those Columbus brought the Catholic church: What is the spiritual status of people, especially of other races, who have long "dwelt in darkness," and what is our responsibility to them and ourselves as we intrude upon them with the version of the gospel of Christ developed in our culture? The Catholic answer was, of course, mixed and in many ways a failure, but Catholic theologians have analyzed that process in ways we can learn from, as they have, as we all now try to do better.

Mormons, of course, agree with Columbus's own conviction that he was inspired and blessed by God in his voyages; because of him and the colonization that followed, the gospel was brought back to Book of Mormon peoples and a way was prepared for the development of the United States, a country sufficiently formed by and respectful of diversity and freedom that the gospel could be restored there and go forth to bless all the world.

But as the revisionist historians of recent years have graphically reminded us, Columbus himself participated in the exploitation and racist violence of the Spanish Conquest he made possible—which was followed by the Portuguese and French and English conquests and participated in by some of our own ancestors. Some Catholics, including Columbus's editor and biographer and champion Bartolome de Las Casas, as well as many heroic and sometimes martyred priests down to the present, strenuously opposed the violence and racism of the Conquest and tried to develop and promote their understanding that the impact of European civilization on others was justified *only* in bringing a non-intrusive and non-judgmental extension of the gospel of Christ to them. And Catholic theologians like Karl Rahner have tried to describe the gains in possible understanding for all of us—the new paradigms made possible—from the mistakes and new perspectives of this crucial historical experience of proselyting Christian cultures colliding with others.

For instance, Rahner has articulated a way of understanding, given God's universal love and power, how Christ's grace must have been operating in non-Christian peoples all along: Christianity cannot "simply confront the member of an extra-Christian religion as a mere non-Christian but as someone who can and must already be regarded in this or that respect as an anonymous Christian. It would be wrong to regard the pagan as someone who has not yet been touched in any way by God's grace and truth."[19] Rahner also asks us to consider what did and what should happen to Christianity itself as it enters into a genuinely loving encounter with others in another culture. He points out that Catholicism was always a world church "in potency," but in the encounter with the New World brought on by Columbus it came for the first time to act, on a huge scale, like an export firm: it exported an essentially "European religion as a commodity it did not really want to change but sent throughout the world together with the rest of the culture and civilization it considered superior."[20] And as a result it has had to face the mistakes and evil that resulted and try to admit that, in a genuine world church, such cultural imperialism must give way to interaction and reciprocal influences in all the non-essentials.

The restored gospel has given us a crucial additional concept to help us improve on the Catholic experience, as we face our own transition into a world church. Alone among Christians, we understand that God did not first reveal Christ's identity and saving gospel at the meridian of time but has done so again and again from the very beginning, in dispensation after dispensation and in all parts of the world. Indeed in the Book of Mormon the Lord declares, "Know ye not that there are more nations than one? Know ye not that I, the Lord your God, have created all men, and that I remember those who are upon the isles of the sea; and that I rule in the heavens above and in the earth beneath; and I bring forth my word unto the children of men, yea, even upon all the nations of the earth" (2 Ne. 29:7).

I can only understand that passage as giving concrete meaning to Karl Rahner's sense that Christ's grace has already come to all God's children. *Every* people has the word of God, much of it in written form, from the Hindu *Baghavad Gita* to the Oglala Sioux *Black Elk Speaks*. Part of our mission is to learn from them and delight in the diversity of revelation God has given.

I do delight in that diversity—even while struggling with its challenges and often failing. I confess I experience the greatest challenge to my faith when I consider the enormous variety of races and cultures and people; then, caught up in the popular Mormon notion that only those who have known Christ through our particular Western Christian and now American Mormon tradition have been "saved" or even experienced life properly, I realize that perhaps less than one in ten of those who have lived have even heard of Christ and only one in a thousand have heard the restored gospel. Consequently I consider, bleakly, that God is terribly inefficient and powerless, wasteful of those billions of suffering lives—and that we must expend even more concentrated, even desperate, effort to save a few more before Armageddon.

In saner moments I remember God's universal love, and I open my imagination to the billions of lives which have experienced that love in many diverse ways and will continue to experience it in the next life, when all the physical and cultural inequities and differences of opportunity will be resolved, so that *all* can truly know Christ and choose to follow him; then I can enjoy being part of a missionary effort that will share what God has given others with what God has given us, with the genuine and joyful anticipation that we can *all* be changed and healed by each other and brought back to him.

Finally, as I face the most difficult and delightful form of diversity, that between men and women, I rejoice in what I believe is the greatest challenge facing our church at present—how to translate the assurance that all are alike unto God, male and female, into a theology of gender and church practices that fully reflect that equality and thus release the enormous spiritual energy and moral impetus that true gender equality and family relationships unfettered by the sinful traditions of the fathers can bring. The most challenging diversity is of course that provided by the partner in marriage, what Michael Novak describes as "seeing myself through the unblinking eyes of an intimate, intelligent other, an honest spouse."[21] And that I believe is what each of us must work through into genuine equality and delight before we can become as the gods in the highest degree of Celestial joy and creativity. We have not yet developed sufficiently the cultural practices concerning gender that will make that possible, and "all the blessings of the gospel" are therefore not yet equally shared. How that will come about I do not know, and it has apparently become a potentially actionable offense to speculate about it. I value my membership in what I believe is Christ's authorized church, led by his apostles, more than I do my speculations, so I will only voice my abiding faith that genuine equality will come in some form and before too long. God is no respecter of persons.

NOTES

1. Lectures on Faith, Lecture 3, in any edition of the Doctrine and Covenants published before 1921; also in *The Lectures on Faith in Historical Perspective*, eds. Larry E. Dahl and Charles D. Tate (Provo, UT: BYU Religious Studies Center, 1990).

2. "The King Follett Sermon: A Newly Amalgamated Verison," ed. Stan Larson, *Brigham Young University Studies* 18 (Winter 1978): 204.

3. See his inclusion, on p. 160 of his *Seventy's Course in Theology, First Year* (Salt Lake City: Deseret News Press, 1907), of a paragraph from William Benjamin Smith's *The Color Line: A Brief in Behalf of the Unborn*.

4. *The Way to Perfection* (Salt Lake City: Deseret News Press, 1931), see chaps. 7, 15, and 16, esp. pp. 43-44 and 105-106.

5. Stewart's book was published by Community Press of Orem, Utah, in 1960, 1964, and 1967, and reprinted by Horizon Publishers of Salt Lake City in 1970. Lund's book was privately printed in 1968.

6. John K. Carmack, *Tolerance: Principles, Practices, Obstacles, Limits* (Salt Lake City: Bookcraft, 1993).

7. Ibid., 64.

8. Bruce R. McConkie, "All Are Alike unto God," speech delivered 18 Aug. 1978, published in *Charge to Religious Educators* (Salt Lake City: Church of Jesus Christ of Latter-day Saints, 1982), 152.

9. *Ensign* 21 (Nov. 1991): 100.

10. Boyd K. Packer, "Address to the Church Coordinating Committee Meeting," 8 Sept. 1987, copy in library, Historical Department, Church of Jesus Christ of Latter-day Saints, Salt Lake City, Utah; cited in Lee Copeland, "From Calcutta to Kaysville: Is Righteousness Color-coded?" *Dialogue: A Journal of Mormon Thought* 21 (Fall 1988): 97.

11. Howard W. Hunter, "All Are Alike Unto God," *Ensign* 9 (June 1979): 72, 74.

12. Lavina Fielding Anderson, "Making the 'Good' Good for Something: A Direction for Mormon Literature," *Mormon Letters Annual, 1984* (Salt Lake City: Association for Mormon Letters, 1985), 163.

13. Yoshihiko Kikuchi, "Breaking Barriers," 1-2, speech delivered at Brigham Young University, 26 Jan. 1993, copy in my possession.

14. *Lighten Up!* (Salt Lake City: Deseret Book Co., 1992), 17.

15. Ibid., 122-23.

16. *Cat's Cradle* (Salt Lake City: Bookcraft, 1993), 65.

17. Quoted in ibid., 85.

18. Ibid., 68.

19. Karl Rahner, *Theological Investigations*, Vol 5., *Later Writings of Karl Rahner,* trans. Karl H. Kruger (Baltimore: Helicon Press, 1966), 131.

20. Ibid., 717.

21. Michael Novak, "The Family Out of Favor," *Harper's*, Apr. 1976, 42.

MONTE CRISTO

I drove from Kaysville and picked up Frank at his mother's home in Ogden at 7:00 a.m. By 7:30 we were well up Ogden Canyon, with the sun full in our eyes each time we made a turn to the east. Frank's body swayed with each turn, and flashes of light crossed his face. By the time we reached Huntsville, the sun was a good four fingers above Monte Cristo, the broad range of mountains where we were heading. The canyon opened out into a wide valley of alfalfa fields, the first crop just coming into bloom, and fields of young wheat not quite headed out. The slanted light glinted from the dew in the fields and from the irrigation ditches. The light caught some of the leaves on the east sides of cottonwood trees in bright green flashes and then cast huge, green-black pools of shadow to the west.

As we curved left around Pineview reservoir and then along the east side of Huntsville, watching for the South Fork turnoff to the right, I asked if we could take time to go by President McKay's old home. "We should be on the river by 10:00, but we're okay for a drive by," Frank said. I turned left at the sign for 500 South, then north again on 200 West to the pioneer home where David O. McKay, president of the Mormon church while Frank and I grew into manhood, had been born and had lived with his parents in the late nineteenth century. Someone was maintaining the tall, gabled, white stucco home and what had been its farmyard, now just grass and rows of huge cottonwoods along the ditch banks. The lawn merged with that of a pioneer rock home to the north, with a lovely, curving, pillared front porch and balcony that shone freshly painted white against the red sandstone blocks.

Just beyond the houses I turned east on First South, which went back across the main highway and then became the South Fork road. After about a mile I saw the sign to the Trappist Monastery off to the right. I wondered what President McKay thought of such a sanctuary in his valley, the monks living more fully than perhaps any Mormon he knew the principle of consecrating all worldly goods to God—and yet they renounced as well the sacred necessity of sex and family. We decided, from what we knew of him, that he probably liked having the monastery there, a hopeful sign of mutual tolerance, a kind of challenge even.

I told Frank about hearing President McKay's last general conference address, in October 1968, when he talked about trying to get a spiritual witness of Joseph Smith's mission when he was a boy here in Huntsville. I pointed at the sagebrush-covered hills to the north. "He said he rode his horse many times out onto those foothills and knelt and begged the Lord for some manifestation, but that when he got up he always had to admit nothing had happened."

"You told us about that in sacrament meeting right after we came to St. Olaf," Frank said. "Joanie and I were both amazed that a prophet had not had a testimony, even when he was a boy, and that he had tried so long without getting one. You were trying to make a point about serving doggedly in the church, but the main thing we felt then was worry. If it was so hard for him, what about us?"

Frank had been hired by the Spanish department at St. Olaf, the Lutheran college in Northfield, Minnesota, a year after I had become its Dean of Academic Affairs and president of the Mormon branch in that area. He and Joan had come from a year in Spain, where there was no Mormon congregation nearby. They had met the year before as students at Weber State in Ogden. Because they had left for Spain right after her conversion and their marriage, they had never really had a "normal" LDS church experience. Both had seemed to me overly precise and self-conscious, emotionally reserved, self-protective. My sacrament meeting talk, I remembered, had been aimed mostly at them, a plea to get involved, to experience church service and communion with common people in common struggles, as well as the study and self-reflection they had focused on in college and in Spain.

President McKay's point, which I had belabored, was that he did not get his spiritual assurance by pleading directly. The witness came later, he said, "as a natural sequence to the performance of duty." After he had gone on a proselyting mission—which was not out of personal conviction but because he had trusted his parents, who said it was right—he received his spiritual manifestation during a missionary conference in Scotland. The guardian angels of the missionaries had become visible to him there, and he suddenly realized that the knowledge he had sought had come, not through seeking but as a gift while he was serving others.

"I probably overdid it," I said, remembering how worried I had been about them both. I had asked them to perform rather humble tasks in the branch, she teaching children in Primary, he advising the young men. They had struggled for a while, trying to do things by the book and in perfect order, and only gradually had learned to relax. Then Joan got to know a red-haired boy in her Primary class whose Irish mother worked all night as a janitor at Carleton College, across the river from St. Olaf, and then came home to care for an abusive, alcoholic husband and get the three children through the day. Frank became friends with another boy, Tim McBride, who at fourteen had left his single mother and the younger children to live in a hotel in Northfield and make it on his own doing odd jobs. One Sunday morning when we met early for our branch presidency meeting, we found him sleeping in the chapel, twenty miles from Northfield. His friends had dropped him off the night before, and he had crawled through a window to be there when Frank came.

Frank and Joan gradually let down their guard and in "natural sequence to the performance of duty" had found themselves loving and being hurt, making mistakes and being forgiven, and having experiences that brought them spiritual conviction. After a while I called Frank as one of my two counselors in the branch presidency, and we became good friends. When I left St. Olaf in 1975, he took my place as branch president, and now, a year later, while he was visiting his mother for a week, he was going to teach me how to fly fish.

He felt the best place was the south fork of the Ogden River, high in the Monte Cristo range where the river was difficult to reach but full of native cutthroat that Frank said were pretty easy to fool. He told me the best time was about at summer solstice, after spring runoff and before the river dried up too much. So he had arranged to visit his mother, who was widowed and living alone, and coordinated this fishing trip.

As we continued up South Fork Canyon, I pointed out, below us to the right, a string of tiny cabins along the river. One belonged to Charlotte's Aunt Annie, and our family had stayed there a few times. I told Frank how one day I was casting a Meps spinner tipped with salmon eggs into a big curving hole back of the cabin, and our children were riding rubber tubes down an easy stretch of water up-river. I had warned them not to float down around the bend where I was because the water swept under a pile-up of logs there, cutting out a huge hole that looked six to eight feet deep. I was having no luck and had just changed to a yellow triple teaser, when I looked up to see my six-year-old daughter, Jane, alone on a small tube, heading into the bend. I froze for a moment, watching her laugh in delight as the tube sped into the current, then launched myself across the hole, fishing vest pulling me down, and just managed to grab the tube and kick backwards before it went under the logs. Jane wasn't frightened until I reached her, then screamed and grabbed my hair. The next morning, our twelve-year-old son, Mark, got up at dawn, took my outfit, the yellow triple teaser still on, and with one cast into the wading pond next to the cabin caught a two-pound German brown.

Right after we passed Aunt Annie's, a road branched off on the right to cross Causey Dam on the South Fork, but we continued up the main road, which follows Beaver Creek and then goes over Monte Cristo into Wyoming, so we could fish South Fork far above the dam. Frank told me how he had grown up fishing the "Narrows" of South Fork, which were not then submerged under Causey Reservoir. Once, right after finals at Weber State, he had gone up early one morning, parked his car on Causey Creek below the Boy Scouts' Camp Kiesel and headed up the trail that followed the ridge on the left, then crossed the creek and went over a hogback down to South Fork above the cliffs of the Narrows. As he got up on the first ridge, he could see flashlights below where the trail ahead of him crossed the creek toward the hogback. He knew a small river like South Fork would be ruined for fly fishing if others got there first, so he went off the trail to the left and walked quickly across a suspended pipeline about 100 feet above the creek, then dashed on up to the trail ahead of the flashlights.

"I was determined—and selfish," Frank laughed. "It's too bad that stretch of South Fork is gone forever. It stayed good most of the summer that far down. Now we have to go up into the headwaters, and it's only good for a bit. I just hope we're not too early in the season to get in. It's been a wet year." Frank was speaking in the way I remembered from first knowing him—quickly, accelerating toward the ends of sentences and dropping his voice a little so you had to listen with increasing focus. When he was hired at St. Olaf, some of the administrators were worried that students would miss what he was saying. I assured them I thought students would make the effort, that they'd find it worth their while.

About five miles up into the foothills of Monte Cristo, Frank directed me onto a logging road to the right. I had offered to drive our new Jeep Wagoneer because Frank was worried that there might still be mud in spots. At first it was easy going, the road mainly graveled, but after about three miles we turned to the right onto a small dirt road and through an open gate and began to find water in all the low spots. I got out and turned the lugs of the front wheels to give us four-wheel-drive, and we did fine for a ways. But then the pools got deeper, some extending for many yards in the two wheeltracks, with deep mud sometimes continuing for a quarter mile through the meadows and even up onto ridges.

Frank looked worried, especially where the wheeltracks had been eroded by the spring runoff to a depth of two feet on the slopes and I had to straddle the ruts and could only make my way from side to side—when I had to avoid trees and bushes that were too close to the road—by finding a place where the ruts were shallow. Each time I turned Frank was thrown along the seat, from my shoulder to the window or back. I pretended to know what I was doing, certain that if we slipped into a rut or high-centered in one of the pools I splashed through, we could be stuck there for a long time. I kept up smalltalk, admiring the flowers and occasional glimpses across meadows and canyons back down towards Huntsville. We had come at the height of the flowering of bluebells, which thickly covered acres of meadow and gradually merged into the early sunflowers bursting out on the dryer hills. We were going downhill, which meant that even if we didn't get stuck, we would not be able to make it back up this slippery road unless there was quite a bit of drying during the day.

Finally, as we came out of a grove of pines onto a rocky, south-facing slope already heating up in the sun, Frank said, "Let's leave the car here. The road goes down towards the river for a ways, but it's too steep to come back up in this mud. I've always walked from here, and it's not too bad." He had fixed a thermos of grape juice and ice, which he put down between the seats out of the sun. "We'll need that when we've hiked back up."

We got our poles and fishing vests and headed out. I had a new Garcia fly rod and a Pfleuger reel, and the evening before Frank had helped me tie the delicate flyfishing tackle and coached me in the basics of casting on his mother's lawn. He had showed me how to tie a "nail knot." It uses a small finishing nail as a base for a series of loops in order to attach line to leader in a continuous curve rather than a hinge and thus transfers the power of a cast smoothly out to the leader. He made up his own nine-foot leader from sections, starting with two feet of .016 inch diameter nylon and stepping down .002 inch of diameter through each of five twelve-inch steps, with a two-foot tippett of .004 inch, two-pound test nylon. He said for these less sophisticated fish I could get by with a 4x tapered leader and a tippet like his.

To connect my tippett, the night before at his mother's home, Frank had showed me the "blood knot" he used between sections of his customized leader. It was beautiful to watch. He took two segments of leader and crossed the ends about an inch over each other to make an X. Holding the X with his right forefinger and thumb, he twisted the short end on the left around the other section about four times and looped it back through. Then he took the new loop between his left forefinger and thumb and twisted the short end on the right around the other section a few times and also pushed it back through the loop. Finally, as he took both short ends between thumb and fingertips and gradually pulled them tight, the knot took symmetrical shape, each

208

end of a section looped around the other a number of times and back through the center in a long, smooth, secure knot that, like the nail knot, did not hinge. It was a delight to work through the steps to what looked like a hopeless tangle of nylon loops—and then, when I had done it right and pulled slowly, to see the blood knot gradually form and tighten up so that when I snipped off the tag ends with my nail-clipper the connection was almost seamless.

Frank had then tied a fluff of wool at the end of each of our leaders and stuck a book under my right arm to teach me how to cast, first by demonstration, then watching and occasionally correcting my arm motion as I practiced. The book kept my elbow in and helped me concentrate on using just my forearm, getting distance through the timing and rhythm of my wrist action. "Accuracy will have to come on the stream," Frank had said. He showed me the flies to buy on the way home to Kaysville, number 16 Renegades and Adamses. The Renegade looks like no insect in the world but is perhaps the best general fly, with a dark green-black body and two hackles sticking out in circular fringes, a white fringe forward that helps novices see the fly well, and a brown one back. The Adams is grey with a brown hackle, a subtler fly, harder to see on the water, but good in most situations, from canyon streams to big, heavy water like the Yellowstone and Madison.

As I was pulling out of his mother's driveway, Frank had told me to get some fly dressing. "They have a liquid form now, a bottle you can dunk the fly in, and even a spray-on, but I prefer the white rub-on paste made by Mucilin." I decided to get that.

My father had fished as a boy in Arbon Valley south of Pocatello, Idaho, where success had meant having something for his pioneering family to eat with their bread and mustard greens. Known all his life as a "meat fisherman," he was effective but unconcerned with style, and that was my legacy, though I was never as effective as he—and my life never so hard that I had to be. Even when we fished for food when I was six and seven during the last years of the Depression, my father could catch limits for both of us. I had seen his beautiful split bamboo fly rod and box of wet flies, including some gorgeous huge concoctions with names like Royal Coachman and Mickey Finn, but had never seen him fish with dry flies. I had learned, by watching, only how to use spinners and simple lures, worms, cheese, and whatever else would get fish on the bank or in the boat the fastest.

I once saw my father, unable to tempt a five-pound brookie in a beaver dam with any of his lures, jump right into the waist-deep water and trap the big fish against the dam's sticks until he could catch it with his hands. I still carry as an emblem, snagged into the two-inch square piece of sheepskin with wool side out on the upper pocket of my fishing vest, one of his specially-designed wet flies that he used his spinning rod to cast out with a bubble on the shore of Strawberry Reservoir—a double Woolly Worm with a huge red spot on its tail.

Frank is a stylist. He learned the techniques and emotions of classic dry-fly angling, partly from his father-in-law, one of the understandably grumpy non-Mormons in the southern part of Idaho where Mormons have become a majority. Some of Parley Wallington's pain in losing his daughter to a Mormon was mitigated when his new son-in-law went flyfishing with him on the large spring creeks coming out of the lava walls of the Snake River Canyon near Twin Falls—and could soon match him in care and skill.

I would go with them the next year, after learning fly fishing at Monte Cristo, when we stopped overnight on our way to Lowell Bennion's boys' ranch in Teton Valley. Parley would give me a few of the flies he had conjured up, using a tiny number 20 hook and bits of black thread and white nylon fluff. It would take me five minutes just to tie on a fly, struggling to get the leader end through the eye and make a reasonable clinch knot in the dying light. Frank and Parley would each catch four or five fish before it was too dark, while I would snap off three flies on back-casts and spend most of the time retying, get two strikes and be too excited when I hooked one and break the leader—landing nothing. Not bad for a beginner, they would say. But I would realize more than before why Frank started me at Monte Cristo.

Leaving the Jeep behind us, Frank and I started down the steep road toward the river from where we had parked. I carried my fly rod as I had learned to carry my casting rod. To save time, I usually just left the tackle on after a fishing trip and broke the rod down into two sections, the lure hooked onto the handle of the reel and the line reeled in a bit to take up the slack. I had carried my rods that way for years—and had lost lures, tangled my leaders, and broken tips. Frank, however, had clipped off his practice "fly" the night before, reeled in his line and leader, and put the reel in his fishing vest pocket. Then he had put the three sections of his rod into an aluminum tube, which was padded with electrician's tape on the end so he could use it for a walking stick.

After about a mile of switchbacks the road angled into a draw and ended at a small man-made pond that collected water for cattle from a spring just above it. When we drank from the spring my teeth ached from the cold water while the sun burned hot on my shoulders. We picked up a small trail down through the aspens at the bottom of the draw and gradually it seemed cooler, the overflow stream from the pond constantly rippling on our right, dew brushing onto our hands from the grasses and small stretches of wildflowers opening up from time to time along the path. The variation of color was startling after the groves of green pines and the masses of bluebells and sunflowers in the higher meadows. There were white-topped yarrow and fluorescent orange Indian paint-brush, large pink penstemons, with an occasional white-flowered variant. In one dry, sunny spot there were two sego-lilies, each just a light green stem and a three-petaled white blossom on top, but then a surprise inside—chartreuse at the heart, with violet stamens, and at the base of each petal a dark purple-black arch, like a heavily painted eyebrow over an eye-spot of green. I wanted to pull one up to taste the bulb that pioneers had sometimes eaten to survive, but it seemed wrong.

After another mile, Frank, who had begun to trot and moved out fifty feet ahead as the path angled up a sidehill, turned back with a smile. His voice was too soft, but I could see his lips forming, "Can you hear the river?" I could only hear the slight wind in the pines. Then as I came up to Frank at the ridge I could see, in the canyon opening below, patches of moving water, light blue-green over the orange bottom, the patches to the east reflecting dots of silver, and could hear the water—just like the sound of the wind in the pines at first but more complex, a mixture of undertones that sorted out into specific tones as we got closer, one for each splashing falls.

Gradually I could see farther up and down the canyon, how the river had slowly cut through a great layer of limestone from the ancient seas as the Wasatch Mountains sheered up from the tectonic plate to the west. Because the rock layers had tilted up from south to north, the north slope had eroded far back from the stream, with a few small grey cliffs but mainly broken rock and topsoil at an angle of repose that allowed scrub oak and grasses and a few pine groves. But I could see that the south slope was much more abrupt, the grey limestone cut straight down for hundreds of feet in places. As we moved down I could see straight across into the cliff face and make out ledges that ran level in both directions out of sight, some of them with water oozing out and down the cliff walls. One ledge brought an iron solution out that had oxidized in long loops of gold down the face.

The trail got steeper, and I began to think of the return hike in the late afternoon sun, but Frank's excitement caught me up and we loped the last hundred yards and out into the river. We knelt right in the water to bathe our heads and necks.

While Frank got his rod set up and his reel and fly on, I tied on a Renegade and practiced casting up the stream into a large hole, where I normally would have dropped a worm. I saw the fly floating on the water a few times, but it usually disappeared when I cast. Frank came up and said, "You're standing right where some of the best fish are—were." He took me upstream and showed me how to cast to eddies along the riffles in the wider, graveled areas of the river, how to see the places where the fish are able to stay without much effort and could watch for food passing by in the current—or for flies landing on the calm water above them. He pointed to a spot about twenty feet beyond us. "See the fish there." I couldn't, but I didn't say so, just watched. He started playing out his line in false casts above the water, pulling from the reel with his left hand as he brought the rod back with his right, then letting the extra line go out with the cast, three feet farther each time. He did this four times, until the fly, which I could barely see looping over at the end of his cast, was stopping about two feet beyond where he had pointed.

On the next cast the fly dropped and floated for a moment on still water and then started going to the right into the current, while the leader and line stayed on the slower water to the left. The fly disappeared in a tiny swirl, and at the same moment Frank's hand jerked slightly back and his rod immediately bent as the orange line moved swiftly across and up the stream. He played the fish back and forth twice across the riffles, then quickly down to a sandy bank just below us. He reeled up and shifted his rod to his left hand to hold the fish in still water while he grasped it in his right hand, just behind the gills.

"Don't want to tire it out," he said, then lifted the fish up and quickly slipped the hook from its gristly upper lip, held it sideways for a moment for me to see the gold and rust-red smudges below each gill that give the fish its name, the same red continuing in a quarter inch band down each side, divided by a dark, blood-red line. As he held the fish in a quiet eddy while it started to breathe water again, I could see the light grey-brown back, mottled with black spots, that made such good camouflage against the sand and gravel of the shallows. When Frank let it go, the fish stayed still for a few seconds, quietly breathing, then suddenly became only a swift flash of shadow up the stream.

Frank looked at my fly and said, "I forgot to tell you about flattening down the barb on the hook so you won't hurt the fish. You'll lose a few but won't leave sores that might get infected. You also need to dress your fly." He took out a pair of needle-nose pliers and showed me how to gently press down the tiny barb without bending and thus weakening the main hook. "If you're not careful, the hook will break off there where the barb was, and then you'll be *too* safe." I practiced on two other Renegades in my flybox and then got out the little round tin of Mucilin fly floatant I had bought. It contained a white paste that looked like Vaseline but wasn't nearly as sticky. Frank showed me how to dry my fly by squeezing it between folds of my handkerchief, then take a little of the Mucilin between finger and thumb and rub it thoroughly over the fly, getting the layer thin enough that it didn't mat down the hackles.

I cast in the riffles without doing any good, while Frank caught two more fish. He said, "Try the lower end of a hole, like the one under that falls, but down at the end of the pool, where the water starts to speed up again. Cast up onto the edge of the current and let it float out into the quiet water." I tried what he said but lost sight of the fly, so when the swirl came to the right of where I was looking, I jerked too late and the fish had already felt the hook and let go. I started to move upstream, but Frank said, "Try it again, there are more fish there. And these cutthroats aren't too smart. He may take it again."

I kept my eye on the fly as it followed the current, trying to learn how to be able to see it after it started floating down. A shadow come up under it, and the fly disappeared. I was surprised but jerked in time and had my first fish.

I caught four or five this way at the lower ends of pools and holes, gradually learning how to see the fly as soon as it dropped, follow it on the current, and set the hook when the fly disappeared. My nerves got set so tight that sometimes I would jerk too quickly, released by the shadowed movement of the fish to the fly, and pull it right out of its mouth. Once, when I did this, I automatically continued the jerk-back into a backcast and then cast out again into the same spot, where another fish took the fly. But I triggered too quickly again and so again continued into a backcast and once more laid the fly out softly. Again the fly disappeared, but I waited a beat and set the hook perfectly.

The fish came straight up out of the water, the largest I had seen that day, maybe eleven inches and thick-bodied, with the red stripe clearly visible. I was so elated that I forgot to strip the line back and keep my rod tip high as the fish made a rush across the stream toward me. The unbarbed hook could only stay in place under pressure, and as the fish moved past me downstream, shaking the slack line, the hook came loose. As I finally pulled the line tight, the fly flipped straight back and hooked into my sleeve.

I sat down on the bank, letting the adrenalin slowly ebb away. Frank had been watching, but merely said, "That was a good fish. Come and try this next hole." He led me through a high mass of willows on the left bank, where we had to hold our rods high and keep ourselves up out of the impossible tangle by pushing over the bigger willow stems with our feet and then stepping on them from one to the next. On the right the south wall of the canyon closed in to the river so that when we came out into a small meadow of grassy sedge and segmented horsetail, we were looking across at a deep hole carved under the rock cliff, which continued up maybe four hundred feet. Pines were growing right down to the water's edge of the left so that the river seemed to come out of a dark cavern, with a sharp line where the sun, now approaching noon, broke straight down over the rock face and across the river.

Frank motioned that the hole was mine but I whispered, "Go ahead," and moved back to his left to watch, feeling a strange reluctance to cast up into the cavern and yet an overwhelming desire to see what might happen. Frank false cast a few times, the tiny grey Adams curving in a fifty-foot figure eight in the sunlight and disappearing further into darkness at the front of each cast. Then he let it drop and began slowly gathering line in his left hand. Just before the fly floated out of the dark into the bright water at the end of the hole, I could see a shadow coming up slowly from nearly four feet below it, then a quick rush the last foot, and Frank struck just as the fish lifted the fly from the water. I knew I would have struck too soon.

While he landed and released the fish, my breathing calmed down, but I wanted to stop for awhile and suggested, "Let's have a sandwich." Since we didn't keep any fish, the large pockets at the back of our fishing vests made perfect lunch baskets, and we each took out cheese sandwiches and apples. A small brook came out of the pine grove to our left and where it crossed the tiny meadow had filled with watercress. I picked some sprigs and put them in the sandwiches, knowing the tang would go well with the mild cheddar. In his vest Frank had a collapsible tin cup, concentric rings of overlapping metal that beaded up with the cold water and leaked slightly, but I lay right down on my belly to drink, putting my face deep into the pool where the brook opened into the river.

After lunch we moved farther upstream, where the river came out from the edge of the wall and was hemmed in by chokecherry bushes on both sides. Frank wanted to teach me to roll cast. We started below the bushes and came up the shallower right side. Frank let out only about fifteen feet of line and leader, with his fly floating to the left and back of him. Then, without backcasting, which would have hooked the chokecherries, he held his rod straight across the stream and with a quick clockwise turn of his wrist flipped the fly upstream into an eddy on the other side. As the fly floated down past him, he moved upstream a few feet, letting his rod tip follow the fly and then, just before it began to drag, he flipped it upstream again, this time into an eddy a few feet higher. He continued this for about five flips and then invited me to try. I was awkward the first few casts, not getting the fly upstream very far, but on the fourth cast the fly disappeared and I struck just right. "Good student," Frank said, clearly surprised, and then left me to continue on my own.

We had decided to quit at 3:00, leaving us time to hike out to the Jeep—and still have plenty of daylight in case we got stuck going up through the mud. Frank had agreed it would be all right to eat two of the fish, so I had brought some tinfoil and some butter that I had left to cool in the river at the bottom of the draw we had hiked down from the car. At 2:00 we agreed to hike downstream from that trail head to where Frank remembered there was a beaver pond and then fish back up.

As we came out of the pines above the beaver pond, a doe was going up a steep trail across from us that led into the cliffs. She turned to face us and calmly watched as we watched back, frozen, hardly breathing. I could see her dark nose and eyes and the huge grey-gold ears turned full toward us, the sun shining through the hair along the edges. Then she turned slowly and walked behind a boulder.

We stood there awhile, watching the fish, who must have been startled by the deer, slowly come back from the river above and from under the banks into the clear, calm beaver pond. We knew they were too spooked to take a fly on such still water, even if we could make a perfect presentation, so we started in the riffles just above the pond and continued back up the river. We took turns with the holes and stretches of riffle, silently leap-frogging, not watching each other fish. The only sound, over the complex roar of the river, was the drone of a jet passing high above toward the Salt Lake City airport.

We got back right at 3:00. Just downstream from the trail head a fallen log had produced a long, narrow hole down the center of the river, with shallow ripples to the left. "Show me what you can do," Frank said, and I ignored the hole, working up the riffles, and landed two nine-inchers in quick succession. As I unhooked each fish, I quickly turned it over in my hand, grasped it upside down with the head protruding out two inches between my middle and forefingers and rapped its nose sharply on a rock. This killed the fish instantly.

Frank continued fishing around the bend that the east ridge of the draw pushed out into the river, while I found a sandy bank and gutted the two fish. With the small blade of my pocketknife, I sliced each open from anus to gills and then stuck the knife upright in the sand to clean later. I hooked my left forefinger through the mouth and my thumb up in front of the gills to close with my fingertip. This gave me leverage to break out the front cartilage, where both sets of gills were attached, using my right forefinger and thumb, and then continue pulling downward to strip out the two front fins just behind the gills and then all the inner organs right to the anus and break off the end of the intestine there. Then I held each fish in my left hand and pushed my right thumb up the backbone, breaking the membrane that covers the main blood vessel and stripping out the blood to the front, continually washing the fish in the stream to take away the clotting blood.

I retrieved the little bottle of butter, kept hard in the cold water, went up on the ridge overlooking the river and built a fire of dead pine branches in a small stone firecircle I had seen there on the way down. While the fire was burning into embers, I poured out flour and salt and pepper onto a square of tinfoil and rolled each fish in it, then watched Frank fishing below me, admiring the intense efficiency of his movements as he looked up river, moved into position, cast and struck, played and released.

I suddenly realized I had for some time needed to urinate but had put it off, driven by the excitement of fishing and the job of preparing the fire and the fish. Now I felt the need intensely, from my belly down through my thighs. I moved over to some low elderberry bushes that hid me from Frank, opened my fly, and let loose with great pleasure. Just as I did so, a hummingbird whirred up the river and hovered directly in front of me, facing me so close I could see glints in his carmine throat and, on the heart-shaped inside of the tail that bobbed up and down to give him stability, black-tipped feathers with an inner ring of white. I stared back at him from a foot away, startled out of time; his head remained perfectly still, the eyes fixed on me, in the midst of the whirring wings and bobbing tail. Then I realized he had mistaken my father's special fly on my vest for a strange new, red-spotted, flower. After a moment, showering glints of green from his back, he whirred off, so fast his wings made a small rattle.

When the fire had burned down to red and white embers and no smoke, I called to Frank to come, spread the butter inside each fish, wrapped it in the foil, and placed it between the embers and a flat rock face at the edge of the firecircle. I gave each fish about two minutes in this little oven and took it out of the foil steaming. I offered a prayer, and we ate with our fingers, licking the little puddles of butter and juice off the foil. The seasoned skin we lifted off first had the strongest taste, the bread-white flesh underneath mild as Dover sole without its sauce. We ate in silence, casting the long-ribbed skeletons, that we lifted out entire, into the bushes behind us, and then licking the foil until it was clean enough to keep.

I felt the danger of not getting out soon and was anxious to leave. But Frank lay back on the needles under a pine and talked about fishing. He told about going to Montana while he was in college and being in camp with a group of world-class fly fishermen, the kind who wrote books and gave expensive lessons and guided excursions. He was just beginning to learn and so one day secretly followed one of the most prestigious anglers as he went out on a large and difficult river. All day he stayed under cover and watched the expert make perfect approaches and presentations, constantly changing his fly patterns and sizes. Frank was astonished at the man's skill, the length and variety of his casts, the softness of the fly descending, even before the line touched the water, the way he could cast across the current to an eddy and still keep a fly in a natural-looking float for five or six seconds, constantly "mending" his line by flipping the floating line deftly back upriver before it could start to drag the fly. But the great angler didn't get a single strike. The fish simply were not taking anything on that day on that stretch of river.

That night in camp Frank overheard the others in the party, who had gone out on the lake, ask how the man had done, and he replied, "Oh, I only got twelve." By the end of the story, Frank's voice had quickened and softened, turned in on itself, so I could barely hear him. "Why couldn't such a good fisherman simply tell the truth?"

We were silent awhile, and I thought about the first time I had watched Frank fish. We had moved from Northfield to a farm house that had been willed to the college along with eighty acres of cornfields and a fifteen-acre wood lot with a small stream running through it all year, enough to support trout, something very rare in southern Minnesota. Right after Frank had joined the faculty I invited him out to fish with me. We each took one side of the stream, fishing with worms, and I moved on ahead but then circled back and hid behind a clump of elderberries in order to watch his meticulous, thorough approach to each hole, different from anything I had seen before.

Frank next told me about a friend he had made that year in Rochester, about sixty miles from Northfield, where Frank, as Faribault Branch president, went for monthly meetings at the church's district headquarters. The man was a counselor in the district presidency and assigned to supervise the Faribault Branch, which meant he interviewed Frank each month and visited the branch often. "He was a gentle man, softspoken. He liked bringing his wife and coming on fast Sunday. We're still keeping up that custom you started of having a potluck lunch to break our fast after testimony meeting. He learned about our problems with a congregation spread out forty miles in every direction and only one or two experienced families, most of the rest new converts.

"As I came to know him better, he invited Joanie and me to stay at their home when we went down for district conference. We met his daughter, a senior in high school and a cheerleader, and he mentioned once that a football player from a broken family had dated her a few times, had gone to church and on a few family outings with them, clearly attracted not only to her but to her secure home.

"Then one Sunday Lynn missed a meeting he should have been conducting. It was announced that his daughter had just died that morning. We learned that she had tried to stop dating the boy and still be a friend, had even kept including him in family doings, but he had persisted, continued to pressure her, then joined the army and went away for a month. That Saturday he had returned on leave and tried to get her to date him, had even parked outside early in the evening until they had the sheriff ask him to leave. Later he called and asked to come by to pick up something he had given her before, and when she let him in he stabbed her and wounded a friend who had gone to the door with her. Then he fled. Lynn took his daughter to the hospital and blessed her, but she had died that morning.

"The next day, on Monday, Lynn and Kathy went to the high school and talked to the students in an assembly about what had happened. They spoke openly about their anger and grief. They also reminded the students that two families were grieving that day, their own and the young man's, and they should remember both. Nearly 2,000 students and town members came to the funeral and the burial. Lynn and Kathy stayed for hours at the cemetery, embracing the students, comforting and being comforted. Lynn told me later, 'I don't want anger to destroy us. I want to forgive.' And they got help—from their own prayers and those of church members and from a psychologist who came and worked with the whole family.

"About a year later I asked Kathy how she was doing. She said, 'I am a happy woman who cries a lot.'"

Frank's voice had become so low he had to repeat that, then coughed and went silent. I waited a while and Frank asked about teaching religion at the LDS Institute at Weber State, his old school. I told him how I had been asked by the bishop of one of my students to speak in sacrament meeting at their Ogden ward. I had talked about how hard it is to accept the modern revelations against materialism, how hard to live the covenants we make in the temple to consecrate everything we have to building the Kingdom of God. I read from sections of the Doctrine and Covenants that announce that the world lies in sin because one person possesses more than another and that we should be equal in temporal things or we cannot be equal in spiritual blessings.

The next week the director of the Institute came out into the reception area where I was checking my box for announcements and said, "I need to talk to you about a complaint about your talk last Sunday." I thought he was joking and joked back and started to leave, but he told me to come into his office. I learned that a member of the ward where I had talked had called church headquarters and tried to get me fired.

The complaint had been referred back to the director.

I told Frank how angry and humiliated I had felt and still did, because that fellow "Saint" had not talked to me but had gone over my head to some authority, clearly interested mainly in punishment—and also because that authority had even listened to the complaint and pursued it, rather than telling the complainer to talk to me. I had described my sermon to the director, who had agreed it seemed to be orthodox enough, but, he finally said, "It's best not to talk about controversial things like wealth."

The director told me the man's name, and I went to see him, defensive and full of desire to condemn him. I found him a very amiable person, a collector of toy soldiers which he displayed in gorgeous arrays all over his house. He said his anger had been aroused at me because his ward, in a declining part of Ogden, was full of widows and elderly couples on fixed incomes, and I had seemed to him to be thoughtlessly accusing them of not doing enough for the church, asking them to sacrifice more.

When we packed up I clipped the fly from my leader, reeled up the line and put the reel in my back vest pocket, and carried the rod carefully in sections. It took almost an hour of hard hiking until we reached the little reservoir and could drink from the spring there. We finished in one long push to the car and then sat on the tailgate drinking Frank's grape juice straight from the spigot of the gallon-size Coleman thermos, looking up at the slopes of Monte Cristo, now turning golden in the westering sun. It wasn't until we put our gear in the back that I noticed I'd left my knife in the river bank.

Frank and I had one more trip to South Fork, the next year. The year after that I tried to take Charlotte and my children in but found the gate locked where we had turned off the upper logging road—I learned later that the Deseret Cattle Company, which leased the land, had decided to keep people out. It was much too far to walk to the river from there, and we turned back. I think often of Monte Cristo and the river that flows on with no human visitation, without the arc of Frank's perfect cast and without his softening voice. I think of deer that come down to the beaver ponds to drink and how they spook the fish, how the hummingbird appears and is gone. I think of those red-throated fish measuring the pools in their shadowed flight, swift as the jet shadows measure, in the silent noons, that continuing valley.

eleven

THE PRINCE OF PEACE

As we meet tonight, on Easter Eve, it is the anniversary of the second night Christ's body lay in the tomb, just before he rose on Easter morning. In this hour I want us to think together of Christ's dead body in the tomb, to soberly consider what led to his death and what resulted. I ask you to pray for me, to extend your faith and love to me, so that my heart will be opened to you and yours to me.

Over fifty years ago I had an experience that became a touchstone for my spiritual life. My father and I were working on our farm in southern Idaho, in June, driving out early in the morning to use our Caterpillar tractor and twenty-four-foot rod weeders to till the half of our land that was lying fallow. On the way we passed our largest field of grain, the one closest to town and lowest in the valley so it ripened first. It was just coming into the boot, as we called it, when you could begin to see what kinds of heads it would form, how many kernels, and thus how good the crop would be. As often happened, my father stopped the truck and we walked out to look at the wheat.

The wheat was about waist high for me, only eight years old, and we walked through it, plucking heads and examining them, me imitating my father. Then something happened that had not happened before. My father knelt in the wheat and asked me to kneel with him. He prayed for the crop and dedicated it to the Lord, consecrated it. He asked the Lord to withhold the wind and hail and fire so that we could harvest that crop, which would be our full year's income and could be lost in a week—or a day or an hour, if conditions were bad—and he promised that he would use all the means from that crop in God's service. I felt something I'd never felt before. I felt a fearful presence that burned deep into my bones, like fire—and yet was peaceful, comforting.

I don't remember if I was fully aware of it then, but as I thought about that experience over the years, refelt it, I became more and more convinced that what I felt was the presence of the Savior, a personal, confirming presence. I came to judge whether something was from the Savior by its resonance with that feeling, on that early morning looking at my father's face as he prayed. That is, I considered whether something made me feel the same as I felt then—and later when I remembered that experience. I probably have not described the event with total accuracy, but I cannot forget the feeling. And I continue to measure all ideas, actions, and expressions, both those of others and my own, by whether they are in harmony with that touchstone.

By the time I was eighteen, ten years after that experience in the wheat field, I was living in Salt Lake City and courting Charlotte. We joined the Salt Lake Oratorical Choir, which existed mainly to perform Handel's *Messiah* each Christmas in the Tabernacle. Some of you will be surprised that I made the choir, because there actually were try-outs. They let Charlotte in because she was a fine alto, trained in the East High School A'Capella Choir under Louise Bowman, and I think they let me in because they wanted to promote romance—wanted me to come with Charlotte to all the rehearsals. We sang that wonderful chorus, "For unto us a child is born, unto us a son is given: . . . Wonderful, Counsellor." Wonderful thing to sing. You remember those amazing, difficult passages on the word "born" for each part, including us tenors, passages that I tried valiantly to manage—usually two notes behind: "For unto us a child is born, unto us a son is given: and the government shall be upon his shoulders: and his name shall be called Wonderful, Counsellor, The mighty God, The everlasting Father, The Prince of Peace" (Isa. 9:6).

I felt again that feeling, that touchstone from my boyhood, when I sang that song, and I knew that there was something right about those names for Christ, something consistent with what I'd felt in that wheat field. I felt that he was indeed the Prince of Peace. I didn't know, really, what that meant. I heard people talk about the gospel of

peace. I read scriptures about God speaking peace to our souls and remembered Oliver Cowdrey's experience when God spoke peace to his
mind. I thought I knew what that felt like.

When we sang, at the beginning of the program tonight, "Jesus,
the very thought of thee, with sweetness fills my breast," I felt the
sweetness I had experienced back in 1953 with Charlotte in the Tabernacle. At that time, under Lowell Bennion at the University of Utah
LDS institute, I was beginning to study the Book of Mormon in detail.
He taught me, for the first time, to understand the Atonement. As I
read and reread the Book of Mormon, I felt increasingly that what the
preface said was true, that it was entirely a witness—to Jew and gentile—that Jesus is the Christ. I came to the point where I could turn to
almost any page and read a few verses and immediately feel the spirit
of Christ—even to the point of tears. I knew, by that childhood touchstone, that the Book of Mormon was from Christ and was true.

But there was a problem with the idea that Christ was the Prince
of Peace. I became aware of it as I read that passage in John 14:27:
"Peace I leave with you. My peace I give unto you, not as the world
giveth, give I unto you. Let not your heart be troubled, neither let it be
afraid." That for me raised a question: "What *kind* of peace, if not
'worldly' peace, is Christ the Prince of?" I heard people say that such
peace had nothing to do with wars between nations, including the Korean War going on then, which I felt was a righteous war and was ready
to fight in.

About that same time Marion D. Hanks was called to be a member of the First Council of Seventy. He was a young man, only thirty,
and Charlotte and I had known him as a seminary teacher and popular
youth speaker in the Salt Lake City area. We listened to him carefully
in his first general conferences, before we were called, right after our
marriage, as missionaries to Samoa, and in one of those addresses he
talked about peace and mercy and told a story about two Latter-day
Saint families who lived near each other. Some offence was committed
by one against the other and for years they were alienated from each
other. No one remembered any longer what the original offence was,
but there was continuing animosity, until finally the one who had first
been offended went to the other and apologized, and the families were

reconciled.

I felt the spirit of my boyhood touchstone again. I felt that little action of apology was one of the things peace is about, the ability to seek reconciliation, even when you're not in the wrong: to extend mercy through some courageous act beyond what justice required. I felt that this was the spirit of the Prince of Peace.

However, my own choices during that time would seem to deny what I had learned. I believed that this concept had to do with personal interactions, nothing beyond that. I'd grown up as an American patriot. I believed World War II was a righteous war. I would have fought in it had I been old enough. When the Korean War came I volunteered for the Air Force college training program, and after our mission to Samoa was sent to MIT for a year's training in meteorology. I then served two years as an Air Force weather officer for a tactical fighter bomber squadron at George Air Force Base in the Mojave Desert. Two or three times in the early 1960s the squadron was alerted for Vietnam. But they didn't go into combat until after I had left the service for graduate work at Stanford University.

At Stanford I had access, through the graduate library, to news and commentary from the international press that began to counter my vision of American righteousness and its use of power. In 1964 quite suddenly I experienced a dramatic paradigm shift, a kind of sea change in my soul. You remember the famous Tonkin Gulf incident, in which it was claimed that North Vietnamese gun boats had fired on an American destroyer. President Lyndon Johnson used that claim as an excuse to bomb Hanoi and to obtain Congressional approval for essentially unlimited power to escalate the war. The sources I had access to convinced me that this incident was a fabrication by the U.S. government, which in fact was later revealed to be the case.

I had grown up believing, connected to my belief that the Constitution was divinely inspired, that U.S. presidents did not lie. When I became convinced that President Johnson had lied, with complicity from his advisors and without significant opposition from Congress, but with such dire results for our country, I crossed some line in my soul. As I thought about it, and consulted the same touchstone I have mentioned, I became convinced that I had crossed to a proper place, to a conviction that the Prince of Peace had to do with peace between nations more than with loyalty to one nation. Since then I've been trying to understand more fully what that means, what the costs of discipleship to such a Prince might be.

I was reminded often of that quest last weekend. A colleague, Bruce Young, and I went to Atlanta to a Shakespeare conference. Before the meetings we visited the Martin Luther King birth place and nearby King Center, saw the memorial, the building, the grave, the beautiful setting there—and the center for training in nonviolent action. I had occasion to think about what it meant for a Christian minister to be committed to the Prince of Peace—and to thus be able to find new means of social change that I think saved our country from violent revolution, and to pay with his life. On Palm Sunday we began the day by going to Ebeneezer Baptist Church, where both Martin Luther King and his father had regularly preached.

Palm Sunday is the day, remember, when Christ came into Jerusalem for the last time. He came nonviolently and ended that week with his death. He came confrontively, not passively. This is one of the things that I've been learning in recent years, that what he taught was pacifist but does not mean passivity. It means something like Martin Luther King's "nonviolent direct action." That is clearly what Christ engaged in that last week of his life. Let me remind you of what happened early in that week, after the triumphal entry on Palm Sunday.

It is a little bit surprising to look at the record again, because it is a record of dramatic confrontation, compared to what we usually think of when we think of Christ. You remember, for instance, that he cleanses the temple, drives out the money changers. Then he tells some violent parables: the one of the landowner who planted a vineyard, hedged it, let it out to the husbandmen, went to another country, and then sent his servants to receive the harvest:

> The husbandmen took his servants and beat one, and killed another, and stoned another. Again, he sent other servants, more than the first, and they did unto them likewise. But last of all he sent unto them his son, saying, They will reverence my son. But when the husbandmen saw the son, they said among themselves, This is

the heir; come let us kill him, and let us seize on his inheritance. And they caught him and cast him out of the vineyard and slew him. When the Lord therefore of the vineyard cometh, what will he do unto those husbandmen? (Matt. 21:35-40)

The normal human reaction, of course, is to think of retaliation: In answer to his question, "They say unto him, He will miserably destroy those wicked men and will let out his vineyard unto other husbandmen, which shall render him the fruits in their season." But Christ doesn't say, "You're right, the Lord of the universe will take revenge." That kind of God is what Christ had come to tell them he was *not*. Often he had reminded his disciples, "They said of old time, 'Thou shalt love thy neighbor and hate thy enemy,' but *I* say unto you."

So, to the chief priests, Christ is direct, unsparing:

Did ye never read in the scriptures, The stone which the builders rejected, the same is become the head of the corner: this is the Lord's doing, and it is marvelous in our eyes. Therefore I say unto you, The kingdom of God shall be taken from you, and given to a nation bringing forth the fruits thereof. And whosoever shall fall on this stone shall be broken: but on whomsoever it shall fall it shall grind him to powder. And when the chief priests and pharisees had heard these parables, they perceived that he spake of them. But when they sought to lay hands on him, they feared the multitude, because they took him for a prophet (Matt. 21:42-46).

From this point on, the chief priests and Pharisees plot how to take Christ's life, but he continues to rebuke them, to expose their basic violence and lack of mercy:

Woe unto you, scribes and Pharisees, hypocrites! for ye pay tithe of mint and anise and cummin, and have omitted the weightier matters of the law, judgement, mercy and faith; these ought ye to have done, and not to leave the other undone. Ye blind guides, which strain at a gnat and swallow a camel. . . . Woe unto you . . . because you build the tombs of the prophets, and garnish the sepulchers of the righteous, And say, if we had been in the days of our father, we would not have been partakers with them in the blood of the prophets. Wherefore ye be witnesses unto yourselves, that ye are the children of them which killed the prophets. Fill up then the measure of your fathers (Matt. 23:13-16; 23-31).

Strong language. Is this the Prince of Peace? I think so. After speaking this violently to religious leaders, he would go nonviolently to his death. Nor would he be a scapegoat, which is what he knew they wanted him to be. Throughout the Old Testament, as he so pointedly reminded them, they had killed the prophets and truthtellers, thinking they could focus their collective national iniquity on one person rather than face their sins individually. He declared his complete innocence. As an innocent victim, he would end the violence by refusing to participate in it, thus stopping the cycles of retaliation.

As we thought about that on Palm Sunday at Ebeneezer Baptist Church, we were reminded that that day was the twenty-fifth anniversary of Martin Luther King's death on 4 April 1968. We thought about his life, what he stood for. And thus we recovered some of the hope of the 1960s that some of you remember—and some of the hopelessness. Then we went to the Martin Luther King Chapel at the college he attended, Morris Brown, which is part of Atlanta University, and saw the huge statue of him there, at least twelve feet high and surrounded by plaques listing his many honors. We gathered with about 2,000 Easter worshippers, all of us black but about ten, and each of us was given a small cross to carry, made of a coconut palm leaf.

They made us visitors feel welcome, had us stand for everyone to see, and then we got hugs from four or five people around us. The young mother sitting next to me with a little child on her lap dropped her baby's bottle and it rolled down the aisle. And Bruce Young, who is a new father and very adept at this, scooted down and retrieved it and felt right at home.

There was some lively music there that you will probably not hear in a Mormon chapel, at least for a while. Then a traditional song we Mormons could relate to. "The Holy City" was sung by the leader of the choir, just the way I'd always heard it in Mormon meetings: "Jerusalem, Jerusalem, lift up your voice and sing. Hosanna, in the highest, hosanna to our King." We drove quickly afterwards to an LDS stake center in time to watch general conference on television. We had the opposite experience there in one sense—two black families among maybe five hundred people. I thought of the gains we have made as a church and people since 1978, and the distance we have still got to go, all of us, to fulfill Martin Luther King's dream.

During that session of conference, Elder Howard W. Hunter spoke on the theme, "Jesus the Very Thought of Thee," interspersing his talk with words from that song. He said: "Surely life would be more peaceful, surely marriages and families would be stronger. Certainly neighborhoods and nations would be safer and kinder and more constructive, if more of the gospel of Jesus Christ could fill our breasts. How deeply, gratefully and adoringly do our lives reflect on his life. How central to our lives do we know him to be." I felt the recognizable spirit of the Prince of Peace as I listened to a modern apostle bear his witness concerning the Savior.

Between sessions of conference we went to the Carter Center, there in Atlanta, and visited the Carter Library and Museum. We went through the exhibits about President Jimmy Carter's life. I was particularly interested, thinking about peace and the struggle for it, in seeing exhibits about his efforts to control the nuclear arms race. In one exhibit was a letter I had remembered reading, long ago, from Robert Milliken and other distinguished atomic scientists, written July 17, 1945. This was after the bomb had been invented by them, before it was used on Japan, and they wrote to President Harry S. Truman, asking him *not* to use it. They reminded the president how they had developed the bomb to counter a possible development of atomic weapons by Germany, but now there was no need to drop it and great danger: "The nation which sets the precedent of such massive destruction of innocence may have to bear the responsibility of opening the door to an era of devastation on an unimaginable scale."

I watched a video and saw exhibits about the Camp David accords that President Carter had worked long and ultimately successfully to bring about in September 1978, achieving finally a peace treaty between Egypt and Israel. He talked on that video about the various times, during that period of weeks that the two leaders struggled there together to come to an accord, when one and then the other would

230

pack up to leave. When Anwar Sadat did that, just as he was leaving Carter met with him and said, "This is a matter of personal trust between us. I'm asking you because of your trust in me to stay." And Sadat did stay and of course eventually paid with his life.

President Carter talked about Menachem Begin, who was also at one point leaving in a huff. Carter arranged to take to him a picture he had been able to get of Begin's grandchildren. Carter had learned their names and he talked with Begin about each grandchild by name, about the kind of world they would live in if he wasn't willing to make some concessions.

One of the things Begin said during those two weeks is that "peace is infinitely harder to make than war." That is true. I feel the spirit of the Prince of Peace when I say that—and I felt it when I watched a video of a devout Baptist, President Carter, talking about his commitment to peace. This past week I have been thinking a lot about Christ and what he stood for. I'd like to share with you some of the scriptures I've looked at as I tried to retrace our knowledge of him from the pre-existence to the second coming.

Dietrich Bonhoeffer, the great Christian minister killed by the Nazis, coined a phrase that sounds right to me. Christ he called "the man for others." I think the appropriateness of that phrase began in the preexistence, when, as modern scripture in the Book of Moses records, Christ offered himself for us, with some knowledge of what it might entail in suffering in this life, so that a plan that did not try to violate agency could be made available. His plan, even before his incarnation, was non-violent. We sometimes forget that the main reason Satan's plan would not work was that it was a plan of violence, a plan of force, which claimed it would "save" everyone through coercion. Christ, the Prince of Peace, chose the more difficult option—but the only one that could actually save us—and thus chose the cost he had to pay.

Mormons understand the "Lord God" who is acting and speaking in the Old Testament to be Christ, Jehovah. This poses some problems when we also think of him as the "Prince of Peace," because of course for many the Old Testament God seems to be a God of violence. Most of the arguments I've heard within the church and in Christianity in general that claim pacifism is not a viable choice for Christians reason that it could not be an option since God is himself not a pacifist. The God of the Hebrews commits acts of violence—which, by definition, cannot be wrong. I think that may be the one major impediment to thoughtful people who might otherwise fully accept Christ as the Prince of Peace. But if we look carefully at the Old Testament that idea, that God himself is violent, can be rejected.

Hosea reports that Jehovah "has a controversy with the inhabitants of the land because there is no truth, no mercy, no knowledge of God" (Hosea 4:1). This seems to connect accepting mercy with a proper knowledge of God, and if we read carefully the literary prophets, as they're called, we find that they are constantly calling Israel to rise above a limited, violent concept of God, which even their prophets sometimes expressed, to a more merciful one.

What the Old Testament makes clear is that God is working with an inherently violent people, even though a "chosen people," who even express that violence sometimes by blaming God for it; God, through his prophets, is trying to move the Hebrews to a higher understanding of what God wants of them. At one point God tells the prophet Ezekiel to no longer accept the saying that "The fathers have eaten sour grapes and the children's teeth are set on edge" (see Ezek. 18:1-4). In other words, he denies that revenge from the Lord goes on into future generations. What makes this so interesting is that the Lord is quoting a previous *scripture*: Before that time, people had accepted that understanding of God's revengeful nature as the word of the Lord, spoken by his prophets. There's no way to interpret that passage in Ezekiel I believe other than to see that God is working with a people whose understanding of God is incomplete, even wrong, and *developing*. Though they have claimed or received some kind of revelation, and have understood it violently, God is trying to lead them beyond that—and succeeds *if* they (and we) will listen to him.

During this time, when God was trying to move his chosen people beyond violence, according to Mormon scripture God appeared to Enoch and showed him the earth's inhabitants:

And it came to pass that the God of heaven looked upon the residue

232

of the people, and he wept. . . . And Enoch said unto the Lord: How is it that thou canst weep, seeing thou art holy, and from all eternity to all eternity. . . . and naught but peace, justice, and truth is the habitation of thy throne; and mercy shall go before thy face and have no end; how it is thou canst weep? The Lord said unto Enoch: Behold these thy brethren; they are the workmanship of mine own hands, and I gave unto them their knowledge, in the day I created them; and in the Garden of Eden gave I unto man his agency; And unto thy brethren have I said, and also given commandment, that they should love one another, and that they should choose me, their Father; but behold, they are without affection, and they hate their own blood (Moses 7:28-29; 32-33).

Enoch is surprised because he had labored under the old conception of God as somehow absolute, in control of humans and thus not capable of that kind of human passion—actually weeping—concerning his chosen people when they exercised their agency and chose violence over the peace he was trying to teach them.

We also learn from the Old Testament something very specific about the Messiah's nonviolence, and Handel made it part of his great oratorio. We're told at the beginning of Isaiah 53, by our modern LDS headnotes, written we understand by Elder Bruce R. McConkie, that "Isaiah speaks messianically." That is, that the person clearly represented here is the Savior:

For he shall grow up before him as a tender plant, and as a root out of a dry ground: he hath no form nor comeliness; and when we shall see him, there is no beauty that we should desire him. He is despised and rejected of men; a man of sorrows; and acquainted with grief: and we hid as it were our faces from him; he was despised, and we esteemed him not. Surely he hath born our griefs, and carried our sorrows: yet we did esteem him stricken, smitten of God, and afflicted (Isa. 53:2-4).

We usually slip by that, but listen to it again: "Surely he hath born our griefs, and carried our sorrows: yet we did esteem him stricken, smitten of God, and afflicted." In other words, we assume that Christ, in the Atonement, was stricken and afflicted by *God*, that God exercises that kind of violence and demands that kind of retribution for our sins. But the passage here tells us we are *wrong*. It is our human projection on God to "esteem" or consider the Messiah to be "smitten of God," afflicted by him. Isaiah goes on to emphasize the point:

> But he was wounded for *our* transgressions. He was bruised for *our* iniquities. The chastisement of *our* peace was upon him; and with his stripes we are healed. All we like sheep have gone astray; we have turned every one to his own way; and the Lord hath laid on him the iniquity of us all. He was oppressed, and he was afflicted, yet he opened not his mouth (vv. 5-6; my emphasis).

Remember, we Latter-day Saints understand this passage is about the God of the Old Testament, who is Christ. He is *not* a God of violence:

> He was oppressed, and he was afflicted, yet he opened not his mouth: he is brought as a lamb to the slaughter, and as a sheep before his shearers is dumb, so he openeth not his mouth. He was taken from prison and from judgement: and who shall declare his generation? for he was cut off from out of the land of the living: for the transgression of my people was he stricken. And he made his grave with the wicked, and with the rich in his death; *because he had done no violence*, neither was any deceit in his mouth (vv. 7-8; my emphasis).

"Because he had done no violence; neither was any deceit in his mouth." How beautiful upon the mountains are the feet of him who publishes peace. I think that is what Christ gives as the Prince of Peace. He rejects the old concepts, even those that may have or seem to have come from prophets.

Now listen to this Messiah in the New Testament as he comes on earth to teach us directly what he and the father are like:

> Ye have heard that it hath been said [and he's quoting scripture here], An eye for an eye, and a tooth for a tooth. But *I* say unto you, That ye resist not evil: but whosoever shall smite thee on thy right cheek, turn to him the other also. . . . Ye have heard that it hath

bcen said, Thou shalt love thy neighbor, and hate thy enemy. But *I* say unto you, Love your enemies, bless them that curse you, do good to them that hate you, and pray for them which despitefully use you, and persecute you (Matt. 5:38-39, 43-44; my emphasis).

We learned much together two weeks ago at the Mormon Peace Gathering in Las Vegas, in presentations, readings and discussions opposing the possible resumption of nuclear testing. In one of our readings, Walter Wink, a Protestant thinker, in an essay from his book, *Violence and Nonviolence in South Africa* (New Society Publishers, 1986), which stirred important debate among Christians in that racially divided country, describes what he calls Jesus's "third way" in the face of violence or oppression—"neither fight nor flight," but non-violent direct action instead. He argues that the passage I have just read from the Sermon on the Mount has been misunderstood: Christ's command to "resist not evil" is assumed to mean we should be passive in the face of evil. Wink points out that that is a bad translation. What it more accurately says is "Do not respond *violently* to violence."

Wink examines the passage on the basis of research into the social and political conditions of the first century in Palestine, pointing out that the prescriptions here, such as "Whosoever will smite thee on thy right cheek, turn to him the other also," "If any man will sue thee of the law and take away thy coat, let him have thy cloak also," and "Whosoever shall compel thee to go a mile, go with him twain," are grounded in the customs and the attitudes and understandings of an oppressed people at that time and did not mean simple acceptance of that oppression. They were forms of pacifism, not passivism.

For instance, Wink points out that in that culture smiting a person on the right cheek was done only to humiliate inferiors and only with the back side of the right hand. The left hand could only be used for unclean tasks, and to actually strike a person, an inferior, directly with a fist would be to recognize them as an equal. So if someone strikes you on the right cheek, turn the other cheek, the left cheek. Now he can neither strike you with his fist nor backhand you with his left hand, which puts him in a remarkably difficult position: even your process of submission becomes a judgment on his violence.

Wink analyzes the other seemingly passive suggestions by Christ in the same way: "Whosoever shall take away thy coat, let him have thy cloak also" relates to the legal requirement that though you could take the outer garment (coat) from an inferior, as security for a loan, it had to be returned by sundown. If you are oppressed by someone taking that coat from you, what Christ is advising you to do is to give your inner garment (cloak) also, and to stand there until sundown naked, as a judgment to embarrass the person who would carry the oppression that far. "Whosoever will compel you to go a mile, go with him twain": The law required conquered peoples to help Roman soldiers carry their heavy packs a mile, but it was against the law, with strong penalties, to compel them to go further. So when an oppressed person said, "No, I'll keep carrying," after the first mile, they put the soldier in the position of begging them to to stop for fear he might be arrested. Wink comments:

> Jesus in effect is sponsoring clowning. In so doing he shows himself to be thoroughly Jewish. A later saying of the Talmud runs, "If your neighbor calls you an ass, put a saddle on your back.". . . Some . . . may object to the idea of discomfitting the soldier or embarrassing the creditor. But how can a people who are engaged in oppressive acts repent unless they are made uncomfortable with their actions? There is, admittedly, the danger of using nonviolence as a tactic of revenge and humiliation. There is also, at the opposite extreme, an equal danger of sentimentality and softness that confuses the uncompromising lover of Jesus with being nice. Loving confrontations can free both the oppressed from docility and the oppressor from sin.

You see Wink's point? There was a wonderful example of this kind of peaceful, non-violent direct action that isn't passive last year at BYU. We had a rape on campus and an outpouring as you might expect of editorials and statements about how terrible that was. One editorial suggested a curfew for women, requiring them to have escorts after a certain time at night, provided by campus ward priesthood quorums. The student women's group, VOICE, thought about this and composed a marvelous form of the nonviolent but confrontive undercutting of stereotype and oppression that Wink argues Christ is advising. They posted around the campus and sent to various people and the press a statement announcing a curfew for *men*. All male students were to be indoors, unless accompanied by two or more females, after 10:00 p.m. If they had any trouble getting escorts, they could call their ward Relief Society president. Well, what did that bit of satire do? It made a powerful point. You can tell how powerful it was by the reaction of some in letters to the editors: the outrage that people "who weren't to blame would be made to suffer," which meant men, of course. But I know the statement made many people think a little bit about our tendency to blame or penalize the *victim* when women are attacked.

We tend to look for excuses for our violence, for evidence God might *allow* revenge. In the 98th section of the Doctrine of Covenants, there is a long passage, laying out what some people see as a justification for retaliation: God seems to be saying, If you've turned your cheek three times, without effect, I can understand your feeling and it is "justified" to use violence. But a more careful look reveals that God is not excusing violence at all but saying, even at that point, when you've been patient three times without response, "If thou will spare him, thou shall be rewarded for thy righteousness and also thy children and thy children's children unto the third and fourth generation" (v. 30). The basic message of that section is

> Verily I say unto my friends, fear not and let your hearts be comforted; yea, rejoice evermore, and in everything give thanks. . . Therefore, be not afraid of your enemies, for I have decreed in my heart, saith the Lord, that I will prove you in all things, whether you will abide in my covenant, even unto death, that you may be found worthy. . . . Therefore, renounce war and proclaim peace, and seek diligently to turn the hearts of the children to their fathers, and the hearts of the fathers to their children (vv. 1, 14, 16).

Such advice about violence ends, "This is the law that I gave unto my ancients, that they should not go out into battle against any nation, kindred, tongue or people, save I the Lord commanded them [which, of course, has *never* happened in the history of our nation]. And if any nation, tongue or people should proclaim war against them, they should first lift a standard of peace unto that people, nation or tongue [which, of course we have not done, either, in our wars of the past fifty years]."

Last Thursday night, when we came down to the San Francisco Bay area, which was our home for eight years in the 1960s and for which we have very tender feelings, we stayed with dear friends near Golden Gate Park. I sat up late reading, thinking about this sermon, and turned to remembering what that Thursday night was—something we Latter-day Saints don't celebrate, don't think about much, at least on that day. But maybe we should make our own celebration then. What is that Thursday before Easter? It is called Maundy Thursday in the Christian calendar, maundy referring to the ancient ceremony of washing the feet of the poor on that day, the day of remembering the institution of the Eucharist at the Last Supper, when Christ washed his disciples' feet.

Why might Latter-day Saints particularly want to celebrate then? We tend to resist celebrating Good Friday, because of our concern with the other costs of the Atonement than those paid on the cross and our resistance to the cross's emphasis on the death. We ought to celebrate Thursday evening, because that time is something we have special understanding of from our modern scriptures. That is when the Atonement really reached its heart and Christ bled in the garden, not from violence from the outside, but in love for us and internal agony over our sins. Many of you are familiar with the crucial passage in Doctrine and Covenants, section 19, about that suffering. It is unique, because anything else we have about Christ's atonement is told by others, witnesses or people who heard about what happened. But here we have Christ telling us himself what it was like to suffer the Atonement on that Thursday evening.

I think we could find ways that on each Maundy Thursday we might gather together, read this scripture and others, and have a unique celebration and sober remembrance. But we could also do it individually as I did last Thursday night. Let me read the passage to you again. Christ is speaking to Joseph Smith, in 1833, 1,800 years after the event—but still feeling it. Can you feel him feeling it? Listen to his language:

> I God have suffered these things for all, that they might not suffer if they would repent. But if they would not repent, they must suffer even as I, which suffering caused myself, even God, the greatest of

all, to tremble because of pain and to bleed at every pore and to suffer both body and spirit and would that I might not drink the bitter cup and shrink—

Now, of course, if you end the passage right there, you have an incomplete sentence. Surely Christ wouldn't speak in incomplete sentences, would he? But he does here. I think he does because, even in the midst of his revelation to Joseph Smith, he feels again the pain of the Atonement in the Garden. We must understand that pain emotionally, feel it in some way for ourselves, I believe, if we are to be moved with faith unto repentance. And if there's any moment at which we can have the most direct access to that pain, it may be at the point of that dash at the end of verse 18. There Christ stops, and after a pause for himself—and us—to reflect, he begins again: "Nevertheless glory be to the Father and I partook and finished my preparations unto the children of men, wherefore, I command you again to repent."

Of course, it's on the basis of the collateral of his suffering, unconditional love for us, while we are still sinners, that he is able to make that command to repent. He is the only person who can offer at the same time the power to do so—what Amulek calls the "*means* unto men that they may have faith unto repentance" (Alma 34:15; my emphasis). That's what he's done for us through the violence he was willing to take on himself. And part of what he was doing was preparing us, I think, to be moved sufficiently that we would not have to engage in violence, whatever our temptation is.

Christ has promised us that we could bring about such a condition of peace in Zion. When he comes again, it will be a time when there is a special situation on the earth: "It shall come to pass among the wicked, that every man that will not take his sword against his neighbor, must needs flee unto Zion for safety. They shall be gathered unto it out of every nation under heaven and it shall be the only people that shall not be at war one with another" (D&C 45:22).

From the beginning to the end, from the preexistence to the second coming, Christ offers himself to us as the Prince of Peace. When I got home from Atlanta, thinking about Martin Luther King, I was motivated to read more about him. One book, *Martin Luther King, Jr.: The Making of a Mind* (Orbis, 1982), by John J. Ansbro, documents the process by which Martin Luther King became convinced that part of his mission, to be consistent with this calling, was to oppose the war in Vietnam and all wars. He studied Gandhi and Reinhold Niebuhr, in theological school and on his own, and at first he was convinced that Niebuhr was right in his criticism of pacifism as being too self-righteous, too unrealistic about the world. But he became finally convinced by Gandhi and by the principles that he saw Christ as clearly teaching, with an additional understanding of what "resist not evil" means: not passivism but, as Wink suggests, active nonviolence.

In fact it is the apostle Paul who makes the requirement, "resist not evil," meaningful. He teaches it this way: "Be not overcome of evil, but overcome evil with good" (Rom. 12:21). And of course nonviolent direct action is exactly that—not ignoring evil, but overcoming it with courageous good. It's out of that kind of conviction that Martin Luther King spoke out at Riverside Church on April 4, 1967, exactly one year before he was assassinated, against participation in the Vietnam War.

As a result, we have now learned, our government tried to undermine his work. Some of that evidence was presented in the newspapers while Bruce Young and I were in Atlanta last week, with headlines that read, "Discovery of Military Spying on Martin Luther King." It wasn't enough that our government did that kind of spying and maligned his character, tried to pin on him the label of communist and philanderer to undermine what he was doing, but there is some evidence of what I immediately suspected and have in my heart felt was possibly true all along, that in fact he was killed because of his opposition to that war in Vietnam, by those who were profiting in some way from that war.

What then, is the connection between the peace that we believe Christ calls us to in our individual relationships, and the violence between nations? I think many of you are aware that the First Presidency in 1981 made that connection clear. Their Christmas message that year addresses directly the question whether Christ is the Prince of Peace only as regards peace between individuals or peace within our own hearts, or does he really have anything to do with nations? The First

Presidency says he does:

> To all who seek a resolution to conflict, be it a misunderstanding
> between individuals or an international difficulty among nations,
> we commend the council of the Prince of Peace, "Love your ene-
> mies, bless them that curse you, do good to them that hate you and
> pray for them which despitefully use you and persecute you: that
> you may be the children of your Father which is in heaven." This
> principle of loving one another as Jesus Christ loves us will bring
> peace to the individual, to the home, and beyond, even to the
> nations and to the world.

That seems to me clear enough. But it is undermined by a mixed history
that we have as Latter-day Saints, because that message has not come
clearly and consistently from our prophets. In the nineteenth century
it did. Joseph Smith, Brigham Young, and John Taylor essentially renounced the wars of our nation, including the Civil War. And it was not
really until 1898 that a dramatic change took place. The evidence is
quite certain that the change came because of our need to accommodate, for survival, to America and it's political system and values.
Thomas Alexander has documented in his biography of Wilford Woodruff how that happened and how Wilford Woodruff was prepared by
the Lord to make that dramatic change in his own thinking, a change
that in fact, quite likely, did enable the church to survive. But at some
cost. This is the way Alexander expresses the cost, when the First
Presidency, quite to the surprise of most people, came out in support
of the 1898 Spanish American War:

> Moving in a direction evident at least since the 1887 Constitutional
> Convention, but nevertheless crossing an immense intellectual ru-
> bicon, Woodruff subordinated the idea of the kingdom of God to
> the idea of loyalty to the United States. In order to prove Latter-day
> Saint patriotism, he proposed to offer the ultimate sacrifice, the
> blood of Mormon youth to the nation.

That is not merely a metaphor. We don't have exact figures but
Mormons have averaged something like one percent of the American

population in the twentieth century, and thus, given our even higher than average degree of patriotic willingness to serve in the armed forces, Mormon youth have suffered at least one percent of the casualties—thousands of deaths. But we Mormons also killed many others—many thousands of Germans and Japanese and Koreans and Vietnamese and Iraqis. And that may be a greater burden for us to bear.

I think it is possible that, as a people, we have been living a lower law in relation to the Prince of Peace, at least for a hundred years, though some individuals have lived the higher law. And the record bears that out in an interesting way. There has been an interesting moving back and forth among the prophets, on the one hand absolutely renouncing the war, including the second world war, and then justifying war in certain conditions. President David O. McKay, at the beginning of World War II, said in General Conference,

> War is incompatible with Christ's teachings:
> War impels you to hate your enemies.
> The Prince of Peace says, Love your enemies.
> War says, Curse them that curse you.
> The Prince of Peace says, Pray for them that curse you.
> War says, Injure and kill them that hate you.
> The risen Lord says, Do good to them that hate you.
> . . . . It is vain to attempt to reconcile war with true Christianity (*Improvement Era*, May 1942, 31).

President McKay then admitted, "In the face of all this, I shall seem inconsistent when I declare that I uphold our country in the gigantic task it has assumed in the present world conflict, and sustain the Church in its loyal support of government in its fight against dictatorship." And he does seem inconsistent, because he must (and does) proceed with a paradox: that Latter-day Saints should, partly because in this real world we are forced to, support the government, even though that means to some extent denying the Prince of Peace. President McKay does, however, lay down some conditions for such war, conditions that can justify our nation's defensive response to the aggression of Germany and Japan in World War II—*but do not justify any of our military actions since then*. He says war is never justified "in an attempt to enforce a new order of government . . . however better the government . . . may be," which is exactly what we were doing in Korea (at least after we crossed the 39th parallel), in Vietnam, in Grenada, in Angola, in Iraq.

There has been a similar equivocation over conscientious objection. At our Mormon Peace Gathering in Las Vegas, one of the participants was a Brother Boyd, who was one of perhaps only three conscientious objectors in World War II and who talked about being sent to a Quaker-run CO camp in California. He told of being aware that his situation was looked into while he was there by President J. Reuben Clark; he wasn't sure why. We know from the research of Michael Quinn that J. Reuben Clark was in the process of becoming a pacifist, which occurred during that war. The reason he was checking on Brother Boyd was to make sure those young Mormons were okay, and in fact after the war he made certain that the Quakers were reimbursed for the cost of the Mormon COs. A statement from the First Presidency was sent to many young men in the 1960s, giving Mormons permission to follow legal procedures in applying for CO status, but on the other hand there is a statement from an LDS church spokeman from 1981 that there is no place in the philosophy of Mormonism for conscientious objection.

So there is an interesting mix of responses, the kind of thing that I think you might expect in a time when generally we are living a lower law and God and Christ and the prophets are trying to bring us, as individuals, to a higher understanding. I think the chief expression of that higher understanding, one that we must look to again and again, is the remarkable editorial by President Spencer W. Kimball in the June 1976 *Ensign*, "The False Gods That We Worship," which states about as clearly as I can imagine it being stated that the ethic of Christ is pacifist. His statement is a ringing indictment of Americans, including Mormons, for failing that ethic:

> We are on the whole an idolatrous people, a condition most repugnant to the Lord. We are a war-like people, easily distracted from our assignment of preparing for the coming of the Lord. When enemies rise up we commit vast resources to the fabrication of Gods

of stone and steel, ships, planes, missiles, fortifications, and depend
on them for protection and deliverance. When threatened we become anti-enemy instead of pro kingdom of God. We train a man
in the art of war and call him a patriot and thus in the manner of
Satan's counterfeit, the true patriotism perverting the Savior's
teaching, "Love your enemies."

What does President Kimball suggest as an alternative to violence?
Certainly not passivism—but nonviolent direct action, taking of the
Gospel of the Prince of Peace to others, both through teaching it and, I
believe, by acting mercifully, constructively, as Christ would, in all we
do to others, including our foreign policy:

> What are we to fear when the Lord is with us? Can we not take the
> Lord at his word and exercise a particle of faith in him? Our assign-
> ment is affirmative, to forsake the things of the world as ends to
> themselves, to leave off idolatry and press forward in faith, to carry
> the gospel to our enemies that they might no longer be our ene-
> mies.

It is interesting to me how that sermon from 1976 has disappeared from Mormon consciousness. How many times have you heard
this important and unique statement by a prophet quoted in a lesson
manual or talk? I never have. I think that disappearance shows our ambivalence as a church in our struggle to live a higher law. But the call
seems to be clear, and it has been reinforced consistently since then, I
believe, by statements of the First Presidency, such as the one opposing the MX, which in its language is clearly not merely an opposition to
that particular form of the MX basing, but to missile systems themselves. But we haven't listened. Our LDS Congressmen haven't listened. Our Presidents of the United States, despite their lip service to
us (claiming to appreciate Mormon leaders and values) have not paid
attention.

The call of the Prince of Peace is to see every individual as Christ
and to do to that person what we would do to Christ. What is the message that our leaders are giving us now? Some of you remember Presi-

dent Hunter's address at the April Conference in 1992, published in the May 1992 *Ensign*. Let me just, as we close, remind you of that. He spoke on the subject, "A More Excellent Way," and quoted Joseph Smith: "If we would secure and cultivate the love of others, we must love others, even our enemies as well as friends. . . . Christians should cease wrangling and contending with each other, and cultivate the principles of union and friendship in their midst." Then President Hunter related a story told him by Vern Crawley, about when he'd been a boy working for his father in a used car lot, strong and young and full of zip and trying to care responsibly for the yard. One night he saw someone stealing something and went out to catch the thief. His father, who had been ill and had just started to come back to work occasionally, just then happened to come along. He put his hand on his son's shoulder and said, "I see you're a bit upset, can I handle this?" He then walked over to the young would-be thief, put his arm around him, looked him in the eye for a moment and said, "Son, tell me why are you doing this? Why are you trying to steal that transmission?" Then Mr. Crawley started walking towards the office, still with his arm around the boy, asking questions about the young man's car troubles as they walked. By the time they arrived at the office, the father said, "Well, I think your clutch is gone and that's causing your problem."

In the meantime Vern was fuming. Who cares about his clutch, he thought, let's call the police and get this over with. His father just kept talking: "Vern get him a clutch, get him a throw out bearing too, give him a pressure plate. That should take care of it." The father handed all of the parts to the young man who had attempted robbery and said, "Take these, here's the transmission too, you don't have to steal young man, just ask for it. There's a way out of every problem, people are willing to help." President Hunter reports that Vern Crawley said he learned "an everlasting lesson in love that day." The young man came back to the lot often and voluntarily, month by month, paid for all of the parts that had been given him, including the transmission. During those visits he asked Vern why his dad was the way he was and why he did what he did. And Vern told him about the gospel of the Prince of Peace, which the young man accepted and changed his life. Vern concluded, "It's hard now to describe the feelings I had and what I went through in that experience. I too was young. I had caught my crook. I was going to extract the utmost penalty, but my father taught me a different way." And President Hunter ends, "A different way? A better way? A higher way? A more excellent way? Oh, how the world could benefit from such a magnificent lesson. As Moroni declares, 'Wherefore, whoso believeth in God might with surety hope for a better world. . . . In the gift of his son hath God prepared a more excellent way.'"

Perhaps we who wish to be peacemakers can learn from President Hunter, learn to speak in parables and tell stories more than speaking out in anger and accusation. That was one way Christ dealt with the problem of social change, and he was a remarkable social revolutionary in his time. Here are two such stories about recent events, parables if you will: A few weeks ago, on April 12, an exhibit of paintings opened at Vincent Catholic Church in Holladay, Utah. These fourteen abstract paintings on the "Stations of the Cross," the main points in Christ's journey to Calvary, were bequeathed to Emma Lou Thayne, one of our finest Mormon poets, by Paul Fini when he died of AIDS in 1985. The two had become friends in March 1983 at a writers and artists retreat when Emma Lou was working on her collection of peace poems later published as *How Much for the Earth?*.

Fini was trying to finish the paintings by Easter that year, as a promise to a friend who had recently died of AIDS. He and Emma Lou became friends and continued to correspond and visit, and she shared his successes with his paintings and his fears when he was himself diagnosed with AIDS. He never sold his paintings, which he saw as personal statements of his Catholic faith, and in 1990 they arrived by UPS on Emma Lou's doorstep. She was moved again by them and began to seek ways to share them, aware that, in Utah, AIDS and abstract art and even Catholicism might be seen as too foreign. She wrote in her journal, "We are messengers of something," and persisted, until now the fourteen paintings, mounted on cross-shaped easels, with explanatory text by Emma Lou, are being donated to the Utah AIDS Foundation for this exhibit and future ones across the country. "What I hope for," Emma Lou says, "is to have the paintings understood and to have Paul understood."

Also this month was the fiftieth anniversary of the completion of the infamous bridge over the River Kwai, part of the "Death Railway" built through Thailand and Burma to supply Japanese troops—where malnutrition, disease, and brutal treatment cost the lives of 116,000 prisoners. This month, in a courtyard at a museum on the river bank, two 75-year-old men shook hands and sat talking for thirty minutes. One was Takashi Nagase, a former Japanese Army interpreter on the railway, who has long been an activist for reconciliation among Pacific war veterans. The other was Eric Lomax, one of the British soldiers working on the railway whom Nagase once interrogated and who had recognized Nagase's photograph in a newspaper article about his work and exchanged letters with him and agreed to meet at the River Kwai.

The Japanese veteran spoke softly to the British one and bowed his head, then sat with him on the bench, tightly holding the other man's hands in his and occasionally wiping his eyes as they talked. Nagase said the meeting freed him of fifty years of guilt and shame: "I apologized to him for what we did during the war," Nagase said. "For me it is a very great sin and a crime against humanity. War makes human beings wild and savage. It makes them devils. The nations of the world must ban war forever."

Banning war will not come easily or soon, but that is, I believe, what the Prince of Peace calls us to—peace "not as the world giveth" but in his own ways, some of which Martin Luther King and Walter Wink and Emma Lou Thayne and Takashi Nagase have shown us. Whatever way we find personally, may we remember the counsel of President Hunter: "If we would secure and cultivate the love of others, we must love others, even our enemies as well as friends. Christians should cease wrangling and contending with each other and cultivate the principles of union and friendship in their midst." And Moroni: "Wherefore, whoso believeth in God might with surety hope for a better world. . . . In the gift of his son hath God prepared a more excellent way."

I bear witness of this to you in the name of the Prince of Peace, Jesus Christ. Amen.